Richard Nixon and Europe

The Reshaping of the Postwar Atlantic World

The U.S.–European relationship remains the closest and most important alliance in the world. Since 1945, successive American presidents each put their own touches on transatlantic relations, but the literature has reached only into the presidency of Lyndon Johnson (1963–69). This first study of transatlantic relations during the era of Richard Nixon shows a complex, turbulent period during which the postwar period came to an end and the modern era came to be on both sides of the Atlantic in terms of political, economic, and military relations.

Luke A. Nichter is an associate professor of History at Texas A&M University – Central Texas and a noted expert on the Nixon tapes. Nichter's books include *New York Times* best-seller *The Nixon Tapes: 1971–1972* (co-authored with Douglas Brinkley) and book-length biographies of Lyndon B. Johnson, Richard Nixon, and George W. Bush for the *First Men, America's Presidents* series. Nichter is a former founding executive producer of C-SPAN's *American History TV,* and his work is periodically reported on by the *New York Times, Washington Post,* and the Associated Press. His website, www.nixontapes.org, offers free access to all 3,000 hours of publicly released Nixon tapes as a public service.

D1617075

For Daniele Struppa —

Richard Nixon and Europe

The Reshaping of the Postwar Atlantic World

LUKE A. NICHTER

Texas A&M University – Central Texas

It has been a pleasure getting to know
you, and I look forward to many further
opportunities to do so. When I need
a trekking partner for my next trip to
Everest base camp I know who to call!

Best wishes,

11/19/2019

CAMBRIDGE
UNIVERSITY PRESS

CAMBRIDGE
UNIVERSITY PRESS

University Printing House, Cambridge CB2 8BS, United Kingdom

One Liberty Plaza, 20th Floor, New York, NY 10006, USA

477 Williamstown Road, Port Melbourne, VIC 3207, Australia

4843/24, 2nd Floor, Ansari Road, Daryaganj, Delhi - 110002, India

79 Anson Road, #06-04/06, Singapore 079906

Cambridge University Press is part of the University of Cambridge.

It furthers the University's mission by disseminating knowledge in the pursuit of education, learning and research at the highest international levels of excellence.

www.cambridge.org
Information on this title: www.cambridge.org/9781107476608

© Luke A. Nichter 2015

First published 2015
First paperback edition 2017

A catalogue record for this publication is available from the British Library

Library of Congress Cataloging in Publication data
Nichter, Luke.
Richard Nixon and Europe : the reshaping of the postwar Atlantic world / Luke A. Nichter, Texas A&M University – Central Texas.
pages cm
Includes bibliographical references and index.
1. United States – Foreign relations – 1969–1974. 2. Nixon, Richard M. (Richard Milhous), 1913–1994. 3. United States – Foreign relations – Europe. 4. Europe – Foreign relations – United States. 5. Europe – Foreign relations – 1945– I. Title.
E855.N425 2015
327.73009′047–dc23   2014048694

ISBN 978-1-107-09458-1 Hardback
ISBN 978-1-107-47660-8 Paperback

To Jennifer and our baby, Ava Anne

Contents

Acknowledgments   *page* ix
List of abbreviations   xiii
Key figures   xvii

   Introduction   1
1 A new dimension of NATO   6
2 Closing the gold window   36
3 The European response   68
4 The Year of Europe   103
5 Europe coalesces   125
6 Britain is out   158
7 Britain is in   183
   Conclusion   216

Bibliography   221
Index   231

The colour plates are to be found between pages 124 and 125.

Acknowledgments

The inspiration for this work is Thomas A. Schwartz's *Lyndon Johnson and Europe*. After reading it, I emailed Schwartz to say that while I came away convinced there are compelling reasons to pay attention to LBJ's European policy in the midst of traditionally more important initiatives such as Vietnam and the Great Society, wouldn't that argument be even more applicable to the Nixon years? He replied that there certainly would be merit for such a study, and he has been an extremely valuable sounding board and source of wisdom ever since.

It was this work that began an unexpected journey with the Nixon tapes that has continued to this day. A decade ago, I discovered that no tapes related to U.S.–European relations had been transcribed or published, so it was essential that I include them. It was a difficult experience obtaining accurate copies of the tapes and the essential ancillaries like the tape logs, time codes, and finding aids, none of which was easy to find. The only way to do such thorough research on the tapes was to visit the National Archives in person in College Park, Maryland. After the time and expense of that experience(s), I made a promise to myself to do something about it when I had the chance. There had to be an easier way.

Starting http://nixontapes.org in 2007 in order to make the complete digitized tapes freely available to anyone in the world was an important step in that direction. More recently, publishing volumes of Nixon tape transcripts with Doug Brinkley has been a way to keep this public service going for many more years. It was a real joy to work with Doug on two volumes of edited Nixon tape transcripts – the first covering 1971–72, and the second on 1973. Doug needed no convincing when it came to the importance of getting these valuable primary sources into the hands of scholars and the public. Without them, a complete discussion of Richard Nixon's presidency is not possible.

I would like to thank those who have read, commented on, or assisted in some way with various portions of the manuscript. Doug Forsyth offered valuable feedback throughout, even when I did not know I needed it. Others who lent me their ears and their time include Doug Brinkley, Irv Gellman, John Gillingham, Gary Hess, Michael McGandy, Rick Moss, Ted Rippey, and Marc Trachtenberg. I must also thank the Nixon-era figures with whom it has been a pleasure to interact in some way during the preparation of this manuscript. They each helped me to gain a better understanding, from their perspectives, of the actions and decisions taken and that are described in this manuscript: Dick Allen, Pat Buchanan, Chuck Colson, Frank Gannon, Steve Hess, Henry Kissinger, Sven Kraemer, Fred Malek, Liz Moynihan, Ray Price, Donald Rumsfeld, Bill Safire, Geoff Shepard, Hal and Marjorie Sonnenfeldt, and Ron Walker.

Thanks are also due to the many helpful archivists who have assisted me along the way. A number of them have moved on from these positions, but it was in these roles that they helped me on this manuscript: Joceline Collonval of the European Commission; Anne-Marie Smith, Johannes Geurts, and staff at NATO; Bruno Galland and staff at the Archives Nationales in Paris; Benjamin Palermiti and staff at the Council of Europe; Knud Piening and staff of the Politisches Archiv des Auswärtigen Amts in Berlin; Agnès Brouet and staff at the Archives of the European Union in Florence; Bruno Derrick, Adrian Jobson, and staff at the British National Archives; Karen Jania and staff of the Bentley Historical Library in Ann Arbor; John Earl Haynes and staff of the Library of Congress Manuscript Division; numerous archivists at the Richard Nixon Presidential Materials Project (later the Richard Nixon Presidential Library), including Greg Cumming, Jennifer Evans, Jon Fletcher, Sahr Conway Lanz, Cary McStay, David R. Sabo, John Powers, Sam Rushay, Allen Rice, and Steve Greene; Stephen Plotkin and staff at the John F. Kennedy Presidential Library; Regina Greenwell, Laura Eggert, Charlaine McCauley, and staff at the Lyndon B. Johnson Presidential Library; Geir Gunderson, Donna Lehman, William McNitt, and staff at the Gerald R. Ford Presidential Library; and Brett Stolle of the Research Division of the National Museum of the U.S. Air Force in Dayton. They are all dedicated professionals, and without their extensive assistance this project would have never got off the ground. The accumulated months I have spent in reading rooms have taught me that befriending archivists may be the single most important act of diplomacy involved in any successful research project.

Finally, I would like to express my appreciation to Lew Bateman and Shaun Vigil at Cambridge University Press. Lew is the best in the business, and it was a pleasure to work with him and his team. In addition, three anonymous readers each offered valuable suggestions that helped to strengthen the manuscript. Many of their good ideas can be found on these pages, whereas all omissions or oversights are mine alone.

Abbreviations

AAPD	Akten zur Auswärtigen Politik der Bundesrepublik Deutschland
ABM	Antiballistic missile
AFB	Papers of Arthur F. Burns
AN	Archives Nationale
backchannel	A method to communicate with a foreign power that bypasses the bureaucracy of a nation
BMS	Papers of Bromley M. Smith
Bundesbank	FRG Central Bank
CAB	Cabinet Room Files
CAP	Common Agricultural Policy
CCMS	Committee on the Challenges of Modern Society
CDU	Christian Democratic Union (West German political party)
CFPF	Central Foreign Policy File
CIA	Central Intelligence Agency
CIEP	Council on International Economic Policy
COE	Council of Europe Archives
COMECON	Council for Mutual Economic Assistance
DI	Directorate of Intelligence
DNSA	Digital National Security Archive
EC	European Community
EEC	European Economic Community
EG	Papers of Emanuele Gazzo
EOB	Executive Office Building
FCO	Foreign and Commonwealth Office

FRELOC	Relocation of NATO forces from French territory following French withdrawal from NATO's integrated command structure
FRG	Federal Republic of Germany (West Germany)
FRUS	*Foreign Relations of the United States*
GATT	General Agreement on Tariffs and Trade
GRF	Gerald R. Ford Presidential Library
HAEU	Historical Archives of the European Union
Herter Committee	Committee led by Christian Herter whose recommendations led to the Marshall Plan
HIA	Hoover Institution Archives
ICBM	Intercontinental ballistic missile
IMF	International Monetary Fund
IMSWM	International Military Staff, Working Memorandum
JCS	Joint Chiefs of Staff
JFK	John F. Kennedy Presidential Library
LBJ	Lyndon B. Johnson Presidential Library
LOC	Library of Congress
MBFR	Mutual and balanced force reductions
MC	Military Committee
Memcons	Memoranda of Conversation
MRL	Papers of Melvin R. Laird
NAC	North Atlantic Council
NARA	National Archives and Records Administration
NATO	North Atlantic Treaty Organization
NIE	National Intelligence Estimate
NPT	Non-Proliferation Treaty
NSA	National Security Adviser
NSC	National Security Council
NSDM	National Security Decision Memorandum
NSF	National Security File
NSSM	National Security Study Memorandum
NTBT	Nuclear Test Ban Treaty
OSD	Office of the Secretary of Defense
OVAL	Oval Office
PAAA	Politische Archiv des Auswärtigen Amts
PREM	Prime Minister's Office Files
PRO	Public Record Office (British National Archives)
Quadriad	Richard Nixon's economic "kitchen cabinet"

Quadripartite Agreement	aka the Berlin Agreement, aka the Four Power Agreement, an agreement among the United States, United Kingdom, France, and the USSR designed to reduce tensions over Berlin
RG	Record Group
RMN	Richard M. Nixon Presidential Library
SACEUR	Supreme Allied Commander, Europe
SALT	Strategic Arms Limitation Talks
SMOF	Staff Member and Office Files
SNIE	Special National Intelligence Estimate
Special Drawing Rights	IMF international reserve asset designed to improve liquidity
SRG	Senior Review Group
Telcon	Telephone Conversation
UN	United Nations
VR	Verbatim Record
Watergate	An umbrella term for a series of scandals that resulted in the resignation of Richard Nixon on August 9, 1974; the location of a break-in at the headquarters of the Democratic National Committee on June 17, 1972
WHCF	White House Central Files
WHT	White House Telephone
ZA	Zwischenarchiv (at PAAA)

Key figures

Acheson, Dean	Former Secretary of State
Agnew, Spiro	Vice President of the United States
Andersen, Knud	Danish Foreign Minister
Annenberg, Walter	U.S. Ambassador to the United Kingdom
Bahr, Egon	State Secretary, FRG Chancellor's Office
Barber, Anthony	British Chancellor of the Exchequer
Barzel, Rainer	FRG CDU Chairman
Bergsten, Fred	National Security Council Staff
Brandt, Willy	FRG Foreign Minister; Chancellor
Brezhnev, Leonid	USSR Communist Party General Secretary
Brosio, Manlio	Secretary General of NATO
Bundy, McGeorge	Former Assistant to the President for National Security Affairs
Burns, Arthur	Chairman of the Federal Reserve Board
Callaghan, James	British Foreign Secretary
Carrington, Peter	British Defense Minister
Chaban-Delmas, Jacques	French Prime Minister
Cleveland, Harlan	U.S. Permanent Representative to NATO
Clifford, Clark	Secretary of Defense
Colson, Charles	Special Counsel to the President
Connally, John	Secretary of the Treasury
Coombs, Charles	Federal Reserve Board official
Couve de Murville, Maurice	French Prime Minster
Cromer, Earl of	British Ambassador to the U.S.
Daane, J. Dewey	Federal Reserve Board official
Davis, Jeanne	Executive Secretary, NSC
Debré, Michel	French Defense Minister
De Gaulle, Charles	French President

Dobrynin, Anatoly	USSR Ambassador to the U.S.
Douglas-Home, Alec	British Foreign Secretary
Ehrlichman, John	Assistant to the President for Domestic Affairs
Eliot, Theodore	Executive Secretary, State Department
Ellsworth, Robert	U.S. Permanent Representative to NATO
Emminger, Otmar	Deputy Director, Bundesbank
Erhard, Ludwig	Former FRG Chancellor
Finch, Robert	Counselor to the President
Flanigan, Peter	Assistant to the President
Foster, John	Director, Office of Defense Research and Engineering, Defense Department
Ford, Gerald	President of the United States
Fourquet, Michel	Chief of Staff, French Armed Forces
Friedman, Milton	Economist; informal presidential advisor
Giscard d'Estaing, Valéry	French Minister of Finance and Economic Affairs
Goodpaster, Andrew	Supreme Allied Commander, Europe
Gromyko, Andrei	Soviet Foreign Minister
Haig, Alexander	Deputy Assistant to the President for National Security Affairs
Haldeman, H. R. "Bob"	Assistant to the President
Harmel, Pierre	Belgian Foreign Minister
Heath, Edward	British Prime Minister
Helms, Richard	Director of Central Intelligence
Hillenbrand, Martin	Assistant Secretary of State for European Affairs
Humphrey, Hubert	Former Vice President of the United States; U.S. Senator (D-Minnesota)
Irwin, John	Deputy Secretary of State
Jackson, Henry "Scoop"	U.S. Senator (D-Washington)
Javits, Jacob	U.S. Senator (R-New York)
Jenkins, Roy	Chancellor of the Exchequer
Jobert, Michel	French Foreign Minister
Johnson, Lyndon	Former President of the United States
Johnson, U. Alexis	Undersecretary of State for Political Affairs
Katzenbach, Nicholas	Former Attorney General
Kennedy, David	Secretary of the Treasury
Kennedy, John F.	Former President of the United States
Kiesinger, Kurt	FRG Chancellor
Kissinger, Henry	Assistant to the President for National Security Affairs

Kosciusko-Morizet, Jacques	French Ambassador to the U.S.
Kosygin, Alexei	Chairman, Soviet Council of Ministers
Laird, Melvin	Defense Secretary
Lemnitzer, Lyman	Former Supreme Allied Commander, NATO
Lodge, Jr., Henry Cabot	Former U.S. Ambassador; former Vice Presidential nominee
Lucet, Charles	French Ambassador to the U.S.
Luns, Joseph	Secretary General of NATO
Malraux, André	French Minister of Cultural Affairs
Mansfield, Michael	U.S. Senator (D-Montana)
McCloy, John	Former U.S. High Commissioner for Germany; informal presidential advisor
McCracken, Paul	Chairman, Council of Economic Advisors
McGovern, George	U.S. Senator (D-South Dakota)
Mitchell, John	Attorney General
Moynihan, Daniel P.	Counselor to the President
Nixon, Richard M.	President of the United States
Nutter, Warren G.	Assistant Secretary of Defense for International Security Affairs
Packard, David	Deputy Secretary of Defense
Pauls, Rolf	FRG Ambassador to the U.S.
Peterson, Peter	Executive Director of the Council for International Economic Policy
Poher, Alain	Interim French President
Pompidou, Georges	French President
Richardson, Elliot	Undersecretary of State; U.S. Ambassador to the United Kingdom
Rogers, William P.	Secretary of State
Rostow, Walt	Former Assistant to the President for National Security Affairs
Rumsfeld, Donald	U.S. Permanent Representative to NATO
Rush, Kenneth	U.S. Ambassador to the FRG; Deputy Secretary of Defense
Samuels, Nathaniel	Deputy Undersecretary of State for Economic Affairs
Sato, Eisaku	Japanese Prime Minister
Scheel, Walter	FRG Foreign Minister
Schiller, Karl	FRG Minister of Economic Affairs; FRG Minister of Finance
Schmidt, Helmut	FRG Defense Minister; FRG Chancellor
Schroeder, Gerhard	FRG Defense Minister

Schumann, Maurice	French Foreign Minister
Schweitzer, Pierre-Paul	Managing Director, International Monetary Fund
Scowcroft, Brent	Deputy Assistant to the President for National Security Affairs
Shriver, Sargent	U.S. Ambassador to France
Shultz, George	Director, Office of Management and Budget; Secretary of the Treasury
Smith, Gerard	Director, Arms Control and Disarmament Agency
Sonnenfeldt, Helmut	National Security Council Staff
Stans, Maurice	Secretary of Commerce
Stein, Herbert	Chairman, Council of Economic Advisors
Strausz-Hupe, Robert	U.S. Ambassador to Belgium; U.S. Permanent Representative to the European Community
Trend, Burke	British Cabinet Secretary
Vance, Cyrus	Former Deputy Secretary of Defense
Volcker, Paul	Undersecretary of the Treasury for Monetary Affairs
Walters, Vernon	Military Attaché at the U.S. Embassy in Paris
Warnke, Paul	Assistant Secretary of Defense for International Security Affairs
Watson, Arthur	U.S. Ambassador to France
Weinberger, Caspar	Deputy Director, Office of Management and Budget
Wilson, Harold	British Prime Minister
Ziegler, Ronald	White House Press Secretary
Zijlstra, Jelle	Dutch Central Banker

Introduction

On January 20, 1969, Richard Nixon's first day as president, U.S.–European relations were at the lowest point they had been at any time since the end of World War II:

- NATO was set to expire in 1969. The North Atlantic Treaty of 1949, its founding document, permitted members to leave after twenty years. While it is safe to say that Atlantic leaders would not have let NATO become obsolete, the situation did not look especially promising. One founding member, France, left NATO's integrated command structure in 1966 and expelled the alliance from French soil. This dramatic move left others to consider whether NATO in an era of détente served the same purpose it did two decades earlier. There were serious doubts, especially after NATO proved unable to agree on a response to the August 1968 Soviet invasion of Czechoslovakia;
- A series of currency crises had plagued transatlantic relations since 1958, when the total number of dollars in circulation eclipsed the amount of gold backing them. This was a major threat to the stability of the Bretton Woods system, which only got worse as the gap grew between dollars in circulation and gold reserves. All that prevented global financial collapse (and a U.S. default) was a continued series of clever American inducements to prevent Europeans from exchanging dollars for gold, a right they had for accumulating U.S. dollars. A day of reckoning neared;
- European integration was stalled. Charles de Gaulle refused British admission to the European Community (EC) twice, blocked procedure

in the European Council of Ministers, and withdrew French forces from NATO's integrated command structure, thus evicting the Western alliance from French soil. The EC teetered on evolving into an anti-NATO, anti-American inward-looking alliance.

Richard Nixon inherited this situation primarily because Lyndon Johnson had spent the bulk of his time and political capital between the Vietnam War and his Great Society initiatives. Nixon made it an early priority of his presidency to redress the situation. Transatlantic relations were one of the few issues other than Vietnam, China, and the Soviet Union handled personally by President Nixon and Henry Kissinger. Both men had long experience with Europe, going back to the Marshall Plan, the founding of NATO, and American support of the European integration movement. They believed in maintaining strong ties with traditional American allies, especially at the beginning of Nixon's presidency, when it was important to show that he would not be obsessed with the Vietnam War. Nixon was eager to demonstrate that the United States could be a force for peace and constructive activity again and that not all of the nation's creativity and imagination had been sapped by the trauma of Vietnam (an average of 200 American soldiers died per week in Vietnam during the second half of 1968). Thirty days into his presidency, Nixon made a tour of West European capitals on this basis and to plan an American foreign policy that – in the future – would not be based around a war in Southeast Asia.

Nixon first publicly provided his vision of a post-Vietnam world in his influential *Foreign Affairs* article "Asia after Vietnam," published in October 1967, more than a year before he reached the White House and even before he was an official candidate for the nation's highest office. Although many observers immediately picked up on a more flexible tone in the article toward the People's Republic of China, he also hinted at the changing nature of the transatlantic relationship. "During the final third of the twentieth century, Asia, not Europe or Latin America, will pose the greatest danger of a confrontation which could escalate into World War III." Nixon signaled that the transatlantic relationship, which had been based on two decades of American assistance and European reconstruction and integration would enter a new phase. The phase was based on an assumption that the United States would soon enjoy a more peaceful era with the Soviet Union, a key feature of the coming détente era.

President Nixon articulated this view further in Guam on July 25, 1969. In an informal session with reporters dealing with questions mainly about Vietnam and China, Nixon made some important revelations about the way he saw the world and how he intended to govern. These remarks, which became known as the Nixon Doctrine, were not limited to simply the way he saw American Pacific interests.[1] They represented the first major revision to the Truman Doctrine in nearly a quarter century: the United States was no longer willing to mobilize forces anywhere to defend against any aggression. The simplicity in his language suggests that the Nixon Doctrine was indeed meant to have application beyond Vietnam. When Nixon said "we, of course, will keep the treaty commitments that we have," and "we should assist, but we should not dictate," he foreshadowed a new phase in transatlantic relations in which Europeans would be expected to take on more responsibility in the areas of their own defense, monetary and economic affairs, and political development. Future American commitments would be appropriated on a more realistic scale commensurate with a new era of reduced Cold War tensions.

Some have said that Nixon had no grand strategy and that the Nixon Doctrine was never intended to be applied universally. These same critics say that his remarks at Guam were intended mainly as a vehicle to articulate his policy of Vietnamization. These are obvious conclusions if one limits one's view of Nixon foreign policy to Vietnam, China, and the Soviet Union. However, to test whether the Nixon Doctrine had application beyond Asia, we can see whether or not the concepts of the Nixon Doctrine were applied to other areas of foreign policy, such as transatlantic relations.

This work is not about every issue that transpired in U.S.–European relations during Nixon's five-and-a-half year presidency. It is, however, about how, under Nixon's watch, the United States' most important alliance evolved during a turbulent period of the Cold War and how the vision of foreign policy provided by Nixon in his *Foreign Affairs* article and Guam remarks played out in terms of policy. In each of the five key facets of transatlantic relations explored in this study – the future of NATO, the collapse of Bretton Woods, the Year of Europe, American

---

[1] Some scholars, such as Jeffrey Kimball, have argued the opposite. See Jeffrey Kimball, "The Nixon Doctrine: A Saga of Misunderstanding." *Presidential Studies Quarterly*, Vol. 36, No. 1 (March 2006): 59–74. Kimball's article was written before the National Archives released Nixon tapes and other records that document how Nixon believed the Nixon Doctrine had application not only to U.S. policy toward Europe, but to other parts of the non-Vietnam world as well. In recent years, a new wave of scholarship is willing to concede more to the idea of a Nixon-Kissinger grand strategy, which "achieved much." For example, see Dan Caldwell, "The Legitimation of the Nixon-Kissinger Grand Design and Grand Strategy." *Diplomatic History* 33:4 (September 2009): 633–652.

support for European integration, and the Anglo-American "special relationship" – Nixon demonstrated a vision, one that was carried out by Henry Kissinger. To show the importance that Nixon ascribed to these issues, they were among the handful of issues – in addition to Vietnam, China, and the Soviet Union – that he and Kissinger handled personally.

In each of these areas of transatlantic relations, Nixon made his mark with a bold new initiative, guided by the principles of the Nixon Doctrine. He made this clear to European leaders a month into his presidency, long before his Guam remarks, and also during his April 1969 address on the twentieth anniversary of NATO:

- After a period of neglect during the 1960s, Nixon came to power and prioritized the strengthening of the NATO alliance. Although formally reintegrating France was not possible, he established bilateral defense ties with France and repaired political relations with Charles de Gaulle. Nixon shifted NATO's purpose from collective defense to collective security with the establishment of the détente era Committee on the Challenges of Modern Society, which remains an important pillar in NATO's structure to this day;
- Nixon was the first president with the boldness to say (and act on it) that the United States should no longer shoulder the financial burden of Europe's monetary system, especially since many European countries had rebuilt to the point of being commercial competitors of the United States by the time of his presidency. As a result of Nixon's direct involvement, the Bretton Woods system and the gold standard were ended, which resulted in the birth of the modern age of globalization;
- In his proposed Year of Europe, Nixon called for a fresh commitment to work toward a strong transatlantic relationship rooted in an American relationship with both NATO and the EC. His guide was the 1941 Atlantic Charter, a statement of democratic principles drafted by Winston Churchill and Franklin D. Roosevelt that served as a blueprint for the postwar world. Nixon wanted the EC to become more outward looking at a time of inward development and expansion. He believed that Europe should play a bigger role in the world, but it should not develop in an anti-American direction;
- Addressing the Anglo-American "special relationship," Nixon believed that Britain was stronger in Europe than out, a key revision of America's closest alliance. He also believed the EC was stronger with Britain as a member due to Britain's longer engagement with the world

than other Europeans. Nixon laid out the vision and then, following his resignation, Henry Kissinger continued his policy under President Ford, ensuring that Britain remained tethered to both the EC and the United States, but especially Europe.

Despite Nixon's better known breakthroughs with adversaries, transatlantic relations were transformed in each of these categories. Although Nixon was not always eloquent and sometimes was guilty of being distracted, rarely does a new presidential administration come to power with such convictions about such a large part of the world. This transformation in transatlantic relations took place according to the principles of the Nixon Doctrine, and Richard Nixon immediately set a new tone in terms of foreign policy during the early days of his presidency.

The structure of negotiations that Nixon and Kissinger used, established as effective with adversaries, did not always work well with allies. Too many times, Nixon and Kissinger saw more exciting opportunities with China or the Soviet Union, and Europe was pushed aside. Because they – and their immediate deputies – handled European issues personally, this resulted in lost opportunities in cases where the State Department and other parts of the civil service could have been better utilized. Many were quick to mark détente as a failed experiment, but, at least in terms of transatlantic relations, the failure was far more often in implementation or execution than in a fault in the original idea. Still, by the mid-1970s, the efforts depicted here resulted in a new era of diplomacy with Europe, one that would not have been possible without the thinking of Richard Nixon and Henry Kissinger.

A new dimension of NATO

"For 20 years, our nations have provided for the military defense of Western Europe. For 20 years we have held political consultations. Now the alliance of the West needs a third dimension."[1] Speaking on NATO's twentieth anniversary, on April 10, 1969, President Nixon challenged Western leaders to give fresh meaning to the defense alliance. Analysts on both sides of the Atlantic wondered whether NATO still had a purpose. One founding member, France, had already left the military alliance's integrated command structure. Statements by leaders of Norway and Sweden added doubt in the minds of others as to the whether a defense alliance was still needed in the détente era.

Nixon shifted NATO's role from collective defense to collective security. "It needs not only a strong military dimension to provide for the common defense, and not only a more profound political dimension to shape a strategy of peace, but it also needs a social dimension to deal with our concern for the quality of life in this last third of the 20th century."[2] To the foreign policy establishment, it was a radical idea that international relations could benefit from a lesson in social or environmental policy. Less than three months in office, Nixon's own centerpiece domestic policies were still largely unveiled, whether concerning the environment (Environmental Protection Agency, Earth

[1] The full text of Nixon's address can be found at Richard Nixon, "Address at the Commemorative Session of the North Atlantic Council," April 10, 1969. Online by Gerhard Peters and John T. Woolley, *The American Presidency Project*. Available from http://www.presidency.ucsb.edu/ws/?pid=1992.
[2] RMN, White House Special Files, President's Personal File, Box 47, "RN's COPY: COMMEMORATIVE SESSION OF THE ATLANTIC COUNCIL, 4/10/69."

Day, Endangered Species Act, Mammal Marine Protection Act), human health and disease (the War on Cancer, Clean Air Act, Clean Water Act), or societal integration (desegregation of southern schools, extending the right to vote to eighteen- to twenty-year-olds with the signing of the Twenty-sixth Amendment, the Equal Protection Amendment, Title IX and preventing gender bias, returning sacred homelands to Native Americans).

Some have rightly questioned whether some of these achievements occurred simply because of a Democratic majority in Congress. On the other hand, for Nixon – who knew more about foreign policy than any of his advisors – to suggest they had application in foreign affairs confirms that he not only supported their passage but also sincerely believed they were the right things to do. In Nixon's view, the philosophy behind his expansionary domestic policy was something that all advanced nations could agree on, even those separated by an Iron Curtain. There was an obvious overlap between domestic and foreign policy making. Free or unfree, all societies faced similar challenges, and we could learn from each other.

But, in April 1969, these were radical ideas to many NATO leaders. Nixon spoke these words in the same room at the State Department that his mentor, President Dwight D. Eisenhower, used to address NATO leaders on its tenth anniversary. It was the same room in which the North Atlantic Treaty was signed in 1949 to create the alliance. This was no coincidence. Twenty years later, an era of reduced Cold War tensions was the reason some questioned the need for a defense alliance. Nixon did not just intend to save NATO from this talk; he planned to transform it beyond a defense alliance. That, he felt, was the best way to preserve NATO for another twenty years.

"We in the United States have much to learn from the experiences of our Atlantic allies in their handling of internal matters: for example, the care of infant children in West Germany, the 'new towns' policy of Great Britain, the development of depressed areas programs in Italy, the great skill of the Dutch in dealing with high density areas, the effectiveness of urban planning by local governments in Norway, the experience of the French in metropolitan planning." Nixon's words marked an intentional departure from his predecessors. American presidents have never been very willing to admit that the United States has much to learn from others. Early in his presidency, this new tone was intended to signal a new era in Washington, an era in which long-standing relationships with allies would be strengthened and new relationships with adversaries would be established.

"On my recent trip to Europe, I met with world leaders and private citizens alike. I was struck by the fact that our discussions were not limited to military or political matters. More often than not our talks turned to those matters deeply relevant to our societies – the legitimate unrest of young people, the frustration of the gap between generations, the need for a new sense of idealism and purpose in coping with an automating world." Nixon's first overseas trip to Europe in late February, only a month after his inauguration, was for the purpose of listening. Conversations with Europeans leaders like Charles de Gaulle, Kurt Georg Kiesinger, Willy Brandt, Harold Wilson, Mariano Rumor, and Manlio Brosio filled Nixon's schedule and covered topics like Vietnam, China, détente with the Soviet Union, European integration, NATO, and bilateral relations with each leader's nation. Upon Nixon's return from Europe, a period of analysis of these conservations helped him to set policy priorities for his presidency. He came away from his European trip convinced that U.S.–European relations lacked a forum to discuss problems other than military or political problems. In the United States, Nixon started the Council on Environmental Quality under Russell Train and the Council on Urban Affairs under Daniel Patrick Moynihan. He thought U.S.–European relations needed something similar, but that the discussion should not limited to problems of the environment or urban areas.[3]

"I strongly urge that we create a committee on the challenges of modern society, responsible to the deputy ministers, to explore the ways in which the experience and resources of the Western nations could most effectively be marshaled toward improving the quality of life of our people. That new goal is provided for in Article II of our treaty, but it has never been the center of our concerns." With arms talks beginning soon with the Soviets, Nixon believed NATO needed to be transformed from an alliance structured during the dangerous years of the early Cold War to an alliance that reflected a détente era of reduced superpower tensions. The likelihood of nuclear war with the Soviet Union was lower than at any point in the postwar period. The nature of the challenges and disagreements within the NATO alliance, as well as between the NATO and Warsaw Pact alliances,

---

[3] Stephen Hess, Moynihan's deputy at the Council on Urban Affairs, proposed for NATO a "Trans-Atlantic Council on Environmental Quality and Urban Affairs." Moynihan approved and sent the recommendation to the president. The name changed several times in the course of speechwriter Ray Price's preparation of Nixon's April 1969 address to NATO, but the concept did not. For more information, see Stephen Hess, *The Professor and the President: Daniel Patrick Moynihan in the Nixon White House* (Washington, D.C.: Brookings Institution Press, 2014).

had evolved. NATO could not be reformed without U.S. leadership, and key allies like France could not be brought back into the Western alliance without being backed by a new era of transatlantic relations and a new tone from Washington.

*** *

When Richard Nixon arrived at the White House in January 1969, he found an Atlantic alliance that had been splintered by the withdrawal of France and humiliated after disagreements among Western leaders prevented NATO from coordinating a response to the Soviet invasion of Czechoslovakia in August 1968. There were serious doubts whether the defense alliance would be renewed beyond its original twenty-year mandate, set to expire in April 1969. Nixon believed that, after the invasion of Czechoslovakia, the Soviet Union desired an improvement in relations with the West in general and the United States in particular. In a top secret report drawn up during the opening hours of the Nixon administration, the Pentagon concluded that the most that should be expected out of the Soviets in the future would be a "nonnuclear attack with limited mobilization."[4] The report also suggested that arms limitations discussions between the United States and the Soviet Union should be revived following the aborted effort by Lyndon Johnson at the Glassboro Summit a year earlier. NATO's role in arms talks should be as an "ancillary and reinforcing forum for consultation, recognizing its limitation." The Nixon administration intended to pursue high-level talks on a bilateral basis but promised European allies that adequate consultation would take place.

Nixon concluded during his 1968 presidential campaign that U.S.–European relations had outgrown the North Atlantic Treaty of 1949.[5] The founding document of NATO permitted members to voluntarily leave after twenty years of membership. France began its departure in 1966, and other members also considered the future of the alliance and their roles in it. The Harmel Report of 1967, a study on "The Future Tasks of the Alliance" commissioned following the French decision to withdraw, proposed several modifications to NATO. These included taking on a greater political role and reshaping NATO beyond simply a defense alliance. However, lack of coordination among Western leaders following the Soviet invasion of Czechoslovakia demonstrated that agreement was lacking on NATO's

---

[4] DNSA, Memorandum from Department of Defense to President Nixon, "Response to National Security Study Memorandum #9, Review of the International Situation as of January 20, 1969, Volume III, Western Europe."

[5] Hoover Institution Archives, Richard M. Nixon Notes, Box 1, Page 3.

future or on the recommendations made in the study directed by former
Belgian Prime Minister Pierre Harmel. West Germany's *Ostpolitik* ambitions were halted.[6] French President Charles de Gaulle expressed doubt
about the role of the United States and NATO leadership.[7] Henry
Kissinger, not yet in government, again called for NATO reform. "In its
first decade and a half, NATO was a dynamic and creative institution.
Today, however, NATO is in disarray as well. Action by the United
States – above all, frequent unilateral changes of policy – are partially
responsible."[8]

At the core of this discussion was a debate within the West over the
reliability of the doctrine of "flexible response," which was NATO's
guiding strategy up to the Nixon presidency. NATO had successfully
prevented a nuclear conflict in Europe, in part, according to the CIA,
because ideology in the Soviet Union was "dead."[9] However, as the
invasion of Czechoslovakia illustrated, a threat of a different kind
remained. Faced with increasingly asymmetric threats, NATO formally
adopted "flexible response" on May 9, 1967:

The Alliance should possess adequate conventional forces, land, sea, and air, many
of which are supported by tactical nuclear weapons. They should be designed to
deter and successfully counter to the greatest extent possible a limited non-nuclear
attack and to deter any larger non-nuclear attack by confronting the aggressor
with the prospect of non-nuclear hostilities on a scale that could involve a grave
risk of escalation to nuclear war.[10]

The adoption of flexible response was not an entirely new concept.[11]
A decade earlier, Harvard professor Henry Kissinger argued for a new
strategic doctrine that would permit NATO to exact extensive but
controllable damage on the Warsaw Pact in his 1957 book *Nuclear
Weapons and Foreign Policy.*[12] A new strategy was needed, he said,

---

[6] James Chance, "The Concert of Europe," *Foreign Affairs* 52 (October 1973): 96–108.
[7] Harlan Cleveland, *NATO: The Transatlantic Bargain* (New York: Harper & Row
Publishers, 1970), 101.
[8] Henry A. Kissinger, *American Foreign Policy: Three Essays by Henry A. Kissinger* (New
York: W. W. Norton & Company, Inc., 1969), 67.
[9] CIA. DI. "Basic Factors and Main Tendencies in Current Soviet Policy." *NIE* 11–69.
February 27, 1969.
[10] NATO, MC, IMSWM-270-68, September 26, 1968, "Memorandum for the Members of
the Military Committee."
[11] Stanley Sloan, *NATO's Future: Toward a New Transatlantic Bargain* (Washington,
D.C.: National Defense University Press, 1985), 44.
[12] Jeremi Suri, Henry Kissinger and the American Century (Cambridge: Harvard University
Press, 2007), 153.

because strategic nuclear weapons were not an effective deterrent if they represented no conceivable military utility.[13] Combining this idea with a reliance on a strong conventional capability, flexible response enabled NATO to prepare for a variety of threats based on the assumption that the primary threat was no longer a nuclear attack. With Richard Nixon agreeing to begin arms talks with the Soviet Union, what role would NATO have, and what strategy would guide it?

On Richard Nixon's 1969 tour of Western Europe, his first stop was NATO headquarters, where he stated that he intended to "reaffirm America's commitment to partnership with Europe."[14] The purpose was both symbolic and substantive: symbolic in that it honored two decades of the transatlantic alliance and substantive for both allies and adversaries in that the new Nixon administration would place a greater importance on that part of the world. Nixon claimed that past American leaders failed to consult adequately with Europe, particularly on NATO and defense matters. "In Europe, NATO is in a state of malaise, accentuated by our shifting policies over the last 10 years," National Security Advisor Henry Kissinger briefed President Nixon.[15]

At NATO, Nixon said that "the era of confrontation" between superpowers was over and that an "era of negotiations" would begin. He repeatedly stressed that the themes of his trip were "cooperation, consultation, and coordination."[16] Nixon also believed that it was time for Europe to bear a greater share of its defense burdens, a key tenet of what would become known as the Nixon Doctrine. By the late 1960s, the United States was paying twice as much on defense as a percentage of its gross national product (GNP) than Europe: 7 percent versus 3.5 percent, respectively.[17] "From the economic and military standpoint we should take a stronger stand on the Europeans carrying a fair share of the load," Kenneth Rush recalled later. "We're in a bad way both in trade and balance of payments. If the Europeans won't take on their share of the

---

[13] On the one hand, the United States built ever larger, ever more expensive, and ever more powerful thermonuclear weapons. On the other hand, foreign policy was formulated to ensure they would never be used. See Henry A. Kissinger, *Nuclear Weapons and Foreign Policy* (New York: Council on Foreign Relations, 1957).

[14] *Nixon: The Second Year of His Presidency* (Washington, D.C.: Congressional Quarterly, Inc., 1971), 58a.

[15] *FRUS*, 1969–1976, Volume I, 39.

[16] *AAPD* 1969, 40; Botschafter Pauls, Washington, an das Auswaertige Amt, "Ueberreichung meines Beglaubigungsschreibens," January 31, 1969.

[17] Richard Nixon, *1999: Victory without War* (New York: Simon and Schuster, 1988), 203–204.

load, they're damn poor partners."[18] Congress and the American public
were becoming more isolationist as a result of Vietnam, causing domestic
pressures to reduce the American commitment to a Europe seen as stable,
peaceful, and, increasingly, a commercial competitor.

President Nixon took the debate over flexible response and the future
of the alliance out of NATO and away from Europeans altogether. Henry
Kissinger's writings in the days following Nixon's European tour illumi-
nated the rationale. "We have not had strong pressure from the Europeans
to increase the size of our strategic forces, and the Europeans have not
opposed our efforts to enter negotiations with the Soviets on limiting
strategic missile systems."[19] Nixon moved such discussions of strategic
doctrine, nuclear weapons, and international security out of multilateral
channels and into bilateral channels. Europeans should be expected to
contribute to discussions of the use of "soft power"; discussions related to
the use of hard power would be left to the United States. Europeans were
also expected to do more for their own defense. "Our position in a nut-
shell is this ... it is essential for Europeans, therefore, to improve their
capabilities," Nixon repeated.[20]

Events leading up to the April 1969 NATO summit in Washington
dealt President Nixon an opportunity to make a major policy address
about the future of the alliance. Sino-Soviet hostilities along the Ussuri
River in March 1969 demonstrated the escalation in tensions that had
developed between the two former communist allies and presented an
opportunity to exploit. At the same time, Nixon announced that he had
decided to ratify the previously dormant Non-Proliferation Treaty (NPT)
as a conciliatory gesture toward the Soviets, removing an obstacle to
starting arms limitation talks.[21] Once Nixon signaled that he expected
those talks to begin in the spring of 1969, some Europeans questioned
whether the United States privileged relations with adversaries over those
with allies. "Although we ... consult with our allies, we should not permit
them to have a veto on our actions provided we ourselves are convinced
they are consistent with allied interests," Nixon said at a National

[18] *FRUS*, 1969–1976, Volume E-15, Part 2, 5.
[19] DNSA, Memorandum from Henry Kissinger to the Secretary of Defense, "Technical Issues Concerning U.S. Strategic Forces," February 3, 1969.
[20] RMN, NSC, Box 1024, Memorandum of Conversation between Prime Minister Heath and President Nixon, December 17, 1970.
[21] DNSA, Memorandum from Henry Kissinger to the Vice President; the Secretary of State; the Secretary of Defense; the Director, Arms Control and Disarmament Agency; and the Chairman, Atomic Energy Commission, "Presidential Decision to Ratify Non-Proliferation Treaty," February 5, 1969.

Security Council meeting held just days before the start of his European tour.[22] The ideological basis that drove this new policy orientation toward NATO later became known as the Nixon Doctrine.

Not everyone agreed with Nixon's proposal to create a committee on the challenges of modern society that he presented in his April 1969 address to NATO. "The president clearly wanted to make the occasion memorable ... the idea that NATO suffered from a deep crisis persisted in the White House," one skeptic remembered.[23] Part of the problem was how the new committee would be named, since it was not clear which part of NATO's military structure would be responsible for Nixon's nonmilitary charge. In addition to Stephen Hess's original proposal, speechwriter Bill Safire proposed a "Council on Modern Life," which Nixon also liked.[24] Henry Kissinger did not approve, so Safire suggested alternate names, including the "Council on the Quality of Life" and the "Council on Social Progress." Nixon formalized the name in National Security Study Memorandum (NSSM) 43, dated April 15, 1969. He called for the "creation of a committee on the challenges of modern society responsible to the [NATO] Deputy Ministers."[25] On November 6, the North Atlantic Council created the "Committee on the Challenges of Modern Society."[26]

The reception to Nixon's proposal was not entirely enthusiastic on either side of the Atlantic. "Expressions of displeasure from the Organization for Economic Cooperation and Development (OECD) in Paris quickly crossed the Atlantic," one observer noted.[27] Many Europeans believed the CCMS would duplicate work being done by other bodies, whether OECD, the Council of Europe, the European Economic Community (EEC), the UN Economic Commission for Europe (ECE), or the new UN Environmental Program (UNEP). The United Kingdom, the closest American ally, was

---

[22] DNSA, Memorandum from Richard N. Moore to Office of Vice President, Office of Secretary of State, Office of the Secretary of Defense, and the Office of the Director, OEP, "NSC Meeting, February 19," February 18, 1969.

[23] Martin J. Hillenbrand. *Fragments of Our Time: Memoirs of a Diplomat* (Athens: University of Georgia Press, 1998), 274.

[24] LOC, Papers of Bill Safire, Box 22, note from April 9, 1969.

[25] Although the CCMS remains an operational NATO committee today, to date, there has been almost no scholarly attention paid to this influential component of the alliance. This gap in the historiography persists because, even as of this writing, the vast majority of records related to the committee's work remain closed to researchers, both at NATO Headquarters and at archives in the United States.

[26] See "NATO Joins the Fights to Save Environment," *New York Times*, November 7, 1969, p. 3.

[27] Hillenbrand, 275.

privately hostile to the idea of a CCMS and risked an open division with the
United States over the matter. NATO Secretary-General Brosio defended
Nixon's proposal and defended its link to NATO's mission. "The aims
of the Committee were seen in the light of Article 2 in the Atlantic Charter
and its setting up as an expression of the notion that security depends
as much on the vitality of the societies united in the Alliance as on the
strength of their armies," Brosio decided.[28] He concluded that there was
sufficient support for Nixon's proposal to merit moving forward with
implementation. A NATO press release reinforced his finding. Member
states, "conscious that they share common environmental problems ...
instructed the [North Atlantic] Council to examine how to improve in
every practical way the exchange of views and experience among the allied
countries in the task of creating a better environment for their societies."[29]

The first gathering of the CCMS was held on December 8–10, 1969, in
the presence of the international press. Pat Moynihan worked for eight
months since Nixon's April announcement to make sure the first meeting
would be a success. "The sessions were lively, friendly, and intelligent,"
Moynihan reported to Nixon.[30] NATO Secretary-General Manlio Brosio
served as chair, encouraging each member nation to propose and carry out
a study related to the committee's charge. The United States proposed
studies including "Disaster Assistance Program," "Road Safety," and
"Air Pollution." Belgium proposed "Open Waters Pollution." Canada
contributed "Inland Waters Pollution." Germany, a strong supporter
from the outset, proposed "The Transmission of Scientific Knowledge
into the Decision-Making Process," and the United Kingdom begrud-
gingly came up with "Individual and Group Motivations in a Modern
Industrial Society – with the Emphasis on Individual Fulfillment." The
purpose of these studies was to stimulate governments to take coordinated
action in these areas.[31] The U.S. Information Office claimed the CCMS as
a triumph of Nixon foreign policy. "The North Atlantic Alliance yesterday took another step to stimulate action by governments to clean up
man's environment ... the Council has now given the 'all clear' for
research by member countries into road safety, disaster assistance, air

---

[28] PRO, FCO 55–408, "Report by the Committee on the Challenges of Modern Society to
the North Atlantic Council, Report by the Chairman," January 15, 1970.

[29] PRO, FCO 55–408, "NATO Press Release (70)1, Challenges of Modern Society,"
January 28, 1970.

[30] LOC, Papers of Steve Hess, Memorandum from Pat Moynihan to Richard Nixon,
December 15, 1969.

[31] PRO, FCO 55–408, "NATO Committee on the Challenges of Modern Society,
Background," January 14, 1970.

pollution and open and inland water pollution."[32] Not all member nations took an active role at first, as Moynihan reported to Nixon, but "toward the end there was a general sense that something might really be happening here: so much so that those who came empty handed seemed almost to regret their judgment that it would not work and was not worth wasting time on."[33]

The reaction of some Europeans, most prominently the British but also others like those from Norway and Sweden, was that they were completely caught off guard by Nixon's CCMS proposal. Although it is true that the environment and urban development did not typically feature prominently in American Cold War foreign policy, both domestic and international observers should not have missed the emphasis Nixon placed on these issues early in his presidency. He established the Council of Environmental Quality (CEQ), the Office of Environmental Protection (later the Environmental Protection Agency), and the National Oceanic Atmospheric Administration (NOAA) in the Department of Commerce. That he would desire to add an international dimension to these efforts through the creation of the CCMS in NATO should not have been a great surprise. That he did so for so little political gain – or even at a political cost – was the surprising aspect, which demonstrated that his belief in environmental protection transcended politics.

From the start, the British government, especially the working level of the Foreign and Commonwealth Office (FCO), was unhappy with the CCMS. The FCO was unimpressed with European prostrations designed to display support for the American initiative. After the first meeting of the CCMS in December 1969, as well as Brosio's obvious support for the idea, the British knew they were on the wrong side of the issue. After Daniel Patrick Moynihan was selected to represent the United States on the CCMS, other NATO members would have no choice but to assign at least a junior minister in order to be respectful. Moynihan, a Harvard professor and intellectual in residence in the Nixon White House, was no typical presidential sycophant. With minimal staff and resources, little to no support from the State Department – which was concerned not with making sure Nixon's CCMS proposal succeeded but that, if it failed, it did not cause a loss of face for the United States – Moynihan was the brains behind the proposal. His ability to channel and bring to bear his boundless

---

[32] PRO, FCO 55–408, "United States Information Office, Atlantic Council Takes Anti-Pollution Stance," January 29, 1970.

[33] LOC, Papers of Steve Hess, Memorandum from Pat Moynihan to Richard Nixon, December 15, 1969.

creativity in establishing a face for Nixon's CCMS in only eight months, between April and December 1969, demonstrated why he was the perfect man for the job.

"I am often asked why NATO has decided to concern itself with questions which seem more properly to belong to other bodies, for example the United Nations or OECD," said Gunnar Randers, Assistant Secretary-General for NATO's Scientific Affairs Division. In response, Nixon advisor Moynihan gave the same justification as Edmund Hillary upon being asked why he endeavored to climb Mount Everest: "There are any number of complex and subtle secondary answers to this query, but the primary answer could not be more direct: because NATO is there." Moynihan, the most liberal among Nixon's top advisers, continued: "Our opportunities are twofold. First we can envisage a kind of trade springing up among the Allies. The law of comparative advantage can come into effect: as one nation learns better to cope with this problem, another with that, these abilities can be exchanged to the benefit of both."[34] The establishment of the CCMS as a permanent part of NATO's structure marked a formal entrance of the alliance into the détente era. With American allies questioning the need to continue a defense alliance, the CCMS was a new approach to bind Western nations together and preserve NATO. As military cooperation expanded to include political cooperation, now the environment and social policy offered new realms for cooperation and partnership both among Western nations and between the East and West.

Whereas the British hoped the CCMS would never get off the ground, Moynihan came away from the first meeting with greater support, especially from Germany. More than any other nation, Germany took the project seriously, and it sent a high-level delegation led by Ralf Dahrendorf, the second-in-command in foreign affairs. Dahrendorf even met privately with Moynihan following the first meeting of the CCMS and stated that Willy Brandt believed that it could be "a major instrument for developing a North Atlantic polity, and also for building East-West bridges."[35] The French also agreed to take part in the CCMS – just as Nixon hoped they could be gradually engaged – despite opting out of NATO's military structure.[36] However, the French were apologetic when

[34] PRO, FCO 55–409, "Committee on the Challenges of Modern Society," NATO Newsletter, January 1970.
[35] LOC, Papers of Steve Hess, Memorandum from Pat Moynihan to Richard Nixon, December 15, 1969.
[36] PRO, FCO 55–408, Telegram from UK Delegation NATO to FCO, "C.C.M.S.," January 28, 1970.

they, in effect, sent no serious government figure to discuss the issue, especially in light of the high-level German delegation.

"It is quite clear that, whatever the skepticism of some member countries, the CCMS has got off to a flying start," admitted one British official, "thanks to a veritable invasion from the United States."[37] Germany also played an important role. "In sum, the German attitude transformed an American initiative into a NATO undertaking," Moynihan reported.[38] According to one NATO diplomat, the position of Richard Nixon was simple. Many of the social problems facing advanced industrial societies were self-inflicted. These same nations were the ones that had the resources to address such global problems, and a forum like NATO was the only one extant in which the United States and European nations could cooperate and in which there existed a twenty-year history of cooperation. Although not spoken by the British and never hinted at by the United States, one could conclude that part of the concern of CCMS skeptics was that it was secretly an American attempt to weaken the European Economic Community and other international organizations in which – unlike NATO – there was no dependence on the United States. In this view, ensuring that nonmilitary problems were dealt with in a forum within NATO was another example of American "empire by integration."[39]

"Did CCMS work, and does it still? Absolutely," NATO diplomat Alan Berlind observed.[40] "In the course of the first two years alone, substantive meetings took place in Venice (flood hazard mitigation), San Francisco (earthquake loss reduction), Indianapolis (problems specific to the urban environment), Brussels (urban transportation), and Dearborn, Michigan (testing of experimental safety vehicles)." The work of the CCMS also quickly spread beyond NATO members to include Sweden, Japan, Yugoslavia, and Mexico. For a committee with members from so many countries, it was a remarkable level of early activity. "We know that

---

[37] PRO, FCO 55–408, Memorandum from J. C. Thomas, FCO Science and Technology Department to D. E. Richards, UK Delegation to NATO, "C.C.M.S.," January 1, 1970 and Memorandum from F. B. Wheeler, FCO Science and Technology Department to A. M. Wood, British Embassy, Washington, "NATO Committee on the Challenges of Modern Society," February 2, 1970.

[38] LOC, Papers of Steve Hess, Memorandum from Pat Moynihan to Richard Nixon, December 15, 1969.

[39] For more information, see pages 1–4 of Geir Lundestad, *"Empire" by Integration: The United States and European Integration, 1945–1997* (New York: Oxford University Press, 1998).

[40] For more information, see "NATO and the Environment," available from http://www.unc.edu/depts/diplomat/item/2009/0103/comm/berlind_nato.html.

President Nixon attaches great importance to the success of CCMS. ... It will be bad for our relations with our Allies in NATO, and with the Americans in particular, if we cannot fulfill this small obligation," the British FCO concluded.[41] The concern that the CCMS duplicated research being done elsewhere was a misunderstanding. The CCMS engaged in very little original research. Its primary purpose was as a forum to pool already existing knowledge and use it for the benefit of all. The CCMS established a degree of openness uncommon even in the West. Meetings were open to the public and the press – unlike the OECD, the Council of Europe, the EEC, or even NATO's North Atlantic Council – and its public reports benefitted skeptics, nonmembers, and nations in the Soviet bloc. The CCMS even welcomed observers from other bodies – including those from the communist bloc – in order to demonstrate that transparency was not a liability.[42]

Despite some initial – even strenuous – resistance, the CCMS took hold and became an important forum for discussion and cooperation between nations. Pat Moynihan updated President Nixon on all that it had achieved on the anniversary of the original proposal. "CCMS is probably now the most active, and productive international activity of its kind. ... We have moved a long way from our shaky beginning," he reported.[43] On the other hand, while progress was being achieved much faster than anyone had anticipated, including the United States government, "everything that has happened has been the result of American push."[44] NATO was simply not organized to think about environmental problems in its first two decades of existence. As Moynihan pointed out, Nixon's call for the creation of the CCMS forced the transatlantic alliance to reorganize, and that was no small task.

At the end of 1970, Pat Moynihan passed U.S. leadership of the CCMS to Russell Train, Nixon's first director of the Council on Environmental Quality. By the mid-1970s, more than 2,000 experts from all fifteen NATO countries and twenty non-NATO nations were participating in CCMS studies. Topics of these studies expanded to best practices related to oil spills, disaster relief, flood mitigation, air pollution, and road safety.

[41] PRO, FCO 55–408, Memorandum from R. Arculus, FCO, to Mr. Hughes, "NATO: Committee on the Challenges of Modern Society (CCMS)," February 5, 1970.

[42] PRO, FCO 55–409, Telegram from FCO to UK Delegation NATO, "CCMS," April 12, 1970.

[43] *FRUS*, 1969–1976, Volume XLI, 44.

[44] LOC, Papers of Steve Hess, Memorandum from Pat Moynihan to Richard Nixon, June 17, 1970.

The CCMS was the vehicle utilized by the United States to reduce Turkish opium production.[45] For Richard Nixon, these international achievements paralleled his own environmental initiatives at home: naming Earth Day on April 22, 1970; the signing of the Clean Air Act (Public Law 91–604), the Water Quality Improvement Act (Public Law 91–224), the Wilderness Act (Public Law 98–625), and the Resource Recovery Act (Public Law 91–512), and the creation of the Environmental Protection Agency.

Although the CCMS was a product of the détente era, it proved to be much more than that. It brought together countries not part of NATO's defense structure – like France – and those with a neutralist outlook, like Sweden. It held together the Western alliance at a time when the growing consensus was that a defense alliance was no longer needed in an era of reduced superpower tension. It provided a new opportunity for U.S. leadership following a difficult period in transatlantic relations during the 1960s. It provided a vehicle to reach out to the Soviet Union and Eastern Europe, and it convincingly showed that the nations of the West could be a force for leadership on social issues relevant to all societies. The CCMS has proved to be useful beyond the end of the Cold War. It has served as a forum for cooperation by nations before joining NATO or the European Union, and meetings have regularly been held in Eastern Europe and even Russia.

* * *

While publicly promoting the CCMS, President Nixon also initiated a much more sensitive effort privately. Because of the sensitivities among NATO allies with respect to French withdrawal from NATO's integrated command structure, Nixon's bilateral discussions with France, the assistance he lent to the *force de frappe*, and his approval of the expansion of the independent French nuclear deterrent remains one of the most controversial aspects of transatlantic relations during the Nixon era. The story begins in the earlier days of the Nixon presidency and was such a closely held secret that absolutely nothing leaked about it for twenty years, until the publication of Richard Ullman's 1989 article in *Foreign Policy* magazine.[46]

---

[45] LOC, Papers of Steve Hess, Memorandum from Pat Moynihan to Richard Nixon, June 17, 1970.
[46] See Richard Ullman, "The Covert French Connection." *Foreign Policy* 75 (Summer 1989): 3–33.1.

Until Ullman's article, the accepted wisdom was that the French nuclear deterrent was entirely homegrown.[47] Ullman had access not to government records, but to interviews with more than 100 officials. In fact, classified material related to the subject did not begin to be released in any quantity until another twenty years after Ullman's article.[48] "Approved for discussion but I'm not optimistic," Secretary of Defense Melvin Laird scribbled on a memorandum concerning the first sign of American movement in the direction of bilateral talks with the French.[49] That is how the process got started during the Nixon administration, although it was not a new idea. Secretary of Defense Robert McNamara had proposed it to French Defense Minister Pierre Messmer in both December 1964 and December 1965, but it did not go anywhere, and, shortly afterward, bilateral relations became too strained to pursue it anyway.

Richard Nixon's thinking was while Johnson and de Gaulle may have had their difficulties, he did not share them. Even while Charles de Gaulle – and successor Georges Pompidou – indicated that formally rejoining NATO's defense structure was politically out of the question due to France's rejection of flexible response, less than a month into Nixon's first term, the French government signaled an interest to discuss bilateral defense cooperation. Informally, discussions started just days after Nixon's election in November 1968, even before he assumed the White House, between Pierre Messmer and U.S. Ambassador to France Sargent Shriver. Instead of the prominent Democrat Shriver, Nixon preferred to utilize his own backchannel source to de Gaulle, Vernon Walters, who reported that "de Gaulle is basically well disposed towards the President Elect. He regards him as a man of strength, courage and

---

[47] For more information on the origins of Franco-American nuclear cooperation, see William Burr, "U.S. Secret Assistance to the French Nuclear Program, 1969–1975: From 'Fourth Country' to Strategic Partner." Wilson Center Nuclear Proliferation International History Project *Research Update* #2 (2011). Available from http://www.wilsoncenter.org/publication/us-secret-assistance-to-the-french-nuclear-program-1969-1975-fourth-country-to-strategic. However, whereas Burr's essay puts the time of the original French request for assistance "by the end of 1969," records recently obtained put the true date more than a year earlier, in late 1968, after Nixon was elected but before he had even assumed the White House.

[48] Many of the records cited here were obtained by the author through dozens of Mandatory Review Requests with the Gerald Ford Presidential Library. At the beginning of this research, in 2006, even the finding aid that listed these records was classified for fear of revealing even the subject of the records it described.

[49] GRF, Papers of Melvin Laird, Memorandum from Paul Warnke to Melvin Laird, "Possible Greater Defense Cooperation with the French," February 6, 1969.

tenacity." In addition, de Gaulle "may make concessions to Mr. Nixon that he would never have made to Mr. Johnson."[50] Why the change of heart? The French also assumed that Nixon would make concessions to de Gaulle that Johnson would not have. Providing assistance to France, and transferring more of Europe's defense burden to Europeans, was also consistent with the Nixon Doctrine.

Following the invasion of Czechoslovakia in 1968 and France's own turbulent domestic unrest that same year, the United States expected a period in which France would more fully enter the Atlantic alliance, even if short of resuming full formal membership in NATO. For Nixon, to reject the opportunity out of hand to offer such assistance to France might even do further damage to bilateral relations at a time when Nixon promised an improved relationship. According to American intelligence sources, the French remained determined to have their own ballistic missile capability, both land and sea based.[51] The election of Richard Nixon created potentially the most direct route to achieve that goal.

Because French nuclear forces remained outside of NATO, the French had few alternatives for such cooperation. American policy makers considered the 1961 Agreement for Cooperation with France to be terminated the moment that France withdrew from NATO's integrated command structure.[52] Any nuclear power large enough to assist France was already part of a bloc, either NATO or the Warsaw Pact, or a signatory to the NPT. By agreeing to bilateral defense assistance, Nixon seized an opportunity to achieve a de facto reintegration of French forces into NATO while not publicly insisting on reintegration. Moreover, defense assistance could yield an even closer bilateral relationship than the one that existed prior to the French withdrawal from NATO. Nixon understood the stakes.

"French defense officials have recently expressed interest in closer cooperation with the United States and NATO on military matters, including nuclear questions," Laird reported to President Nixon on February 20, 1969.[53] The British government was aware of de Gaulle's interest in cooperation with the United States, but Prime Minister Wilson

---

[50] RMN, NSC, Box 1, Memorandum from Vernon A. Walters to Henry Kissinger, "France," December 31, 1968.

[51] GRF, Papers of Gerald Laird, Box C18, Memorandum from Dave Packard to Henry Kissinger, "US/French Interchange in Area of Ballistic Missiles," February 20, 1970.

[52] GRF, Papers of Gerald Laird, Box C18, Memorandum from Dave Packard to Henry Kissinger, "US/French Interchange in Area of Ballistic Missiles," February 20, 1970.

[53] GRF, Papers of Melvin Laird, Box C13, Memorandum from Melvin Laird to President Nixon, "NATO Defense Issues," February 20, 1969.

was assured by the American government that such talks would not go forward. "In the autumn of last year, French spokesmen, including General de Gaulle, let fall various hints which suggested that France might be looking for some form of closer nuclear relationship with the Americans, possibly extending to the UK. We agreed then with the Americans that nothing whatever should be done to encourage these ideas," a top secret British study reported.[54] However, American efforts to hold such talks with the French clearly went forward.

Nixon, expecting arms reduction talks with the Soviets to begin soon, saw the importance of timing in assisting France. Any eventual arms limitations agreement reached – including the planned ratification of the Anti-Ballistic Missile (ABM) Treaty – would impose limits on American and NATO forces. Assisting the French was a way to hide American capabilities in a place outside of the scope of such a treaty since France's nuclear deterrent was independent of NATO, and Charles de Gaulle had previously rejected the ABM treaty. For Nixon, it would also be easy to deny that Franco-American defense cooperation was in the works because such a reversal in American policy would have been unthinkable just a few years earlier at the height of de Gaulle's obstructionism.

After a delay resulting from de Gaulle's resignation, Franco-American defense talks were initiated during President Georges Pompidou's February 1970 visit to the United States. It was Henry Kissinger who subtly raised the subject during a Paris meeting with Pompidou to plan the agenda for the summit. "When I asked whether he could discuss defense matters on his visit, President Pompidou said, 'I can and I want to,' " Kissinger reported to Nixon.[55] The French and American militaries had already initiated talks on their own. In December 1969, the French Minister of Armaments Jean Blancard made a request to the Pentagon that the United States provide the French "technical assistance in the development of their ballistic missile program."[56]

These friendly French overtures to the United States were Pompidou's way of signaling a new era in French foreign policy. The departure of Charles de Gaulle removed the barrier to progress in the European

---

[54] PRO, PREM 13–2489, TOP SECRET "Anglo-French Nuclear Cooperation in the Defense Field: Memorandum by the Foreign and Commonwealth Office and Ministry of Defense," undated.

[55] RMN, NSC, Name Files, Box 816, Memorandum from Henry Kissinger to President Nixon, "Summary of My Conversation with President Pompidou," undated.

[56] RMN, NSC, Name Files, Box 816, Memorandum from Helmut Sonnenfeldt to Henry Kissinger, "Memo from Deputy Secretary of Defense on Assistance to France on Ballistic Missiles," January 23, 1970.

Community (EC), including an expansion in its membership, and, through The Hague Summit in late 1969, brought France brought back into good standing with both its EC and NATO partners. Although France had no plans to formally rejoin NATO, it was now open to a bilateral defense alliance. For Nixon, despite the difficulties in providing assistance, it was essential to demonstrate that his relationship with France would be different from that of his predecessors. "Nothing established more clearly for the French our willingness to turn the page on the past record, particularly because we did not seek any immediate quid pro quo," Secretary of Defense Mel Laird wrote to President Nixon.[57]

In early 1970, the French military assistance request set off a flurry of American activity as to whether such assistance was in American interests and whether such assistance was legal according to export limitations. Henry Kissinger was concerned that things were moving too quickly. He also wanted to make sure that the White House got credit for any breakthrough, emphasizing that the Foster-Blancard channel "might be one means to do so" but certainly not the preferred one for either Nixon or Kissinger.[58] Both governments were newly in power, and neither had precedent to guide them. "The French program is the worst nuclear program in the world. The Chinese one is the best," Foster said.[59]

Kissinger aide Helmut Sonnenfeldt advised that such cooperation was not in American interests at the working level unless it was preceded by a specific Nixon-Pompidou understanding. The United States had little to gain from providing defense assistance, unless it was linked to something political in return. "Given current French policy, it continues to be in this government's interest not to contribute to or assist in the development of a French nuclear warhead capability or a French national strategic nuclear delivery capacity," he suggested.[60]

Military assistance to France was also forbidden according to Johnson-era National Security Action Memorandum (NSAM) 294 of April 20, 1964. There was little ambiguity in the ban, which included "exchanges of information and technology between the governments, sale of equipment, joint research and development activities, and exchanges between industrial and commercial organizations, either directly or through third

[57] *FRUS*, 1969–1976, Volume E-15, Part 2, 304.
[58] GRF, Papers of Gerald Laird, Box C18, Memorandum from Henry Kissinger to Dave Packard, "Assistance to the French Missile System," January 27, 1970.
[59] *FRUS*, 1969–1976, Volume E-15, Part 2, 312.
[60] RMN, NSC, Name Files, Box 816, Memorandum from Helmut Sonnenfeldt to Henry Kissinger, "Military Cooperation with the French," February 28, 1970.

parties, which would be reasonably likely to facilitate these efforts by significantly affecting timing, quality or costs or would identify the U.S. as a major supplier or collaborator."[61] None of this mattered to the French, who not only lacked such a prohibition of their own but also had no intention of signing the NPT. However, following the ban, the French were able to get assistance only through unofficial channels, such as licensing agreements through American corporations likes Lockheed and Boeing, but even then France had to agree that any assistance received would not be used for military purposes.

Although many of the records related to American military assistance remain classified, several tangible results came from the Nixon-Pompidou meeting in February 1970. Kissinger went into action, first with General Andrew Goodpaster, then Supreme Allied Commander, Europe. "Following his conversations with President Pompidou, the President wishes you to resume contact at an early opportunity with the French Chief of Staff [General Fourquet]," Kissinger instructed. "These actions should, until further instructions, be conducted on a US EYES ONLY basis and should be given maximum security classification and be made known to US personnel on the most restricted need-to-know basis."[62] Nixon and Pompidou agreed that cooperation should move forward and that they would personally review progress on a periodic basis.[63] Negotiations with the French posed special problems. For example, when the United States first shared Polaris submarine technology with the British in 1963, a result of the Kennedy-Macmillan Nassau meeting the year before, it did so on the basis that all future British systems would be available to NATO.[64] Similar understandings were reached with Italy and Turkey. However, when it came to sharing Poseidon technology – the successor to Polaris – France remained outside of NATO's command structure.

Cooperation with the French proceeded with scientific collaboration at first, including isotope separation, a process that refines natural uranium into weapons-grade uranium. Although such uranium was needed for French nuclear power stations, its dual use could have implications

[61] GRF, Papers of Gerald Laird, Box C18, Memorandum from Dave Packard to Henry Kissinger, "US/French Interchange in Area of Ballistic Missiles," February 20, 1970.
[62] RMN, NSC, Name Files, Box 816, Memorandum from Henry Kissinger to Andrew Goodpaster, "Further Contact with French Military Authorities," undated.
[63] RMN, NSC, Name Files, Box 816, Memorandum from Helmut Sonnenfeldt to Henry Kissinger, "U.S.-French Military Relations – Your Talk with General Goodpaster," April 1, 1970.
[64] GRF, Papers of Melvin Laird, Box C18, Memorandum from Melvin Laird to Richard Nixon, "Modification of SSBN Commitments to NATO," August 27, 1971.

for weapons systems, too. France relied on nuclear energy – a state-run industry – for a significantly greater portion of its domestic energy needs than any other Western nation. It was a large enough sector, and secretive enough, that development of dual-use technology could be concealed. American cooperation brought French praise and dismissal of the British. "Unlike the British government, which has ceased to manifest any interest in the gaseous diffusion method, the French government is continuing its research in this method, in the belief that it can still be greatly improved. The experience acquired by the Americans in this field is very wide, while that of the French is more limited although far from negligible," the French Ministry of Foreign Affairs publicized in March 1970, a month after the Nixon-Pompidou summit.[65]

After these first steps, Franco-American defense cooperation continued but was uneven. Henry Kissinger doubted the usefulness of such cooperation to long-term American interests absent any tangible political inducement. Nonetheless, by mid-1970, defense cooperation expanded to a variety of other fields, including stationing French military personnel in Germany, French involvement in NATO's Nuclear Planning Group, the sale of advanced computers for French nuclear weapons, and assistance to the French ABM shield after President Nixon authorized Pentagon official John Foster and top-level personnel from the Polaris and Minuteman programs to travel to France during June 1970.[66] "Largely as a result of the President's [February 1970] meeting with Pompidou, we have begun a number of efforts to establish closer cooperation with France on military matters," Helmut Sonnenfeldt summarized.[67] When John Foster, the Director of Defense Research and Engineering and one of the Pentagon's negotiators with France, returned from a trip to Europe in December 1970, he noted "I can confirm ... that there has been marked progress in U.S.-French relations in recent months."[68] In fact, bilateral relations had progressed a little too quickly for some.

---

[65] RMN, NSC, Name Files, Box 816, Report by the French Ministry of Foreign Affairs, "Outlook for Franco-American Cooperation in the Field of Isotope Separation," March 16, 1970.

[66] RMN, NSC, Name Files, Box 816, Memorandum from Henry Kissinger to President Nixon, "John Foster's Trip to France to Explore US Assistance to French Ballistic Missile Program," June 23, 1970.

[67] RMN, NSC, Name Files, Box 816, Memorandum from Helmut Sonnenfeldt to Henry Kissinger, "Franco-American Military Relations," August 3, 1970.

[68] GRF, Papers of Melvin Laird, Box C18, Memorandum from John Foster to Melvin Laird, "Trip to France and England 18–19 December 1970," December 21, 1970.

One reason Henry Kissinger had reservations about Franco-American defense cooperation was because it could potentially damage relations with other Europeans. The United States and France were barely on speaking terms only a few years before, when de Gaulle's obstructionism in the EEC made him a pariah among Europeans. Kissinger approached Nixon with a concern that a more coherent transatlantic policy was needed. "The entire question of nuclear doctrine and deployments remains an area of great concern to you because of the ambiguous nature of our agreement with the allies as well as the rationale behind our own plans," he wrote.[69] Kissinger worried specifically that the British had already discovered that Franco-American defense cooperation had been going on. "If any progress occurs in U.S.-French military relations it will quickly become apparent within our government and on the ground. The British will recognize that this did not just happen overnight but was the result of detailed explorations and negotiations over a period of time. They will assume that this was a product of the Pompidou visit."[70]

Although Kissinger's concern did not halt Franco-American defense cooperation, it did temporarily apply the brakes. In a memorandum from Kissinger to Nixon during March 1971, he noted the stalled French requests for advanced computers, the French ABM shield, and nuclear safety. The first two requests had been held up since the previous summer, when Kissinger first expressed his concern.[71] Meanwhile, in other areas of cooperation with France, Kissinger was more agreeable, especially with regard to matters that were not national-security classified. But the French pressed for greater access.

When a legal determination found that the export of advanced computers was forbidden according to Congressional restrictions, Kissinger suggested that the White House should "redefine advanced computers." On Kissinger's suggestion, Nixon approved "limited assistance" to the French ballistic missile program and opened exchanges on nuclear safety. "I favor moving more openly as V. Nam winds down," Nixon scribbled at the bottom after checking off his approval.[72] However, also at Kissinger's

---

[69] RMN, NSC, Name Files, Box 816, Memorandum from Henry Kissinger to President Nixon, "Your Meeting with General Goodpaster, Tuesday, August 4, 1970."

[70] RMN, NSC, Name Files, Box 816, Memorandum from Henry Kissinger to President Nixon, "Your Meeting with General Goodpaster, Tuesday, August 4, 1970."

[71] Kenneth Weisbrode, *The Atlantic Century: Four Generations of Extraordinary Diplomats Who Forged America's Vital Alliance with Europe* (New York: Da Capo Press, 2009), 257.

[72] RMN, NSC, Name Files, Box 816, Memorandum from Henry Kissinger to President Nixon, "Military Cooperation with France," March 25, 1971.

urging, Nixon rejected a $20 million French computer request, agreeing to supply certain computer parts instead.[73] Then, the American policy reversed again. On June 5, 1971, Nixon withdrew his objection to the sale of computers, but only after the issue became an "irritant" to Pompidou.[74] The lifting of this prohibition permitted the French to purchase all but the most advanced and largest computers without a French assurance of nonmilitary use. These included the sale of the IBM 360 series (but not the 370) to the French, a state-of-the-art mainframe developed in 1964 that was capable of a vast eight megabytes of main memory.[75]

Even this modest degree of assistance to France was soon put on ice. By the summer of 1971, Congress indicated an interest in holding hearings on the legality of American defense assistance to France. The Joint Committee on Atomic Energy initiated an investigation into whether American defense cooperation with France was congruent with the NPT, which strictly regulated the transfer of nuclear technology.[76] In addition, Senator Mansfield insisted on withdrawing American troops from Europe. "Mansfield could kill us," Kissinger stated to French Defense Minister Michel Debré at Nixon's Western White House in San Clemente.[77] Congress also raised the thorny issue of settling FRELOC, the costs incurred by the United States for relocating NATO forces to Belgium after being expelled from French territory by Charles de Gaulle. Henry Kissinger attempted to resurrect Franco-American defense cooperation in 1973, but such efforts faltered due to a deterioration of Franco-American political relations during the Year of Europe.

Whereas strategic moves like the creation of the CCMS and defense cooperation with France were clearly designed to hold together the Western alliance at a time when it was strained, other aspects of Nixon's

---

[73] RMN, NSC, Name Files, Box 816, Memorandum from Henry Kissinger to President Nixon, "French Proposal to Manufacture Transistors in Poland," June 2, 1971.

[74] RMN, NSC, Name Files, Box 816, Memorandum from Henry Kissinger to President Nixon, "Your Meeting with Ambassador Arthur K. Watson, June 15, at 3:30 p.m. for ten minutes," June 14, 1971.

[75] RMN, NSC, Name Files, Box 816, Memorandum from Helmut Sonnenfeldt to Henry Kissinger, "Your Meeting with Debré Friday, July 6, 10 a.m.," July 5, 1972.

[76] RMN, NSC, Name Files, Box 816, Memorandum from Theodore L. Eliot, Jr. to Henry Kissinger, "Joint Committee on Atomic Energy Hearings on Projected Nuclear Safety Talks with the French," November 16, 1971.

[77] RMN, NSC, Name Files, Box 816, Memorandum of Conversation between Henry Kissinger and Michel Debré, "Meeting Between French Minister of Defense Michel Debré and Dr. Kissinger, Friday, July 7, 1972, 9:50 a.m. at the Western White House," July 11, 1972.

NATO policy were disappointing. After his well-received address to the North Atlantic Council during late February 1969, Nixon left his ambassadorial selection in abeyance until May. Then, rather than appointing an expert with a deep commitment to the Atlantic alliance, Nixon appointed campaign aide and former Congressman Robert Ellsworth.[78] The post became vacant again in 1971 for the better part of a year. Ellsworth pleaded with Nixon that the administration needed a real expert at the post and not another political appointee.[79] Kissinger attempted to fill the spot with a serious figure, including begging John McCloy to take the job, without success.[80] Due to a limited pool of acceptable candidates, Kissinger considered merging one or more of the three American diplomatic posts in Brussels (to Belgium, to NATO, and to the EC). He assigned Ambassador to Belgium Robert Strausz-Hupe to conduct a feasibility study. Strausz-Hupe confirmed the need to reform representation at NATO: "NATO's need for reorganization is long standing. It is now a Vatican, top heavy with military-political Titular Bishops without sees. It is a paper mill that grinds slowly." Strausz-Hupe recommended against a merger of any sort.

Richard Nixon and Henry Kissinger preferred bilateral negotiations and backchannels to multilateral forums. After first-term breakthroughs with adversaries China and the Soviet Union, NATO allies accused the Americans of neglecting transatlantic relations. Privately, Kissinger did not completely disagree with that assessment. "We're going to Moscow, but Japan is a mess. Western Europe is a mess. We've given up our friends to our enemies," he stated.[81] After McCloy declined the ambassadorial post to NATO, Nixon gave consideration to the youngest member of his cabinet, Donald Rumsfeld, but for the wrong reasons. Rumsfeld, as Kissinger explained to President Nixon, had no previous foreign policy experience except that which he had obtained as a former member of the U.S. House of Representatives.[82] In a private meeting with Nixon in the Oval Office, Rumsfeld expressed interest in the post but did not want to be seen being "dumped" at NATO as Ellsworth had been. After Rumsfeld exited the Oval Office, Nixon told Bob Haldeman that he intended to dump Rumsfeld at NATO. The president also decided on Rumsfeld for the post because Nixon was concerned that he had been making "political

[78] RMN, HAK Telcons, Box 1, February 4, 1969, 9:50 p.m.
[79] RMN, Nixon Tapes, White House Telephone 595–007, October 18, 1971.
[80] RMN, Nixon Tapes, White House Telephone 014–062, November 11, 1971.
[81] RMN, Nixon Tapes, Executive Office Building 295–14, November 16, 1971.
[82] RMN, Nixon Tapes, Oval Office 542-005, July 22, 1971, 11:36 a.m.–12:28 p.m.

speeches" around the country. With more than one contemporary sug-
gesting the young, charismatic Rumsfeld as Nixon's running mate in
1972, Nixon preferred to get Rumsfeld out of town (it was an ages-old
Washington practice to exile potential rivals). Once Rumsfeld arrived at
NATO in 1973, he performed admirably, although Nixon recruited
Andrew Goodpaster on more than one occasion to "have a long talk
with Ambassador Rumsfeld" and to "take a personal interest in
Rumsfeld and teach him the facts about NATO relationships."[83]

While Nixon reshaped long-term NATO strategy for the détente era,
the lack of proper day-to-day policy management of NATO policy had
consequences beyond a deterioration of European confidence in the
United States. Nixon also competed against an hourglass of rising isolationism. This losing battle to keep the United States outwardly focused
gave administration rivals, particularly in Congress, room to maneuver
and in which to propose their own policies. One such rival was Senate
Majority Leader Mike Mansfield. A Democrat from Montana, Mansfield
was generally supportive of Nixon foreign policy moves such as the Nixon
Doctrine and the scaling down of troops deployed to Southeast Asia.
However, in May 1971, Mansfield called for a halving of American forces
in Europe.[84] Known as the Mansfield Amendment – because of the threat
that it could be attached to almost any Senate bill – it caused panic for
Henry Kissinger, who immediately commenced on a massive bipartisan
effort to defeat Mansfield. McGeorge Bundy and Kissinger assembled a
group of bipartisan foreign policy figures to speak out against Mansfield,
including Cyrus Vance, Henry Cabot Lodge, Jr., Dean Acheson, Lyman
Lemnitzer, and Nicholas Katzenbach.[85]

Unwilling to speak to Mansfield directly, Kissinger obtained a summary of Mansfield's demands from Senator Jacob Javits. To Kissinger's
surprise, they were not that much different from current White House
policies or the tenets of the Nixon Doctrine, although Mansfield's
demands were arranged according to an accelerated time schedule. "The
President is requested to negotiate within NATO for the assumption
of greater troop levels by the other NATO members and financial arrangements consistent with the balance of payments situation of the United
States; and, to withdraw U.S. forces in Europe to the extent made
possible by such negotiations. The President shall report to the Congress

---

[83] GRF, NSA, Memcons, Box 1, Conversation among President Nixon, General Andrew
Goodpaster, and Brigadier General Brent Scowcroft, February 15, 1973.
[84] Weisbrode, 254.
[85] RMN, HAK Telcons, Box 10, May 12, 1971.

in 90 days, and each 90 days thereafter, on the progress of such negotiations," Javits reported. Kissinger was dumbfounded. "At the end of a year
where we got the Europeans to commit themselves to strengthen their
forces, and at a time we are entering negotiations with the Russians ... we
find it hard to understand."[86] Bundy assured Kissinger that many influential Democrats did not support Mansfield's proposal. However, they
were not willing to take on one of their own until the White House
communicated a clear policy with respect to NATO. "You have a lot of
friends on your fight, but they have got to get a signal ... they want
something the White House is backing," Bundy stated.[87]

Rather than formulate a clear policy, the White House dispatched
various administration officials to testify at nearly every venue deemed
of value. Secretary of Defense Melvin Laird asked the House Committee
on Armed Services, "Why do we need 310,000 troops in Europe 25 years
after the end of World War II? The Warsaw Pact maintains over 55
divisions in Germany, Poland, and Czechoslovakia, most of which could
be combat read in less than 2 days ... on military grounds alone the risk to
NATO is greater now than it was 5 or 10 years ago."[88] Laird understood
that he was fighting a rising tide of American isolationism. According to a
Pentagon briefing memorandum Laird received earlier, "it is clear ... that
the U.S. is in a mood and on a course of military retrenchment and
withdrawal, while the Soviets are in the opposite mood and course of
build-up and expansion. This divergence will expand Soviet political
options while constraining ours. If it goes far enough we risk a Soviet
mood like that of Hitler and Tojo, only worse."[89]

On President Nixon's orders, Kissinger called former President
Johnson for help in convincing prominent Democrats to speak out against
Mansfield. "The president has lined up all former secretaries of state,
secretaries of defense (except Clifford), SACEURS, etc., to support that
statement. He would also like to have the two living ex-Presidents go
along with it." Johnson was willing to help, and did, but he was cautious
about taking a public stance against a prominent member of his own
party. "I have very strong feelings about the NATO forces, as I expressed

[86] RMN, HAK Telcons, Box 10, May 12, 1971.
[87] RMN, HAK Telcons, Box 10, May 13, 1971.
[88] GRF, Papers of Melvin Laird, Box A81, "The American Commitment to NATO: Report
     of the Special Subcommittee on North Atlantic Treaty Organization Commitments of the
     Committee on Armed Services, House of Representatives, Ninety-Second Congress,
     Second Session, August 17, 1972."
[89] GRF, Papers of Melvin Laird, Box A81, Memorandum from John H. Morse, Deputy
     Assistant Secretary, European and NATO Affairs, to Mr. Nutter, November 25, 1970.

all during my administration, but to go to writing letters and making statements, if I do that I'll have everyone in my party calling me, as they do all the time, asking me to make statements some in favor, most against the president," he said.[90] Walt Rostow reported to Kissinger that Johnson was willing to release a statement in support of the Nixon White House. "Henry, I have something that President Johnson dictated," he said. "He dictated the following statement: 'I have seen the President's proposed statement opposing at this time a unilateral reduction of military forces maintained in Europe for the common defense. I am totally in accord with that statement.' "[91]

With such broad bipartisan consensus, the Mansfield Amendment was defeated on May 19, 1971, on a vote of 61–36. The following day, Kissinger called Dean Acheson to thank him for his support. "I just wanted to tell you what privilege it has been to be associated with you and wanted you to know that if what you did was overkill we can't have enough of it. ... I think your idea of assembling these people was the turning point."[92] However, the fight was far from over. During remaining years of the Nixon presidency, the White House faced an unprecedented number of attempts by Congress to expand its authority over wartime decision making. These included the McGovern-Hatfield Amendment (1970), the Cooper-Church Amendment (1970), the repeal of the Tonkin Gulf Resolution (1971), and the Case-Church Amendment (1973). These attempts culminated with the 1973 War Powers Resolution, but did not stop there. Further efforts, such as the Jackson-Vanik Amendment (1974) and the Jackson-Nunn Amendment (1974), came even after the formal end of the Vietnam War.

Struggles between the Nixon White House and Congress put even more strain on transatlantic relations. The British were especially concerned, as seen in Prime Minister Heath's briefing papers for a meeting with President Nixon:

On the American side, there has been recent evidence that less attention is being paid to consultation with NATO. This has encouraged a suspicion on the part of their Allies that the Americans attach more importance to their bilateral relations with the Soviet Union than to Allied interests and susceptibilities.[93]

---

[90] RMN, HAK Telcons, Box 10, May 14, 1971.
[91] RMN, HAK Telcons, Box 10, May 15, 1971.
[92] RMN, HAK Telcons, Box 10, May 20, 1971.
[93] PRO, FCO 41–987, "Proposed Meeting Between Prime Minister of United Kingdom and President of United States: Defense Questions," undated.

Although American forces in Europe had remained steady over the previous years, actually increasing from 300,000 in 1970 to 320,000 by 1972, these figures were still dramatically off the peak of 434,000 in 1964. During a July 1972 summit between American and British leaders, Nixon offered reassurance. "The main thing I want you to assure the Prime Minister, I don't give a damn if we lose the election, we are not going to cut the defenses, we are not going to turn back on our European policy, we are not going to turn isolationist in this country," he stated. "In Europe, if we start to back down, in my view, you've just opened the floodgates for a massive Soviet incursion."[94]

Additional confusion stemmed from a multitude of American and European initiatives related to transatlantic relations or NATO, many of which overlapped in some way. Between 1969 and 1974, these included the NPT, Strategic Arms Limitation Talks including SALT I and II, the Conference on Security and Cooperation in Europe (CSCE), a proposal for a European Security Conference, and Mutual and Balanced Force Reductions (MBFR). This list does not reflect other related undertakings such as the Quadripartite Agreement, discussions related to "burden sharing" bilateral offset agreements, or the body of treaties that became known as *Ostpolitik*. Regarding CSCE and MBFR, an exasperated British Foreign Secretary Alex Douglas-Home stated in a private NATO meeting during December 1972, "we are now embarked on two negotiations even more ambitious and complicated that anything this Alliance has seen before ... we must be seen to be doing two different things and it presents the dilemma; we must be seen genuinely to be seeking an end to the division of Europe. We can only do it step by step, that is the lesson of the last 25 years as to how to deal with the Russians."[95]

Europeans sensed a growing American disengagement in Europe by the end of 1972. One State Department cable noted, "two prominent Dutch parliamentarians ... said they detected significant shift in thinking of U.S. Congressional delegation in favor of unilateral reduction of U.S. troop strength in Europe outside of MBFR framework."[96] At a time when the Soviets were extracting concessions from the Germans in the course of discussions related to *Ostpolitik*, the need for a clear transatlantic policy was especially acute. One of the concessions that

---

[94] RMN, Nixon Tapes, Oval Office 756-021, July 28, 1972, 2:09 p.m.–2:42 p.m.

[95] NATO, C-VR(72)60, Verbatim Record of the Meeting of the Council held on Thursday, 7 December, 1972 at 9:30 a.m. at NATO Headquarters, Brussels.

[96] NARA, RG 59, CFPF, Telegram from U.S. Mission The Hague to Secretary of State, "U.S. Troops in Europe," May 24, 1973, The Hague 2381.

Egon Bahr made to the Soviets was his promise of West German support for a Soviet-proposed European Security Conference. The Soviet proposal envisioned a time when Europeans were totally responsible for their own security, an arrangement that included the Soviet Union but not the United States or NATO.

When word of the "Bahr plan" leaked, naturally, the United States was greatly alarmed because the proposal was interpreted as the plan for the dissolution of NATO. The plan had been worked out between Bahr and the Soviets directly through his backchannel to the KGB.[97] According to the version of the Bahr plan obtained by the American Embassy in Bonn, the West German proposal for the dissolution of NATO could be achieved in three steps. Both Germanies would first agree to a treaty. Second, they would agree to a treaty with the Soviet Union. And finally, the parties would negotiate reductions in forces stationed in Germany on their own, without input from the United States.[98] NATO Secretary-General Joseph Luns told Henry Kissinger of his reaction to the Bahr plan. "I had a long talk with Bahr, and I talked to the Chancellor. . . . I then said it was not very wise to say the things he was saying. He then talked about other possibilities: the dissolution of NATO, that there would no longer be two military blocks in Europe, and some arrangement to make this possible." Henry Kissinger dismissed such wild plans, although privately the White House was concerned: "They always have romantic ideas . . . the Germans are really insane. They have nothing to offer the Russians. The only thing they have left to offer the Russians is to wreck NATO."[99]

***

All outstanding issues and policy ambiguities in transatlantic relations were to be rolled into one initiative, the Year of Europe. The 1973 proposal was intended to be just as bold an assertion of American foreign policy creativity as the secret overtures to the Soviet Union and China had been and would be conducted with a similar reliance on secrecy and backchannel communications. Some critics have suggested that the swing in Nixon's attention back to Europe beginning in 1973 was a reaction to criticism that he had ignored Europe too often during the previous four years.

---

[97] Weisbrode, 221.
[98] NARA, RG 59, CFPF, Telegram from U.S. Embassy Bonn to Secretary of State, "Bahr Plan," April 6, 1973, Bonn 5129.
[99] RMN, NSC, Box 1027, Memorandum of Conversation between Joseph Luns and Henry Kissinger, April 13, 1973.

The renewed American interest in NATO came too late. The U.S. Congress had become more isolationist after the protracted end to American involvement in Vietnam and the struggle over maintaining promised U.S. forces in Europe. The ambassadorial post at the U.S. Mission to NATO had remained vacant or was not taken seriously for too long. NATO allies not privy to Nixon's secret overtures to China and the Soviet Union felt abandoned, and, by the time American attention was again turned toward the needs of NATO early in Nixon's second term, there was little hope for improvement. Congress was hesitant to appropriate the necessary funds to improve American forces stationed in Europe and was more interested in limiting growing executive power, especially while the growing Watergate probe took shape in the spring of 1973. European allies had become disenchanted with an American policy-making process that they felt had relied too much on secrecy and too little on consultations with allies before making important agreements that affected Europe.

In addition to the other challenges faced during the Year of Europe, discussed later, American policy makers knew as early as April 1973 that a complete overhaul of American NATO policy would not be possible. A National Security Council workgroup set up to study the problem informed Henry Kissinger on April 4 that resolving the outstanding disputes with France and the Germans "could be a determining factor in influencing those 30–40 Congressmen who may determine the outcome of the troop deployment debate in Congress." However, the tenets of the Nixon Doctrine could not be implemented quickly enough for Nixon's Congressional critics. "It is the consensus of the Working Group that *we cannot expect to get our Allies to increase their efforts to improve their forces and at the same time give us a genuine better deal on balance of payments offsets.*"[100]

Although the Nixon administration enjoyed some success in starting the CCMS and fending off the strongest isolationist threats at home, the White House was not successful at using the CCMS to articulate a coherent, comprehensive statement of policy vis-à-vis NATO. President Nixon utilized the CCMS primarily as a vehicle to hold the alliance together at a time when even long-standing allies questioned the need for a costly defense alliance in the détente era. He did this by expanding NATO's role into political affairs and social and environmental policy and by

---

[100] Emphasis original. DNSA, Memorandum from Phil Odeen to Henry Kissinger, "NSSM 170 – Offsetting the Balance of Payments Costs with NATO," April 4, 1973.

satisfying a sufficient number of French requests for American military assistance. These efforts removed doubt from NATO's future and removed France as the greatest European critic of American foreign policy. These policies were carried out consistent with the Nixon Doctrine, which itself was designed to address the rising tide of American isolationism. The insistence of Nixon and Kissinger on implementing so many foreign policy decisions under conditions of maximum secrecy – without the help that could otherwise have been marshaled by members of Congress and the foreign service – ensured that policies like the CCMS were not as successful as they could have been.

2

Closing the gold window

When President Nixon took office on January 20, 1969, the Bretton Woods system was severely distressed. Consistent with his predecessors, he chose not to act for fear of damaging the international economic position of the United States. Yet, less than three years later, Nixon's bold announcement of his New Economic Policy on August 15, 1971, placed the system on a path toward its dissolution, one of the most important economic events in postwar history. Bretton Woods was never meant to be permanent, although Americans and Europeans feared that restructuring or removing the global monetary pivot risked another Great Depression. Even in 1971, Nixon was reluctant to act, but he ultimately saw little choice when the pressures to do so reached a critical point: an acute shortage of American gold reserves, a need for a monetary system that required less manipulation, pressure from the conservative wing of his party to respond to increasing American isolationism, and the desire to do something politically advantageous in the area of economic policy in advance of the 1972 presidential election.

Designed during World War II to provide economic stability and foster postwar recovery, the system's collapse was the result of a long and ultimately unsuccessful struggle to sustain the currency regime past its useful life span. Framed to meet the needs of the 1940s, Bretton Woods in the 1970s appeared out of step, unnecessarily unstable due to innumerable ad hoc adjustments, and not in sync with the liquidity demands of the Nixon era or reflective of the altered economic landscape. Nixon's blueprint to end Bretton Woods was part of a broader, more isolationist economic policy consistent with the Nixon Doctrine, which said that Europeans should take greater responsibility for their own needs.

The collapse of the system marked the end of the postwar era[1] and of the golden age of capitalism itself, in which American gold and economic assistance were prerequisites to European recovery following World War II.

The Bretton Woods system was set up during an economic conference attended by forty-four nations and held at Bretton Woods, New Hampshire, July 1–22, 1944.[2] John Maynard Keynes and Harry Dexter White drafted the proposals beginning in 1941 that would form the basis of Bretton Woods. Negotiations on these proposals began during September 1943 and were capped by a summit at Atlantic City in June 1944.[3] The final act of the Bretton Woods conference, signed on July 22, created the International Monetary Fund (IMF) and the International Bank for Reconstruction and Development (later the World Bank). In addition, the conference set up a new world currency system of gold-based "fixed but moveable" exchange rates.[4] Adjustments to the system were supposed to be made in consultation with the IMF. This system stood in contrast to the rigid interwar "pure gold" exchange rate system that had contributed to the Great Depression because its inflexibility inhibited central bankers from taking necessary action to expedite economic recovery.[5] Bretton Woods was a welcome transition that returned

[1] The early 1970s is also where Eric Hobsbawm subdivides his *Age of Extremes*; the postwar era came to an end due to the economic and social crises of the early 1970s. Tony Judt, in *Postwar: A History of Europe since 1945*, uses a similar periodization. See the discussion in Hartmut Marhold, "How to Tell the History of European Integration in the 1970s: A Survey of the Literature and Some Proposals," *L'Europe en formation no. 353–354 (automne-hiver 2009)*: 13–38.

[2] The State Department released two volumes of proceedings and documents associated with formation of the Bretton Woods agreement in 1948. Due to the sensitivity that still existed at the time, they were prepared in a way that did not link decisions and statements with individuals, and no one was quoted directly. For more information, see *Proceedings and Documents of the United Nations Monetary and Financial Conference: Bretton Woods, New Hampshire, July 1–22, 1945* (Washington, D.C.: Government Printing Office, 1948). Transcripts, which contain such personal identifying information, were discovered by the Department of Treasury only in 2012. Until the discovery, historians were unaware that they existed. The Center for Financial Stability, a nonpartisan think tank, has made copies of the transcripts available from http://www.centerforfinancialstability.org/brettonwoods_docs.php

[3] PRO, PREM 15–309, undated summary.

[4] Joanne S. Gowa, *Closing the Gold Window: Domestic Politics and the End of Bretton Woods* (Ithaca: Cornell University Press, 1983), 36.

[5] For a discussion on the origins of Bretton Woods and the Anglo-American effort beginning in 1942 to construct a postwar international monetary system that was designed to ameliorate the problems of the interwar gold standard, see Benn Steil, *The Battle of Bretton Woods: John Maynard Keynes, Harry Dexter White, and the Making of a New World Order* (Princeton: Princeton University Press, 2013).

currencies to a quasi-flexible gold standard after a hiatus during the war. The system allowed the recovering economies of Europe to accumulate U.S. dollars as a result of market exchanges, including postwar American aid such as the Marshall Plan, which could be converted to gold at the rate of US$35 an ounce, guaranteed by the gold reserves in the United States Treasury at Fort Knox.[6] The American guarantee was maintained in exchange for other countries' obligations to ensure monetary discipline at home.

The United States did not have this same discipline imposed upon it; American debts could be paid by issuing new currency. During the late 1950s and 1960s, this occurred with greater frequency as a result of ballooning American foreign aid programs, Lyndon Johnson's Great Society initiatives, and the funding of growing American involvement in Southeast Asia.[7] A significant turning point was 1958, when the total number of dollars in circulation eclipsed the amount of gold held in reserve, a violation of a key tenet of the Bretton Woods system. As a result, the United States experienced increasingly larger balance of payments deficits and ever shrinking gold reserves, which ultimately set in motion a series of monetary crises in the 1960s.

American policy makers took these crises seriously, yet no long-term solution emerged. After a gold crisis in 1960, the Eisenhower administration worried that the entire Atlantic alliance might collapse if the payments deficits were not corrected. President Kennedy indicated that payments deficits worried him more than nuclear weapons, in particular after another nagging session by his father, Joseph Kennedy.[8] President Johnson was concerned that he might be blamed for a global economic depression.[9] French President Charles de Gaulle blasted reckless American policy and the Bretton Woods system and accused the United States of exporting inflation. As nations accumulated excess dollars over time, confidence in the dollar and American monetary policy eroded. Such

---

[6] Further information can be found in Bretton Woods Agreement Act, 59 Stat. 512, July 1945.

[7] Michael Kreile, "The Search for a New Monetary System: Germany's Balancing Act" in Helga Haftendorn, et al., eds. *The Strategic Triangle: France, Germany, and the United States in the Shaping of the New Europe* (Washington, D.C.: Woodrow Wilson Center Press, 2006), 151.

[8] George Ball once said about Kennedy, "every weekend he went up to Hyannis Port he came back absolutely obsessed with the balance of payments." See LBJ, Transcript, George Ball Oral History Interview II, July 9, 1971, by Paige E. Mulhollan, page 19.

[9] Francis J. Gavin, *Gold, Dollars, and Power: The Politics of International Monetary Relations, 1958–1971* (Chapel Hill: University of North Carolina Press, 2004), 197.

deterioration was also painful for American consumers. Expansionary monetary policies without a devaluation of the dollar attracted imports, caused inflation, increased prices, reduced exports, and put pressure on employment. Additional factors worldwide that undermined the Bretton Woods system included a lack of wage discipline, the underdevelopment of institutions for coordinating reforms, and rising capital mobility.[10]

Knowing that American gold reserves could not withstand a mass conversion of dollars into gold, throughout the 1960s American policy makers created a series of political inducements to compel Europeans to hold onto their dollars rather than exchange them for gold. Beginning in 1961, the United States negotiated "offset" agreements with West Germany, in which the German government received American munitions in return for the increased foreign exchange expenses of American troops stationed in Germany. This was actually an ingenious, if somewhat sinister, scheme by the U.S. government. It worked like this: there were more dollars in circulation than gold sitting in Fort Knox beginning sometime after 1958. The United States was financing overseas American military involvement, in part, by printing more currency. European governments complained that the dollar was overvalued. With a worsening American balance of payments, nations like Germany accumulated dollars. The Americans blamed their poor balance of payments situation, in part, on the foreign exchange costs of stationing American GIs in Germany. Offset agreements with the German government assisted with the American balance of payments situation, which meant that the Germans would buy an agreed-upon amount of American military equipment using dollars. Loose American fiscal policy was corrected by implementing a system in which the United States harvested Germany's excess dollars.

On one occasion in 1973, Secretary of Defense James R. Schlesinger explained this scheme to Henry Kissinger. Schlesinger described it as "a system that insulates the Defense component of the balance of payments from the rest of the balance of payments," which would "get that monkey off our backs." Kissinger replied that the scheme was "masterful."[11] As might be expected, over time, this arrangement became unpopular for some Germans who became convinced they were paying the "occupation costs" of American troops stationed in Europe. Alternative solutions were elusive. In 1963, the Group of Ten leading industrial nations began

---

[10] Barry Eichengreen, *The European Economy since 1945: Coordinated Capitalism and Beyond* (Princeton: Princeton University Press, 2007), 242. This trend became known as the "Triffin Dilemma," which is defined here: http://lexicon.ft.com/term?term=triffin-dilemma.

[11] RMN, HAK Telcons, Box 21, July 15, 1973, 12:25 p.m.

discussions to develop a new monetary system, but without success. In the mid-1960s, to allay European fears, the United States loosened the Federal Reserve requirement to hold gold reserves.[12] In 1968, Special Drawing Rights were created in an attempt to meet shortages in liquidity, and President Johnson himself took a personal role in their negotiations.[13] The West was simply unable to cope with an unparalleled rise in international trade, one that accelerated during the 1960s.[14] These political efforts were merely a temporary patchwork attempt to keep the flawed Bretton Woods system alive. The world was moving beyond the postwar era into a more global era, and the Bretton Woods system was not flexible enough to grow with it.

This was what Richard Nixon inherited in 1969. Having a background in neither economics nor a desire to immerse himself unnecessarily in a difficult policy issue about which even experts were undecided about to what to do, Nixon ignored the advice given to him in late 1968 and early 1969 from experts such as Milton Friedman, Paul McCracken, and Paul Volcker. This advice was that the change in administration in January 1969 marked an ideal time to implement major overhauls to Bretton Woods. Friedman even proposed an entirely different monetary system to replace Bretton Woods.[15] Although there had always been some academics in favor of floating exchange rates, these views did not approach the mainstream until the Nixon administration.[16] Robert Ellsworth summed it up for Nixon on November 30, 1968: "There is a great deal of talk in Europe, in the press and elsewhere, about the need for a world monetary conference, a latter day Bretton Woods. No one, however, claims that there is any agreement or consensus about what direction that conference should move in."[17] Therefore, the American policy remained in defense of the status quo, emphasizing the "great merit and

---

[12] 79 Stat. 5, March 1965 (An act to eliminate gold reserves against Federal Reserve Deposits), and 82 Stat. 50, March 1968 (An act to eliminate the gold reserve against Federal Reserve notes).

[13] LBJ, Transcript, Dean Rusk Oral History Interview IV, March 8, 1970, by Paige E. Mulhollan, page 24.

[14] Harold James, *International Monetary Cooperation since Bretton Woods* (New York: Oxford University Press, 1996), 150.

[15] Hoover Institution Archives (HIA), Papers of Milton Friedman, Box 33, "Confidential – A Sketch of a World Monetary System."

[16] Paul A. Volcker and Toyoo Gyohten, *The World's Money and the Threat to American Leadership* (New York: Times Books, 1992), 38.

[17] RMN, NSC Box 1, Memorandum from Robert Ellsworth to President-Elect Nixon, "European interests in U.S. policy," November 30, 1968.

strength" of the Bretton Woods system.[18] Privately, however, the same economic advisors referred to Bretton Woods as "the villain." "The system is now so rigid" that "the need for greater flexibility" was a unanimous view among experts.[19]

On January 18, 1969, Arthur Burns called Nixon's attention to a report that highlighted the growing American balance of payments problem as well as the de facto inconvertibility of the dollar to gold.[20] Burns, who did not support floating rates, was concerned about "an entirely new problem – namely, a sizeable inflation in the midst of recession."[21] Three days later, Henry Kissinger issued National Security Study Memorandum (NSSM) 5, which included the president's request for a review of American international monetary policy.[22] This was a shock to numerous experts within the government, such as Paul McCracken and David Kennedy, because monetary policy had never been handled by the National Security Council before. "It should be absolutely clear that economic and financial policies in this administration are not being determined by the military – directly or at one remove," McCracken wrote.[23]

The academic economists were particularly forceful, not wanting to lose influence on the issue. Milton Friedman advised that the day was near when the instabilities built into the Bretton Woods system must be reconciled. That was a frightening thought, and a task that no one wanted. The need for increasing liquidity to meet ballooning capital movements could not remain. The dollar must be set free from the burden it carried, Friedman argued unsuccessfully.[24] He maintained this position throughout the 1968 election cycle, during which he served on various economic policy committees for the Nixon campaign.[25] Only over time did

---

[18] GRF, Papers of Arthur Burns, Box A9, Statement of Paul W. McCracken, Hendrik S. Houthakker, and Herbert Stein, Members of the Council of Economic Advisers before the Joint Economic Committee, February 17, 1969.

[19] Bentley Library, Papers of Paul McCracken, Box 14, Memorandum from Paul McCracken to President Nixon, "Who is 'The Villain' in International Monetary Disturbances?" February 1, 1969.

[20] *FRUS*, 1969–1976, Volume III, 1.

[21] GRF, Papers of Arthur Burns, Handwritten Journals, 1969–1974, Box 1, November 23, 1970.

[22] *FRUS*, 1969–1976, Volume III, 20.

[23] Bentley Library, Papers of Paul McCracken, Box 14, Memorandum from Paul McCracken to David Kennedy, February 1, 1969.

[24] Larry Ebenstein, *Milton Friedman, A Biography* (New York: Palgrave Macmillan, 2007), 186.

[25] GRF, Papers of Arthur Burns, Box B115, Memorandum from Arthur Burns to Rose Mary Woods, April 22, 1969.

Friedman's ideas began to receive more serious consideration, usually when similar points were raised with Nixon by others, such as during a visit to Washington by former German Chancellor Ludwig Erhard on May 5, 1969.[26] However, Nixon could not become sufficiently interested in the problem. Modest efforts to improve liquidity, such as Secretary of the Treasury David Kennedy's "crawling peg" simply reinforced the view that piecemeal attempts to reform Bretton Woods would never be enough to overcome the system's flaws.[27]

Despite ignoring advice to act in 1969, by the summer of 1971, Richard Nixon spent a significant amount of his time immersed in the details of economic and monetary policy. His announcement of the New Economic Policy on August 15, 1971, considered the mortal blow to Bretton Woods, suspended the conversion of dollars into gold and included a host of other domestic initiatives and international programs that were in the spirit neither of Bretton Woods nor of Nixon's conservative beliefs. Nixon's new policy went well beyond simply fixing the immediate problem of gold. What explains this complete policy reversal only two years after Nixon expressed almost no interest in tackling the problem?

President Nixon's direct involvement in the issue began during April 1971. On April 9, he called Chairman of the Federal Reserve Board Arthur Burns to compel him and his staff to hear a briefing that Nixon had heard.[28] The presentation was conducted by the chair of the recently formed Council on International Economic Policy (CIEP), Pete Peterson.[29] The CIEP was established on January 19, 1971, and, as one of its first tasks, studied the issue of the future competitive position of the American economy in the world.[30] The very first study memorandum issued by the CIEP called for a "complete analysis of the issues ... we should begin intensive planning for a major international initiative on a broad range of international economic problems focusing on the U.S.-EC-Japan relationship."[31]

---

[26] *AAPD* 1969, Botschafter Pauls, Washington, an Bundeskanzler Kiesinger, May 5, 1969, 144.

[27] William Glenn Gray, "Floating the System: Germany, the United States, and the Breakdown of Bretton Woods, 1969–1973." *Diplomatic History*, Vol. 31, No. 1 (April 2007): 300.

[28] RMN, Nixon Tapes, White House Telephone 001–063, April 9, 1971, 1:47 p.m.–1:54 p.m.

[29] RMN, Nixon Tapes, Cabinet Room 052-001, April 8, 1971, 10:40 a.m.–12:17 p.m.

[30] GRF, Papers of Arthur Burns, Box B115, White House press release, January 19, 1971.

[31] GRF, Papers of Arthur Burns, Box A24, Memorandum from Peter G. Peterson to Council on International Economic Policy, "CIEP Study Memorandum #1: Development of an International Economic Strategy for 1971–1972," March 8, 1971.

Peterson convincingly argued that the future ability of the United States to compete commercially against Western Europe and Japan was in jeopardy. There were no clear objectives in the American balance of payments policy or in international economic and trade policy more generally. There was also no reason why the United States should continue to act as the pivot of a monetary system designed to stabilize Western Europe, when some European nations had already become commercial competitors of the United States. Although American exports had increased 100 percent since 1964, West Germany's had increased by 200 percent and Japan's had grown by more than 400 percent.[32] The previous month, Germany surpassed the United States as the largest accumulator of currency reserves.[33] Peterson introduced a new idea: he established a link between economic and monetary policy and foreign policy, and he challenged his audience to consider how American foreign policy could be used to promote the nation's foreign economic interests.

The briefing had a profound impact on Nixon, who otherwise seemed unmoved by Paul McCracken's third "inflation alert" on April 13, following the previous alerts of August 7 and December 1, 1970.[34] Nixon, having no great background in economics – he certainly did not make such reforms an underpinning of his 1968 campaign – became convinced that the future prosperity of the U.S. economy demanded better planning.[35] It was the underlying message of the need for greater American leadership in the world that resonated with him, as well as the need for Europeans to assume greater responsibility for their own monetary policy, an idea consistent with the Nixon Doctrine. Nixon believed that the briefing would force those around him to have a broader view of the world and the role of American economic and foreign policy. Although focused on secret negotiations with China and the Soviet Union, in 1971 Nixon sought a foothold in the domestic economy in advance of the 1972 election, when it was anything but clear that he would win reelection.

Nixon was convinced that the Peterson briefing would impact Burns as much as it had himself, so he leaned on Burns to make sure all senior

[32] Richard Reeves, *President Nixon: Alone in the White House* (New York: Simon and Schuster, 2001), 340.

[33] Gray, 308.

[34] Bentley Library, Papers of Paul McCracken, Box 15, memorandum from Paul McCracken to President Nixon, "Meeting with Paul McCracken, April 13, 1971," April 12, 1971.

[35] Herbert Stein, *Presidential Economics: The Making of Economic Policy from Roosevelt to Clinton* (Washington, D.C.: American Enterprise Institute, 1994), 138.

policy makers at the Federal Reserve heard it. "I thought so much of it myself that I am having it given to the rest of the cabinet, and the whole White House staff," Nixon said. He believed the White House and the Federal Reserve should work more closely in formulating the nation's monetary policy. Insiders at the Federal Reserve were already privately referring to the monetary situation as being in "a crisis of confidence in the dollar."[36] Arthur Burns, who enjoyed quasi-celebrity status in Washington as the government's top inflation fighter, agreed to hear the briefing but raised the point that some could interpret it as White House interference with Federal Reserve neutrality.[37] Nixon often made proclamations about the importance of the Federal Reserve's independent status. "Arthur speaks only to God and me – mostly to God, since his position is independent – as it should be," he once said.[38] Privately, because of Nixon's experience in the 1960 presidential election, he could never permit a truly autonomous Federal Reserve.[39]

The monetary crisis of the summer of 1971 began in May. With the United States unwilling to modify its monetary policy to support the dollar against Europe's currencies, capital fled the dollar for the West German deutschmark at an unprecedented rate. Senior economic advisors had actually been expecting a German revaluation any day, which some said could also include the Dutch, Belgian, and Swiss currencies.[40] Nixon met with his economic team – George Shultz, Arthur Burns, Paul McCracken, Paul Volcker, and John Connally – for two hours on the afternoon of May 4. According to Arthur Burns, the current crisis was the result of "loose talk by German politicians about revaluing the mark,"

---

[36] GRF, Papers of Arthur Burns, Box E5; report by Robert Solomon, March 21, 1971.

[37] William Greider, *Secrets of the Temple: How the Federal Reserve Runs the Country* (New York: Simon and Schuster, 1987), 66.

[38] GRF, Papers of Arthur Burns, Handwritten Journals, 1969–1974, Box 1, December 16, 1972.

[39] Rowland Evans and Robert Novak wrote that Eisenhower-appointed Secretary of the Treasury Robert B. Anderson talked then Senate Majority Leader Lyndon B. Johnson out of an emergency tax cut as a result of the 1958 election. The Federal Reserve under William McChesney Martin concurred, as did business leaders, who were more concerned about a federal balanced budget than a short-term stimulus. The issue enabled John F. Kennedy to convincingly argue that the Republicans were no longer the party of prosperity during the 1960 presidential election. The episode hardened Nixon's views toward the Federal Reserve, and Nixon replaced Martin as soon as he had the opportunity, in 1970. See Rowland Evans and Robert Novak, *Nixon in the White House: The Frustration of Power* (New York: Random House), 1971, 370.

[40] Bentley Library, Papers of Paul McCracken, Box 15, memorandum from Herb Stein to President Nixon, "Weekly Report on International Finance," April 2, 1971.

which stimulated an influx of dollars into Germany.[41] Burns's assumption was confirmed in a telephone call between Burns's assistant J. Dewey Daane and Bundesbank deputy Otmar Emminger the same day.[42] This was not the first time that German rumors had prompted an international monetary crisis, which had also occurred in 1968.[43]

These moments of crisis in Europe often became opportunities for progress on the European Monetary Union (EMU), a long-standing project associated with the European integration movement and the desire of some Europeans to remove the dollar as the pivot of the international monetary system.[44] The purpose of Nixon's May 4 meeting was to "consider more fundamental questions" about the monetary system. Nixon said he wanted to "shake the system up." From a political standpoint, 1971 was the year to do it since it was not an election year.[45] Burns suggested the possibility of holding a weekend conference with the Europeans to work out the details. Nixon said he thought it was a good idea and that he would send John Connally to Europe for such discussions.

It was not soon enough. In an emergency measure, the German markets closed on May 6 "until further notice" while the government devised a plan to reduce the growing short-term speculative capital movements that threatened international monetary stability.[46] More than a billion dollars flooded the German foreign exchanges within the first fifteen minutes of their opening the preceding day.[47] Declaring the American dollar overvalued while tip-toeing around the categorical American refusal to devalue the dollar, the German government believed that it was time "to close the gold window."[48] These views were conveyed at a ministerial meeting of European Community members on May 9. The West German government urgently sought a currency regime with "greater flexibility." Without immediate action, the current trends projected that the problem would only become more severe. Chancellor Willy Brandt defended his

[41] GRF, Papers of Arthur Burns, Handwritten Journals, 1969–1974, Box 1, May 4, 1971.
[42] GRF, Papers of Arthur Burns, Box B65, Memorandum from J. Dewey Daane to Arthur Burns, "Notes on Conversation with Emminger," May 4, 1971.
[43] HAEU, Papers of Edoardo Martino, Box 101, Report by Monetary Committee, European Economic Community, "Avis au Conseil et a la Commission," October 25, 1969.
[44] HAEC, BAC 3–1974 30, Report by European Parliament, "La creation d'une union économique et monétaire," September 29, 1970.
[45] RMN, Nixon Tapes, Oval Office 490-024, May 4, 1971, 3:07–6:19 p.m.
[46] PAAA, B52/III/A1, Telegram from der Bundesminister für Wirtschaft an das Auswärtige Amt, "Schliessung der Deutschen Devisenbörsen," May 6, 1971.
[47] GRF, Papers of Arthur Burns, Box B65, "Conversation with Dr. Klasen," May 5, 1971.
[48] PAAA. B52/III/A1, "Sitzung des Bundeskabinetts am 7. Mai 1971," May 6, 1971.

government's position in a nationally televised address on the same day, noting that "in recent days we have all witnessed the struggle for our currency ... the Federal Government is not responsible for the inflows of dollars."[49]

On May 11, Brandt wrote Nixon to inform him that the monetary crisis was causing the German government great difficulties.[50] Fearing inflation, the German government ceased further intervention in the markets and allowed the deutschmark to float upward. After the Bundesbank's currency reserves had spiked to DM 69.5 billion (US$18.7 billion), Bundesbank deputy Otmar Emminger argued that the mark should be permitted to temporarily float in order to relieve the flight of capital from the dollar.[51] The Bundesbank was "drowning with dollars," according to German Ambassador to Washington Rolf Pauls.[52] However, Germany's political leaders were restrained from advocating for a floating deutsch-mark, even temporarily, due to the refusal of France. It was unknown what impact floating European currencies would have on the Common Agricultural Policy (CAP), one of the core pillars of the European Economic Community (EEC).

For Brandt, avoiding a break with France was the paramount consid-eration. The German government faced "violent criticism" for its decision to allow the mark to float upward during May. The four-pronged French criticism included that there had not been substantive consultations, that the agricultural markets were disturbed, that any European moves toward EMU were now delayed, and that the German decision threatened the foundation of the EEC.[53] The French also accused the Germans of attempting to please the United States, absent any American effort to address the monetary crisis. West Germany Ambassador to Washington Rolf Pauls was concerned that a "dangerous crisis" could form with the United States if the problem was not settled quickly, especially since the U.S. Senate continued to threaten passage of the Mansfield Amendment.[54] Washington remained silent on the German actions. Europeans read such

[49] PAAA. B52/III/A1, Telegram from the Foreign Office to German Embassy Washington, Brussels, Paris, London, and Rome, "sicherung der wirtschaftsstabilitaet in europaeischer verantwortung," May 9, 1971, 4744.

[50] *AAPD* 1971, Bundeskanzler Brandt an Präsident Nixon, 162.

[51] Gray, 308.

[52] PAAA, B31/332, Telegram from German Embassy Washington to Foreign Office, "Bundeskanzlerbesuch," June 1, 1971, 1206.

[53] PAAA, B52/III/A1, "Währungs- und stabilitätspolitische Maßnahmen der Bundesregierung," May 12, 1971.

[54] *AAPD* 1971, Botschafter Pauls, Washington, an das Auswärtige Amt, 175.

silence as ignorance, or, worse, that the United States believed the deutschmark was overvalued.[55]

On May 11, Treasury Secretary John Connally gave President Nixon and his cabinet a briefing on the German actions. Connally advised Nixon to do nothing, to "sit and wait." That was also the advice of Milton Friedman. "People are concerned about paper tigers, not real ones," he said.[56] "I don't think we're hurtin' one bit," Connally argued. He was relieved that the blame the United States ordinarily received for its monetary policy from France was being projected on to the Germans.[57] Connally, a prominent Democrat and former LBJ aide, was a controversial figure. He was among Nixon's closest economic advisors yet virtually unknown in the world of finance. Arthur Burns asked his diary: "Is Connally a spender like [Lyndon] Johnson, despite his 'conservatism'?"[58] Paul McCracken was critical of Connally. "There is a widespread feeling in Europe that we have no interest or concern about the international financial and economic system. Some assume that we are wholly absorbed in domestic matters."[59]

On May 28, Connally gave a major address in Munich at the International Banking Conference of the American Bankers Association. The event was Connally's introduction to the world's most influential international monetary experts because he had only been appointed to the Treasury in February. Connally took the unusual step of remaining for all meetings and meals during the conference.[60] In previewing possible responses to the growing monetary crisis, Connally hinted at possible unilateral American action. "No longer can considerations of friendship, or need, or capacity justify the United States carrying so heavy a share of the common burdens ... no longer will the American people permit their government to engage in international actions in which the true long-run interests of the U.S. are not just as clearly recognized as those of the

[55] HAEC, BAC 3–1978 556, Telex from European Commission Liaison Office Washington D.C. to European Commission, "Position du Secrétaire américain à la Trésorerie sur la politique commerciale des Etats-Unis et l'amélioration de la balance des paiements," May 18, 1971.

[56] HIA, Papers of Milton Friedman, Box 179, Letter from Friedman to George Shultz, May 3, 1971.

[57] RMN, Nixon Tapes, Cabinet Room 056-004, May 11, 1971, 9:30–9:45 a.m.

[58] GRF, Papers of Arthur Burns, Handwritten Journals, 1969–1974, Box 1, December 20, 1970.

[59] Bentley Library, Papers of Paul McCracken, Box 15, memorandum from Paul McCracken to President Nixon, "The Recent International Monetary Disturbances and Some Suggestions," May 17, 1971.

[60] Volcker and Gyohten, 74.

nations with which we deal."[61] Although consistent with the Nixon Doctrine, the abruptness of his remarks was not consistent with the collegiality normally present in gatherings of finance ministers and central bankers.

Europeans at the conference were not without a response. Vice Chancellor Walter Scheel reminded American Deputy Undersecretary of State for Economic Affairs Nathaniel Samuels that the German people would not support linking monetary reform with American troop commitment to Europe. That aspect of the Nixon Doctrine would not be tolerated. This would be seen by the German people, Scheel argued, as paying the American "occupation costs" (*Besatzungskosten*). Samuels was also reminded that the previous German government under Ludwig Erhard collapsed in part due to an impasse over similar negotiations with the United States, which resulted in the loss of an important American ally.[62] Connally, even while he threatened unilateral American action, stated that his position was the status quo, including convertibility and the preservation of Bretton Woods. Although such a statement helped to calm the currency markets, it was not a solution. "Can it be that, despite all appearances to the contrary, Connally is not really a leader?" a confused Arthur Burns wondered.[63]

Nixon became restless as the crisis stewed. On June 2, Chairman of the Council of Economic Advisers Paul McCracken informed the president that "we have just muddled through another international monetary crisis ... however, we cannot be sure of having escaped entirely or permanently." McCracken recommended action. "I believe a decision has to be made urgently on the direction in which we would like the international monetary system to develop."[64] In a meeting on June 8 with Chief of Staff Bob Haldeman, Assistant to the President for Domestic Affairs John Ehrlichman, and Office of Management and Budget Deputy Director Caspar Weinberger, Nixon commented on the recent comments by Arthur Burns in the press. Burns was known for freely and publicly offering unsolicited opinions, especially at after-hours social settings.[65] In the past two months, since Nixon encouraged Burns to hear the April briefing, "Arthur changed from a total optimist two months ago, and now he's a total pessimist ... because he's been over to Europe.

---

[61] *FRUS*, 1969–1976, Volume III, 155.
[62] *AAPD* 1971, Ministerialdirektor Herbst an die Botschaft in Washington, 187.
[63] GRF, Papers of Arthur Burns, Handwritten Journals, 1969–1974, Box 1, May 22, 1971.
[64] *FRUS*, 1969–1976, Volume III, 157.
[65] RMN, Nixon Tapes, Oval Office 514-007, June 8, 1971, 11:06 a.m.–12:00 p.m.

These international gangsters – that's what they are – vampires sucking the blood out of every transaction. They want instability." Nixon "read the riot act" to McCracken, Shultz, Volcker, Flanigan, and Peterson, according to Ehrlichman's diary. Connally was to be the administration's sole spokesperson on economic and monetary affairs to reduce confusion.[66] "Or else quit," Nixon ordered.[67]

During the summer of 1971, Henry Kissinger's office also became increasingly concerned about monetary affairs insofar as the effect the crisis could have on foreign policy with Europe. "Any new action in this field – including no action – will have major consequences for overall U.S. foreign policy," NSC staff Ernest Johnson wrote on June 23.[68] On June 29, in a meeting with John Connally and George Shultz, President Nixon again expressed concern that the country did not do enough long-range economic planning and that it was time for that to change.[69] This theme was the cornerstone of the Nixon's speech in Kansas City on July 6, which foreshadowed that major economic policy changes were on the horizon.[70] These anticipated reforms would be based on tenets of the Nixon Doctrine.[71] Although Nixon understood he had a problem that required his direct attention, his lack of expertise on the subject matter inhibited him. He still considered monetary policy to be a technical – not a foreign policy – problem. Although the distressed foreign exchange markets of May settled during June, volatility again increased at the end of July.

On the afternoon of July 21, Nixon met with Paul McCracken on the subject of American economic competitiveness. Toward the end of the meeting, Nixon picked up the Oval Office phone and called John Connally, Nixon's closest cabinet member and preferred presidential successor:[72]

---

[66] Before Connally became Nixon's official spokesperson on economic as well as fiscal matters, the administration had a "babel of voices" on the subject, including George Shultz and Arthur Burns. See Jules Witcover, *Very Strange Bedfellows: The Short and Unhappy Marriage of Richard Nixon and Spiro Agnew* (New York: Public Affairs, 2007), 212.

[67] HIA, Papers of John Ehrlichman, Box 2, "June 1971 diary: Pentagon Papers, JC to be Econ Spokesman."

[68] *FRUS*, 1969–1976, Volume III, 160.

[69] RMN, Nixon Tapes, Oval Office 530-003, June 29, 1971, 8:32 a.m.–10:07 a.m.

[70] RMN, White House Special Files, President's Personal File, Box 67, "Remarks of the President, Media Briefing on the President's Media Briefing on the President's Domestic Policy Initiatives, Holiday Inn, Kansas City, Missouri."

[71] Dennis Merrill and Thomas G. Paterson, *Major Problems in American Foreign Relations, Volume II: Since 1914* (Boston: Houghton Mifflin Company, 2005), 456.

[72] RMN, Nixon Tapes, White House Telephone 006-183, July 22, 1971, 11:32 p.m.–11:35 p.m.

NIXON: Hi John, I'm just completing a meeting with Paul McCracken –
CONNALLY: Yes, sir.
NIXON: – and, one of the subjects, or major subject, that we've talked
    about that is extremely intriguing to me is, with regard to our
    international competitive position, and it has to do, of course, with,
    a part that we were not discussing, and that is, our monetary thing,
    how we might do something there. I would like if you would talk to
    [Paul McCracken] –
CONNALLY: Yes, sir.
NIXON: – but without your [Under Secretary of the Treasury for
    Monetary Affairs], without [Paul] Volcker. [. . .] I think you and
    I have got to put ourselves in the top of this heap, listen to everybody,
    and then, frankly, decide what we're going to be.
CONNALLY: All right, sir. I'll –
NIXON: – and so, do it, approach it with an open mind, if you will.
CONNALLY: Oh I will, don't you worry.[73]

The following day, on July 22, Nixon assembled his economic kitchen
cabinet – the "Quadriad" – composed of John Connally, George Shultz,
Arthur Burns, and Paul McCracken. Although Quadriad meetings started
at the very beginning of the Nixon administration (and accomplished
minimal aims, such as continuing the import tax surcharges left by the
Johnson administration), the Quadriad became greatly enhanced in 1971
when its newest member, John Connally, had the ear of the president.[74]
This group was charged with the task of studying overhauls of American
economic and monetary policy. Nixon chose these aides because they
were not, as he saw them, among the "ideologues who grew up with
Bretton Woods and just don't want anything to change." Nixon was not
afraid to make bold decisions; witness his work in other areas of foreign
policy. "Goddamn it, my view is why be bound by all that stuff in the
past?" he said.[75] The purpose of the Nixon Doctrine was to improve the
position of the United States. Treaty commitments would be honored, but
helping others was secondary to helping the United States. "This is not

---

[73] Connally noted in his memoirs that "I had no sooner taken office than we had to confront
    a very hostile international monetary system. [. . .] Throughout 1971, the U.S. economy
    was in such distress, and the world monetary picture so volatile, that comparisons were
    being made to 1933." See John Connally, *In History's Shadow: An American Odyssey*
    (New York: Hyperion, 1993), 236.
[74] GRF, Papers of Arthur Burns, Box A8, Memorandum from Paul McCracken to Secretary
    Kennedy, Director Mayo, and Counselor Burns, March 20, 1969.
[75] RMN, Nixon Tapes, Oval Office 542-004, July 22, 1971, 10:51 a.m.–11:36 a.m.

going to be comfortable for other people, but it might be very damn helpful for us." For some of Nixon's aides, it was shocking to hear this. "I am convinced that the President will do anything to be reelected," Arthur Burns wrote in his diary.[76] Paul McCracken became so frustrated that he told Nixon he intended to resign and desired to return to the faculty at the University of Michigan at the end of the year.[77]

Arthur Burns had strong views on any proposed reforms to international monetary policy, and Nixon knew he must play a part in the solution. Burns had long desired to end the American balance of payments problem by increasing the official price of gold while still preserving convertibility, believing that the result would be stable currencies to promote international trade and investment.[78] He told Nixon previously that if it became necessary to end convertibility, "we should do all we can – both substantively and cosmetically – to make it appear that other governments have forced the action on us."[79] According to Burns's diary, he was called into the Oval Office on July 8 and threatened by Nixon and Connally. "The president stated that 'I too will be expected to conform to publicly announced admin- istration policies.' "[80] Nixon had several ways to influence Burns, including threatening to alter the size of the Federal Reserve Board, leaving vacancies on the Board unfilled, and withholding salary increases from Burns. Burns's salary was an especially delicate matter. He made a recommendation in 1970 that the Chairman of the Federal Reserve Board be paid a salary equal to that of cabinet members. Burns claimed that he intended the increase to take effect with his successor.[81] On July 24, in a meeting with Bob Haldeman and John Ehrlichman, Nixon asked, "now what do you want to do with Arthur Burns, give him that raise?"[82] "No," Haldeman responded, "you were going to meet with Burns." Nixon noted, "well,

---

[76] GRF, Papers of Arthur Burns, Handwritten Journals, 1969–1974, Box 1, March 8, 1971.

[77] Bentley Library, Papers of Paul McCracken, Box 15, Memorandum from Paul McCracken to President Nixon, "Meeting with Paul W. McCracken, July 22, 1971, 10:45 am," August 4, 1971.

[78] Wyatt C. Wells, *Economist in an Uncertain World: Arthur F. Burns and the Federal Reserve, 1970–78* (New York: Columbia University Press, 1994), 37. Critics of such views, Wells argues, such as George Shultz and Milton Friedman, pointed out that the defense of fixed exchange rates often required domestic policies that were otherwise inappropriate.

[79] GRF, Papers of Arthur Burns, Box N1, Memorandum from Arthur Burns to President Nixon, May 19, 1971.

[80] GRF, Papers of Arthur Burns, Handwritten Journals, 1969–1974, Box 1, July 8, 1971.

[81] GRF, Papers of Arthur Burns, Box K32, Letter from Arthur Burns to Caspar Weinberger, December 2, 1970, and to George Shultz, December 29, 1972.

[82] RMN, Nixon Tapes, Oval Office 545-003, July 24, 1971, 12:36 p.m.–1:03 p.m.

I think we've changed our mind. You call Connally, and say that . . . I just feel I ought to let Burns cool his heels for a few more days. It doesn't mean we should fight him openly, but [Connally] believes the cool treatment is necessary at this point." Haldeman concurred. "I'm not so sure I would stop there, but I agree with at least that much."

"I have no problem just not having [Burns] around," Nixon said. "And I'll tell you another thing that will get to him, John – just not give him that raise. Could you get [a] story leaked through the [Counsel to the President Chuck] Colson apparatus on Arthur? Connally suggested two things as a matter of fact. One is that 'recommendations are being made among the president's economic advisors that the Federal Reserve Board membership [is to] be increased because it's having so many problems these days.' That's point one, and [that] 'this is a matter that will be recommended.' The other one is that 'a recommendation has been made that in view of the fact that the president has responsibility for full employment, the president is considering legislation to reform the Federal Reserve. The Fed has got to be brought in [to the Executive Branch].' " As the saying goes, Washington is the only vessel to leak from the top.

Nixon continued: "The independence of the Fed . . . ," but Ehrlichman finished his sentence, " . . . is seriously in question because of the [poor] economic results of the last year." Nixon knew the impact of such a leak. "It would worry Arthur a little."[83] A UPI article appeared in the *Washington Daily News* on July 28, and related articles appeared in the *Wall Street Journal* and the *Washington Post* on July 29.[84] Burns deeply resented the false stories in the press. "The harassing of the Fed by the president and his pusillanimous staff will continue and may even intensify. Fortunately, although I am no longer sure whether the President fully knows this, I am still his best friend. By standing firm, I will serve the economy – and thereby also the President – best."[85] Bill Safire, who had been utilized by Nixon to rankle Burns in the past, wrote Bob Haldeman to say the leaked stories were "stupid" and "vicious, mean, and infuriating."[86]

As the media speculated on which monetary reforms the White House was considering in response to the crisis, Nixon demanded absolute secrecy

[83] H. R. Haldeman. *The Haldeman Diaries: Inside the Nixon White House* (New York: G. P. Putnam's Sons, 1994), 331–332.

[84] GRF, Papers of Arthur Burns, Box B117, "Nixon Weighs a Double-Size Fed: Burns Denies Pay Request," July 29, 1971.

[85] GRF, Papers of Arthur Burns, Handwritten Journals, 1969–1974, Box 1, March 8, 1971.

[86] LOC, Papers of Bill Safire, Box 33, Memorandum from Bill Safire to Bob Haldeman, August 3, 1971.

on the part of the Quadriad. In a conversation between President Nixon and Pete Peterson on July 26, the president was still elated from his July 15 announcement that he would be the first American president to visit the People's Republic of China, the result of months of secret negotiations. Nixon similarly recommended keeping monetary policy discussions "top secret, involving only [John] Connally and a few deputies, on a top secret basis, to keep from a half dozen reporters in two weeks [from] knowing we're doing this."[87] It was as though he wanted the high he felt for catching everyone off guard on China to never end. "I would not under any circumstances inform [Arthur] Burns. Burns has nothing good to say about the economy. Every time he speaks he says 'everything is a failure.' " To that, Peterson responded:

PETERSON: I guess what I'm asking for is authority to do a top secret thing on a bold approach to this problem, looking toward an August announcement, if it all works out well, with Connally, Shultz, and I'll add McCracken, and then just keep everybody else out.

NIXON: I think this is a good idea ... The key man in this play is Connally, because he understands politics, and he is also the Treasury man. When I get him in tomorrow, you come in, and let's just bless it right there ... Something has to be done, doesn't it? Part of the problem, you know Pete, is not one that is created by anything that we've done. This problem, ever since about 1961 or -2 has been covering a lot of it up through all of our international manipulations.

"You go to work immediately on a covert basis, and I'll get Connally, and we'll talk about this thing," Nixon concluded. "I don't want it too big. You really have to have people who contribute to the dialogue. I don't contribute much except a deep-seated ignorance."

The next day, President Nixon had renewed concerns about secrecy. In a meeting with Peterson and Connally, the president emphasized that, "in view of the high sensitivity of this, if we ever have anything secret in this damn government, this, next to China, has got to be secret."[88] Connally disagreed:

CONNALLY: Frankly, I think we ought to tell Arthur Burns. The problem with Arthur, and I sounded him out last night. He's not thinking in terms of as bold a step as Pete or I are.

NIXON: Will he keep quiet?

[87] RMN, Nixon Tapes, Oval Office 546-002, July 26, 1971, 4:32 p.m.–5:19 p.m.
[88] RMN, Nixon Tapes, Oval Office 547-009, July 27, 1971, 12:15 p.m.–1:09 p.m.

CONNALLY: Yes, he will, provided we bring him in the issue. The danger is that without him there, he's going to be hot.

PETERSON: And perhaps with good reason.

NIXON: One way to work Arthur on this, knowing his ego, is to get him to think the idea was his.

CONNALLY: We need to lay out the alternatives for you. . . . The figures are coming out tomorrow on our June balance of trade. And we've got a negative balance of trade of $360 million. April and May were over $200 million deficits in each of those months. This was the third successive [record deficit] month in a row. Big story in the [*Washington*] *Post* this morning, "Reserve assets in the United States are at their lowest since 1938." Now we've got to pay out another $800 million. The gold [reserves] will be below $10 billion for the first time. These are basic facts. I draw one conclusion: if we have the defense of the dollar, I don't think we can hold it until the election of '72, plus the fact that as things stand now, we have approximately $10 billion in gold to satisfy $30 billion worth of commitments [in circulating dollars]. If we try to defend the dollar between now and next year, which we can do, it's one of the alternatives, but it's going to take some drastic action on your part regardless.

PETERSON: John tells it how it is. We need bold action soon.

CONNALLY: . . . Here's what you want to do, is to write a letter. You write to the International Monetary Fund, it's a very simple thing. It's a letter of two paragraphs. The first paragraph in effect says that you no longer will convert dollars to gold. You do that with one sentence. Secondly, you say, assuming you want to go this route, you say you no longer will support the fixed exchange rates section of the International Monetary Fund. That means you're going to float.

With his customary abruptness, Connally recommended what would be one of the most important economic events of the postwar period. With the gold reserves at a critical point, Nixon had no other choice. He hoped to avoid taking major action until after the 1972 election, but Connally convinced him that major action would be needed before the election even to preserve the status quo.

There were still deep differences among Nixon's aides over monetary policy. Nixon sent Pete Peterson to Camp David to offer his earlier April briefing to an expanded group, including representatives of the departments of State, Commerce, Labor, and Treasury; the Council of Economic Advisers; and the National Security Council. The result was not quite what the president had hoped for. "You know what happened at Peterson's Camp David sessions? He pulled all the Under Secretaries groups of his Council [on International Economic Policy] for two days, and he got a cleavage right smack down the middle," Bob Haldeman told Nixon. "State, and the Council of Economic Advisers, and the guy from the NSC who was there, said 'there's no problem. What's all this shouting about? We've seen this trend before. Your charts are misleading, and you can always rape statistics, and so on.' And Commerce, Labor, and Peterson's group, and Treasury, said 'there's a hell of a problem. We're going down the tubes here.' And there was a two day battle."[89] The episode demonstrated that even as the United States moved closer and closer to taking action, there was no consensus. Preservation of the Bretton Woods system had been American policy for a quarter century. The impact of a major policy change had unknown domestic and international consequences across a range of government agencies.

As Nixon neared a decision, meeting with the Quadriad occupied a growing amount of his time. During a four-hour session in the Oval Office on August 2, 1971, the main issue was whether any proposed reforms required Congressional approval.[90]

CONNALLY: Seems to me there are two essential problems here. . . . One is an international problem. Two is a domestic problem. . . . In the international field, [it's] convertibility of dollars into gold. And we're going to have to stop that at some point. Most people seem to think that $10 billion in gold [reserves] is a point below which we should not go. We can stop convertibility very easy, by just saying so. The next thing is, you ought to float. . . . Whatever we do in the international field ought to be coupled with action on the domestic front, so they tend to shield each other. . . . But then you say you recognize we have problems at home, and coupled with that, you're going to put a ceiling on spending in the Congress. Say you want to reduce [the federal budget by] ten billion dollars. So this gives you a strong position of fiscal responsibility. Then you say "I'm going to impose a ten percent border tax on all imports into this country until such time as we renegotiate our currency . . . because we are non-competitive."

NIXON: That requires Congressional action.

---

[89] RMN, Nixon Tapes, Oval Office 549-007, July 28, 1971, 10:20 a.m.–11:16 a.m.
[90] RMN, Nixon Tapes, Oval Office 553-006, August 2, 1971, 9:58 a.m.–2:05 p.m.

CONNALLY: No it doesn't. . . . Then you got to put on a 90 to a 120 day
freeze. Not "wage and price controls," [but] a "freeze." Every field,
for 90 to a 120 days, until we have time to renegotiate on the
international field, and [during this] time we can see what impact
these things are going to have. . . . It'll stimulate the hell out of your
economy. . . . You can't force countries to devalue, but you can take
them off the gold standard.

NIXON: I tend not to be as persuaded by the international monetary
arguments as I am by the domestic arguments. So therefore I am
inclined to think that we should consider doing all those things
domestically which would also have a good effect internationally, and
as a last resort do the international thing, except of course floating.
The floating thing I think is so goddamned confusing that nobody's
going to understand. Closing the gold window sounds as if the dollar
is going to hell, that's to the average person.

Connally's protectionist domestic proposals were a direct appeal to
Arthur Burns, who was less comfortable with the international actions
proposed, such as closing the gold window. Whereas devaluing the
dollar's value in relation to gold required Congressional approval,
Nixon was relieved to hear that ending the link between the dollar and
gold did not. Nixon feared a public relations nightmare if the measure
were put to Congress, which could hold weeks of hearings and attach
hundreds of amendments to it.

Connally pushed Nixon even harder for action in the Oval Office on
August 6. Nixon was interested primarily in the domestic consequences of
any proposed actions and especially the effect they would have on his
image and electoral chances. "It's basically psychology. The country needs
a psychological lift. And the psychological lift can only come from doing
something," Nixon said.[91] "I agree with that one thousand percent. You
have to do something. You have to jerk this country up . . . so that they say
we've got a leader here," Connally appealed to Nixon's ego. The relationship between domestic policy and international economic policy was
finally clear to Nixon. "If we put this wage price thing on, we've got to
shake the country and say 'look, you people have got to get off your ass
and go to work. We've got to be more competitive. It's time for America to
be more competitive in the world.' " Paul McCracken made a similar
appeal on August 9. "No nation with a weak currency and a weak

[91] RMN, Nixon Tapes, Oval Office 556-004, August 6, 1971, 10:34 a.m.–11:38 a.m.

competitive position can exercise strong international economic leadership. Indeed, history is quite clear that a country with a weak currency and
a weak international economic position will find its political leadership
also impeded," McCracken wrote.[92] That was an argument tailor-made
for the way Nixon saw the world.

On August 12, 1971, although Nixon knew a decision would have to
be made soon, he still delayed. Paul Volcker called a vacationing John
Connally to tell him that gold reserves had reached another new low.
In addition, Great Britain planned to submit a massive request to convert
US$3 billion into gold.[93] The request was received by Charles Coombs of
the Federal Reserve Bank of New York on August 13, while visiting the
Treasury Department in Washington.[94] The British request caused panic
in the Treasury and prompted Connally's early return to Washington. The
request indicated that the British government presciently understood that
the time for remaining gold conversions was short. The United States was
forced to act. Should the British request be granted, the publicity of such a
large transfer of gold would cause a European run on the Federal Reserve
at the worst possible moment. Should the request be denied, would that
signal – or, worse yet, *confirm* – that the Americans were about to enact
major international monetary reforms. With less than 10 billion in gold
reserves before the British request, an American default loomed.

Nixon called his Secretary of the Treasury. Connally explained his
decision to cut his vacation short and return to Washington immediately.
"We expect a bad day tomorrow [for the gold reserves] ... we're constantly losing the initiative, I'm afraid." He recommended immediate
action. Due to the dire international situation and rapidly declining
American gold reserves, "the least we could do is to move on the international front this afternoon ... or early in the morning, just close the

---

[92] Bentley Library, Papers of Paul McCracken, Box 15, memorandum from Paul
McCracken to President Nixon, "Memorandum for the President," August 9, 1971.

[93] RMN, Nixon Tapes, White House Telephone 007–112, August 12, 1971, 12:01 p.m.–
12:12 p.m. There is some dispute over whether the British request ever occurred. This is a
critical dispute because American policy makers believed it occurred, and, subsequently,
they were driven to the actions taken during the weekend of August 15. The request is
mentioned in multiple memoir accounts, including Connally, 237; Haldeman, 340; Stein,
167, and William Safire, *Before the Fall: An Inside View of the Pre-Watergate White
House* (Garden City, N.Y.: Doubleday & Company, 1975), 509. The British denied the
request was ever made. In a letter on August 13, 1971, from Alan Bailey, Office of the
Chancellor of the Exchequer to Robert Armstrong, 10 Downing Street, Bailey stated "at
no time did the Bank of England ask for conversion of U.S. dollars into gold; nor is there
any basis for a figure of $3 billion." See PREM 15–838.

[94] Volcker and Gyohten, 77.

[gold window]." The remaining domestic reforms could be put off, if desired, he said. "We wouldn't have to move on the domestic front until, say, Monday [August 16], which would give you all weekend [August 13–15] to firm up the details. ... The thing that worries me is that I don't want to leave the appearance that we've reacted in haste, or that we were unprepared." Nixon agreed. It was time to be decisive.

Nixon called Arthur Burns to tell him this news. Burns was greatly disappointed that Nixon planned to end convertibility of the dollar to gold, but prepared his staff for the possibility that it would happen. "Advocates of closing the gold window seem to be overlooking at least one disastrous consequence of such action. This would be the massive destruction of international liquidity that would inexorably follow ... closure of the gold window would pull out the cornerstone of the IMF and immediately paralyze any lending operations by that institution," Burns deputy Coombs wrote on August 13.[95] A similar view was also expressed by Paul McCracken. Even George Shultz was nervous about ending the gold window so suddenly, even though he believed it was the right thing to do in the long run. Burns provided an apocalyptic reflection in his diary. "My efforts to prevent closing the gold window ... do not seem to have succeeded ... we now have a government that seems incapable, not only of constructive leadership, but of any action at all."[96]

Virtually all accounts of the American decision to close the gold window focus on the weekend that Nixon and his advisors spent at Camp David, which preceded Nixon's televised announcement on August 15. The summit at Camp David was simply so that everyone felt that they participated in the historic decision. It was also important to get everyone in the room at the same time and go over the details while the markets were closed for the weekend in both the United States and Europe. The decisions were made during two back-to-back meetings in Nixon's hideaway office in the Executive Office Building on the afternoon of Thursday, August 12. Both were captured by Nixon's White House taping system, which best demonstrates Nixon's calculations and thinking. The first determined the procedure for taking final action, whereas the second meeting decided the action itself. The meetings also carefully choreographed the weekend of August 13–15 at Camp David where it is traditionally understood that these decisions were finalized.

---

[95] GRF, Papers of Arthur Burns, Box B65, Memorandum from C. A. Coombs to Arthur Burns, August 13, 1971.

[96] GRF, Papers of Arthur Burns, Handwritten Journals, 1969–1974, Box 1, August 12, 1971.

In the first meeting, Bob Haldeman suggested how to communicate Nixon's decision to everyone affected.[97] "Let a few people in on it. Tape 'em all, the people you let in, maybe half a dozen. Go up to Camp David, where they're locked up and can't talk to anybody, and just sit there and just grind the thing through, through the weekend, and [announce the result] on Monday [August 16]."[98] Nixon still hoped to take no more action than was necessary to solve the immediate crisis. "I think the domestic [action] would be much better coming on the seventh [of September, when the Congress reconvened]." He feared the consequences of announcing too many domestic reforms without input from Congress. He was more comfortable about acting unilaterally to close the gold window. He had no choice.

The second meeting that afternoon decided the action to be taken. Nixon approved Haldeman's suggestion to go to Camp David for the weekend. Now he needed to secure Connally's support. George Shultz also took part in the meeting that changed postwar economic history. "In order to stop the crisis, if we look at the international monetary thing, all that is needed is to close the gold window. That stops the crisis, right?" Nixon asked.[99]

CONNALLY: That stops the crisis from our losing assets, but in effect it may create a crisis in terms of the international money markets. It'll leave them in a chaotic state until something else happens, in my judgment.
NIXON: You have to say of course, that when you do this ... that the United States was taking action to preserve the dollar ... and that we were temporarily closing the gold window, and that we would be prepared now to discuss with ... nations around the world ... a better, more stable system. ... I would not have you do it ... at prime time [for television viewers] at night. There's no use to stir up a lot of people about things they don't understand. ... Now, the question is, if we do the whole thing at one time, could we do it now, tonight? I don't think so ... well, I guess we could start burning the coal and we could get it by tomorrow night. But I don't see any damned advantage

---

[97] RMN, Nixon Tapes, Executive Office Building 273-007, August 12, 1971, 3:11 p.m.–4:20 p.m.
[98] Haldeman assigned Larry Higby of his staff to inform those involved to be available the weekend of August 13–15 for an unspecified length of time on an unspecified topic and not to inform anyone – including spouses – of their destination. Bill Safire comically recalls being summoned in a similar fashion in *Before the Fall*, 509.
[99] RMN, Nixon Tapes, Executive Office Building 273-020, August 12, 1971, 5:30 p.m.–7:00 p.m.

of that. In my view, if we do don't it tonight, John, then if we're thinking of doing the whole package, what I was thinking we would do is call the whole working group together, and we could whip up to Camp David tomorrow, and spend Friday, Saturday, and Sunday. Now that's one thing we could do, go for the whole ball on Sunday [August 15].

SHULTZ: I was going to say, I think that the closing of the gold window and the impact of that has already been taken into account in the marketplaces.

CONNALLY: Well, they're all predicting, all the professionals think it's coming.

NIXON: That may be one of the reasons everybody's so jittery.

CONNALLY: Well, sure it's why it's jittery, that's why it's going to remain jittery. I don't really think we ought to be concerned about that. I think we ought to primarily be concerned about how you can most effectively convince the American people that you, number one, are aware of your economic problem, number two, that you have thoughtfully considered them not as an piecemeal emergency stop-gap measure, but that you have analyzed them in depth, and that you have dealt with them in a substantive matter. ... The problem of doing it piecemeal is, number one, everybody's going to be saying, well, "what's–he's got to do something else. What comes next?"

NIXON: Yeah.

CONNALLY: And beyond that, they start speculating. Then everybody starts trying to jump the gun on you, you get a bunch of leaks, you get a bunch of Congressmen, and they all want to be holding [hearings] to show how smart they are. ... I agree with you completely that if you can wait until September seventh to do it, no question whether that's the wise thing to do, no question in my mind that if you do the whole package, the impact will be infinitely greater than the sum of the parts.

NIXON: Yeah.

CONNALLY: But the main thing is, I don't think you can wait that long in terms of the international money market. We've lost since August, in the twelve days in August, the foreign governments have acquired over three billion dollars [in gold] –

NIXON: Yeah.

CONNALLY: – three billion, six hundred, and ninety-four million dollars [in gold], just since the last twelve days. Today was a billion dollar day, tomorrow might be three billion [if the British request is approved]. We could ride it out, but when you consider what debts we have and the –

NIXON: Well let me now ask this, John, just so we can see what our options are in terms of doing it all in one package. Let me see if I can get this correct. You would have doubts about closing the gold window, and then doing the rest of it on September the seventh. That doesn't sound good to you.

CONNALLY: I don't think it's the best solution . . . I think the net effect of that is, that number one, the impression is that you were forced to do it by what's happened in Europe in the last two weeks. And secondly, that you didn't know what to do, it took you from now, from tomorrow, to September the seventh to figure out what to do, and that you were merely reacting. . . . You don't have a good situation. Polls indicate you're taking a whipping on this economic issue. . . . What the hell do we have, six or ten billion [dollars in remaining gold reserves]. . . . We owe thirty billion [dollars in overseas commitments] . . . we can't pay it . . . you can just say, "I'd hoped that I might wait, but the situation has reached the point where I think I must say to the nation and the world now what my plan is . . . the situation is such that I think damage would be done to the international monetary stability as well as the domestic economy to wait further." I'm not going to say that you can't stand it until September, but . . . we're not ready for it, we can't go tomorrow, we're not ready for tomorrow.

NIXON: George . . . let's come back to Arthur [Burns]'s view. Arthur's view is that we should do it all at once.

SHULTZ: His program [is] to do these domestic type things, including the border tax, and see if that doesn't handle the gold crisis, [and] don't close the gold window, and carry on these discussions that are essentially aimed at changing the price of gold.

CONNALLY: I just don't see the point. Hell, if you're going do all this domestic stuff, let's close the gold window, so we don't have the rest of these guys just keep nibbling at us. Because if they keep nibbling, if the announcement of the domestic program doesn't work, then next week you got to close the gold window, and I think that's a –

NIXON: I think he has a point there.

CONNALLY: – I think that's a risk you don't have to take.

NIXON: As a matter of fact, George, as we look at your analysis, we really ought to close the gold window, shouldn't we?

SHULTZ: Sure, I believe as a long-run proposition that we ought to close it and keep it closed.

NIXON: John, one thing that you and I, on a political matter, in talking to the Quadriad, have to remember, is this: our primary goal must be a continued upward surge in the domestic economy. And we must not, in order to stabilize the international situation, cut our guts out here.

SHULTZ: On the wage price thing, a freeze of no longer than 120 ... days.

NIXON: Well, the shorter it is, the simpler it can be ... But for a short freeze, what the hell, anybody can suffer for 60 days, or 90 days, 120 maybe [*laughs*] ... I think we ought to go Monday [August 16], with the whole ball. I would suggest, and this is one way we can keep it closely held, a meeting in Camp David over the weekend, and have everybody locked up up there ... I want to [say], in not wanting to appear to panic ... [that] we have been meeting for a long time on this subject ... I think we can just go out and say that we are taking these steps because we think it is time now for the United States to do this. Crack it out there, very central, not too much explanation ... I think this is something ... it's like the China announcement, where action is hard, the words should be very brief.

CONNALLY: You want ... to show that we've been deteriorating [under the present system] for twenty-five years, and that you're the first president that's had the guts to take this comprehensive action.

NIXON: I would say that for the past twenty-five years we've seen a gradual deterioration of our position, and ... we've had these monetary crises and so forth, and it's time now to call it off.

SHULTZ: I was just going to ask. Suppose you could have it either way, unilateral through the president, or through the Congress, would you have a preference?

CONNALLY: Oh, unilateral would be the preference.

NIXON: I prefer the unilateral thing for another reason, that the Congress is likely to hedge it with so many restrictions –

CONNALLY: That's correct.

NIXON: Well now John ... I think we can go Monday. ... Putting it in the context of the China thing, I did that with great surprise, and we could, when we brief on Monday [August 16], we'll say the president has had this under consideration for, which is actually true, [Pete] Peterson wrote me a memorandum months ago.

CONNALLY: It'll be the shot heard around the world, you can be sure of that. [*laughs*] It'll be [heard] in every town and hamlet.

NIXON: I would say that we set our [Camp David] meeting for three o'clock tomorrow afternoon.

CONNALLY: Yes sir.

NIXON: The thing is, John, I personally have pretty much decided what I want to do anyway. . . . I'm pretty well decided. . . . That's really the way I tend to operate anyway, and everybody knows it. I usually don't horse around and say, "let's take a vote."

SHULTZ: The markets will boil Friday afternoon, and on Monday they'll know what happened. There'll be a tremendous amount of speculation about what was in those meetings. Perhaps there's an advantage to saying, either making your statement, or issue a statement Sunday night.

NIXON: . . . I see your point about Sunday night. Well, if we can get ready, that would be better, then we wouldn't screw around and have Monday to lose another billion dollars [in gold reserves].

SHULTZ: . . . Beginning about midnight Sunday night, in other words, the markets in Brussels, the European market, with the time difference, this kind of speculation is going on beginning about midnight on Sunday . . . I think it's the biggest economic policy since the end of World War II.

CONNALLY: I can say in twenty-five years, no question about it. . . . I think it gives you an opportunity. . . . I think this might put your critics so far behind the eight ball that they're not going to know what to do.

NIXON: This is fine. Listen, John, it occurs to me, hell, we don't have to screw up the market tomorrow . . . [by announcing] we're all going [to Camp David]. We won't announce a goddamn thing. . . . I go to Camp David regularly. The rest of you happened to come up, that's all. . . . The main purpose of going to Camp David [is that] I can take people up there and they don't need to know a hell of a lot about it. The main purpose of going to Camp David, frankly, is to get everybody in there where they're not going to talk to anybody.

CONNALLY: Right.

NIXON: Where everybody keeps their damn mouth shut, and there's no papers, I know there's going to be stories in *The New York Times* on Sunday about the administration going out. That is what I don't want. But we meet for three days, get the job done, and come back. And I can keep 'em up there, too, until I get back. You see what I mean? Without any leaks. That's the way I do it. But we won't say everybody who's going. You can . . . say "look, the president's inviting you up for the weekend, inviting you up to Camp David for the weekend."

The solution was decided. Nixon was the first leader who had the boldness to end the failing Bretton Woods system, even though his methodology was unnecessarily abrupt. The gold window would be closed but negotiations could take place with European allies. Nixon also agreed to various protectionist measures, including an import tax, promotion of "made in America" products, and wage and price controls. He went against his own economic philosophy to ensure the support of Arthur Burns, the right wing of the Republican Party, and isolationists in Congress who would otherwise criticize Nixon's unilateralism. The protectionist measures were also a direct appeal to the American electorate, who Nixon hoped would see he was looking out for them. It was one of the most controversial decisions of Nixon's entire presidency.

Arthur Burns described the long weekend at Camp David as "peaceful and harmonious – as such things go."[100] The substantive decision had already been made, and Burns got what he wanted. His notes, not recorded in his diary until August 22, as well as Bill Safire's, remain the best records of that weekend.[101] The tenor of both records is that everyone involved knew they were making historic decisions, and a commensurate amount of security veiled the process. "This is the most important weekend in economics since March 4, 1933," Herb Stein said. There was a concern that no foreign policy advisors were present at any point during the meeting. Security seemed to be a greater concern. Stein joked to Safire that the commandment for the weekend was "there shall be no phone calls out of this encampment."[102]

Nixon reminded everyone of this several times over the weekend. "There is to be absolutely no call made out of here ... between now and Monday night. Everyone here is to button his lip." All participants were given VIP treatment by Nixon, including Camp David jackets. Attendees, who understood that history was being made, signed a log to record their attendance, and a photograph was taken. For some participants, such as Arthur Burns and Paul McCracken, the weekend marked a zenith in their influence on monetary policy. McCracken left the administration, whereas Burns stayed on but became increasingly miserable. For other advisors, such as George Shultz, the weekend marked an ascendancy of

[100] GRF, Papers of Arthur Burns, Handwritten Journals, 1969–1974, Box 1, August 22, 1971.
[101] Expansion of the Nixon taping system to Camp David did not occur until 1972, at a great loss to history.
[102] LOC, Papers of Bill Safire, Box 22.

power and influence.[103] Throughout the weekend, secrecy was essential until the final decision was announced. "Fortunes could be made with this information," Paul Volcker told Bob Haldeman. "How much is your budget deficit?" Volcker asked George Shultz. "23 billion," Shultz said. "Give me a billion and a free hand on Monday, and I'll make it for you on the money market," Volcker quipped. "We are releasing forces that we need not release," Burns wrote in his diary.

Nixon preempted the popular Western program *Bonanza* at 9:00 p.m. on Sunday, August 15, to suspend convertibility of the dollar in a live, nationally televised address. When he was criticized by the press for not providing the text of the speech in advance, Nixon responded "why, you dumb bastards, if we told you, you would have told the world and we would have lost all our gold."[104] He informed only select Congressional leaders, by telephone, at 7:30 p.m. "That's the way we did the China thing," Nixon reminded himself.

Although historians have concurred that the Bretton Woods system had been "on death watch" for many years, it was Nixon who dealt the mortal blow to the system. "The time has come for a New Economic Policy for the United States," Nixon said. "Its targets are unemployment, inflation, and international speculation."[105] This action was intended to produce major improvements in the American balance of payments and trade deficit, the first since 1893, while an import surcharge was to be a bargaining lever against any foreign resistance or retaliation.[106] Wages and prices were frozen for 90 days, while both federal taxes and government expenditures were cut.[107] The policies took effect almost immediately. John Connally informed Chairman of the IMF Fund Pierre-Paul Schweitzer on August 15. "This is to notify you that, with effect August 15, 1971, the United States no longer, for the purposes of international

---

[103] In not only the United States, but also in Europe and Japan, the collapse of Bretton Woods led to the rise of a new generation of officials with expertise in monetary affairs. Several served as finance ministers during the collapse of Bretton Woods and became close to each for the remainder of their long careers due to the experiences of shared crisis. In addition to Shultz, this group included Helmut Schmidt, Valery Giscard d'Estaing, and Takeo Fukuda. To ensure they could meet without attention from the press, they called their gatherings a meeting of the "Library Committee."

[104] LOC, Papers of Bill Safire, Box 22.

[105] RMN, White House Special File, President's Personal File, Box 68, "The President's Reading Copy, The Challenge of Peace."

[106] David P. Calleo, *The Imperious Economy* (Cambridge: Harvard University Press, 1982), 62–63.

[107] Otmar Emminger, *D-Mark, Dollar, Wärungskrisen* (Stuttgart: Deutsche Verlags-Anstalt, 1986), 190–195.

transactions, in fact, freely buys and sells gold under the second sentence of Article IV, Section 4(b)."[108]

August 15, 1971, marked a "definitive and decisive turning point in the President's state of mind."[109] He came to believe that if the United States was not a world power economically, it could not be a world power politically or militarily.[110] Nixon's action gave him new confidence to act in the economic sphere. On the evening of August 15, Nixon made a series of phone calls to notify administration officials of his decision. "We're going for the wage price freeze ... we're going to float the dollar ... we're going to invest in tax credits, we're going to repeal the excise tax on automobiles, the personal income tax exemption, we're going to cut the budget. It's quite a bundle. It's going to have quite an impact. We're describing the New Economic Policy.[111] But it'll be quite something. It's going to really pull the rug out from underneath everybody concerned," he said to Attorney General John Mitchell.[112]

Although Nixon deserves credit for taking the difficult action that no one before him would, his methodology was not without flaws. Nixon's greatest oversight that weekend was underestimating the impact his decisions would have on American foreign policy. In the photograph of those who met at Camp David over August 13–15, 1971, arranged by Bill Safire "for history's sake," not a single foreign policy advisor was present. "A decision of major foreign policy importance had been taken about which neither the Secretary of State [William Rogers] nor the national security advisor had been consulted," Henry Kissinger wrote in his memoirs, even though he was out of the country for secret negotiations with the Vietnamese that weekend.[113] Arthur Burns was even more critical.

---

[108] GRF, Papers of Arthur Burns, Box B65, Memorandum from John Connally to Pierre-Paul Schweitzer, August 15, 1971.

[109] GRF, Papers of Arthur Burns, Handwritten Journals, 1969–1974, Box 1, October 14, 1972.

[110] Pascaline Winand, " 'L'année de l'Europe' of Henry Kissinger et les Européens," in Andreas Wilkens, ed. *Willy Brandt et l'unité de l'Europe: de l'objectif de la paix aux solidarités nécessaires* (Bruxelles: P.I.E. Peter Lang, 2011), 381.

[111] In a letter to the author on May 1, 2009, William Safire noted, "I see you refer to the New Economic Policy, which was the original name of the Camp David 'shock' announcement of wage and price controls, suspension of the convertibility of the dollar into gold, etc. As I was doing the final draft of Nixon's speech, I learned from someone with a sense of history (it may have been Arthur Burns) that the phrase had been used before – by Lenin about one of his 5-year plans. I cut it out with alacrity." Yet, use of the title continued.

[112] RMN, Nixon Tapes, Executive Office Building 273-026, August 15, 1971, 5:04 p.m.–5:10 p.m.

[113] Henry Kissinger, *The White House Years* (Boston: Little, Brown, and Company, 1982), 954.

"The weekend confirmed my growing feeling that the President needs to act in a way that satisfied his hunger for drama and novelty, that he lacks true self-assurance and that therefore requires some dramatic act to convince himself that he is a strong leader," Burns recorded in his diary.[114]

August 15, rather than being a conclusion to the monetary crisis that had built up steam over the summer of 1971, marked the beginning of a new era. It was a new era not just for monetary policy, but also for diplomatic negotiations that would occupy much of Nixon's time for the remainder of the year. Initially concluding that the actions of August 15 had primarily domestic consequences, he was not prepared for the European response that began almost immediately and continued until they culminated in the Smithsonian Agreement of December 1971. Although Henry Kissinger and other foreign policy advisors were not involved in monetary policy before August 15, they were integral to building European consensus and calming international tensions thereafter.

---

[114] GRF, Papers of Arthur Burns, Handwritten Journals, 1969–1974, Box 1, August 22, 1971.

3

The European response

Following the August 15, 1971, debut of Nixon's New Economic Policy, he went on the offensive during the fall of that year to explain his bold, sudden announcement. Undersecretary of the Treasury for Monetary Affairs Paul Volcker traveled to London on August 16 to calm representatives of France, Germany, Italy, Japan, and the United Kingdom.[1] "I arrived in London on Monday, August 16, to meet with my counterparts to explain our approach, including our unwillingness to change the price of gold," recalled the number two man at the Treasury. Volcker sensed European anguish over the American actions.[2] Bretton Woods had been the lynchpin of the world economic system since 1944.

Nixon's announcement clearly divided Europeans, a fact that was evident to Volcker. Whereas Bundesbank deputy Otmar Emminger stated how impressed he was at the comprehensive nature of Nixon's program, many European leaders were concerned with how the markets would react once reopened. Most West European nations closed their markets on August 16 and kept them closed at least a week.[3] With the current fixed parities no longer operational, the negotiations to establish a new currency system could take a year or two.[4] They would involve not just the top political officials from each European nation, but also central bankers, European Economic Community (EEC)

---

[1] RMN, NSC, Box 678, Telegram from Secretary of State to American Embassy Paris, August 16, 1971, State 149438.
[2] Volcker and Gyohten, 81.
[3] GRF, Papers of Arthur Burns, Box B54, "Chronology of Official Actions taken Abroad since August 15 that have affected the Foreign Exchange Markets," undated.
[4] FRUS, 1969–1976, Volume III, 170.

leaders, industry, and labor.[5] Nixon's decision to end the system may have been accomplished in a twenty-minute speech, but the rest of the world now had months or even years of work to do.

At the time of Nixon's surprise announcement, many European leaders were in the midst of their August vacations and had no advance notice other than previous public remarks by officials like John Connally.[6] Henry Kissinger was also caught off guard while out of the country. When he reached Nixon by telephone on the evening of August 16, he congratulated his boss on "another coup." "So many have said that it was like the China news. It reminds people of that again," Nixon said, recalling his previous "Nixon shock" on July 15, when he announced that secret negotiations had been taking place with Communist China and that he would be the first president to visit the nation.[7]

Volcker wrapped up his meeting in London, but then made a controversial stop in Paris on August 17 to offer a special explanation for Nixon's announcement to the French government. This was a privilege that was not extended to any other European country, which reflected the fact that President Pompidou was the most knowledgeable on monetary policy of any head of state.[8] It was a stop Nixon insisted on since Pompidou had been helpful in ensuring the logistics necessary for Henry Kissinger to carry out secret negotiations with the North Vietnamese in Paris. Meeting with French Finance Minister Valéry Giscard d'Estaing, Volcker offered reassurance that American policy makers still agreed with the basic principles of Breton Woods. Giscard stated the French concern that everything the United States had achieved over the past twenty-five years in terms of monetary stability was now in jeopardy. Volcker defended Nixon's actions by noting that there was an even greater danger of growing protectionism in the United States that only drastic monetary reform could prevent.[9]

When EEC ministers held extended meetings in Brussels the following week, they had difficulty agreeing on common action.[10] This was the first

[5] PRO, FCO 49–337, "A Chronology of Events following the Nixon Economic Measures announced on 15 August, 1971," August 16, 1971.
[6] RMN, NSC, Box 678, Telegram from American Embassy Paris to Secretary of State, "Personal Message from President Nixon to President Pompidou," August 16, 1971, Paris 13910.
[7] RMN, HAK Telcons, Box 11, August 16, 1971, 10:15 p.m.
[8] GRF, Papers of Arthur Burns, Box G8, "Memorandum of Discussion, Federal Open Market Committee, 8/24/71," August 24, 1971.
[9] FRUS, 1969–1976, Volume III, 171.
[10] Bentley Library, Papers of Paul McCracken, Box 15, memorandum from Herb Stein to President Nixon, "Monetary and Financial Developments," August 20, 1971.

time that Europeans had to concern themselves with creating a currency system independent of the United States. Up to that point, they had always relied on the U.S. dollar and the ease of either saving dollars or converting them into gold reserves. Europeans were particularly caught off guard by Nixon's actions, coming as they did from "an administration that was up to this point asleep on this problem."[11] "The intrinsic weakness of the dollar combined with international speculation" were to blame for Nixon's drastic moves.[12] In an extraordinary session of the EEC Council of Ministers, Europeans agreed to a series of piecemeal emergency measures, as put forth by a German proposal. These measures included limiting exchange bands to 1.5 percent, more closely coordinating central bank actions, avoiding excessive capital movements, and European governments agreeing to harmonize economic and financial policies.[13]

These small defensive steps were the origins of the European Monetary System, from which a common currency was created. Europeans shared a fear that these steps would not be enough, especially if the American measures were tightened even further.[14] The markets were in bad shape across Europe. According to minutes of the first Federal Reserve Open Market Committee meeting following August 15, "The markets had construed the developments of last week or so as a breakdown of international cooperation . . . there was grave apprehension of deepening political conflict, spreading protectionism, and exchange controls."[15] That was not a positive review of Nixon's announcement, which was designed to strengthen the international position of the United States.

On September 7, 1971, Congress returned from its August recess. As expected, Nixon was sharply criticized for taking unilateral action in its absence, criticism that focused especially the domestic portions of his announcement, which could have been done through legislation. Nixon told John Connally to ignore the criticism. "I feel so strongly that . . . we don't want to . . . rescue this international monetary thing too soon. Let it

---

[11] HAEC, BAC 3–1978 556, Telex from European Commission Liaison Office Washington D.C. to European Commission, "mise en place difficulte de la nouvelle politique economique du president Nixon," August 19, 1971.

[12] HAEC, BAC 3–1978 556, "TRES URGENT" Telex from European Commission Liaison Office Washington D.C. to European Commission, "La nouvelle politique economique du President Nixon et ses implications internationales," August 18, 1971.

[13] *AAPD* 1971, Ministerialdirigent Bömcke, Brüssel (EG), an das Auswärtige Amt, 276.

[14] HAEU, Papers of Robert Triffin, Box 24–25, draft of article, "The Community and the World Dollar Problem," August 28, 1971.

[15] GRF, Papers of Arthur Burns, Box G8, "Memorandum of Discussion, Federal Open Market Committee, 8/24/71," August 24, 1971.

stew," he said.[16] Connally admitted that negotiations with Europeans to settle the problem "may go on for a year." Nixon did not seem to be very concerned about the bad press he was receiving. "I won't foreclose a damn thing . . . having taken this enormous risk, which many thought, well, you remember the dire predictions. We've now bought the time, and we're going to use it." Nixon was not going to let a little European criticism bother him.

Criticism from within his administration was another matter. Some advisors who, like George Schultz, were in support of the international changes, such as ending dollar convertibility, were critical of Nixon's protectionist proposals, such as wage and price controls. Other advisors, like Arthur Burns, were in support of the domestic aspects of the New Economic Policy but were critical of ending the gold standard. On September 11, Nixon met with John Connally and Arthur Burns, two figures vitally important to the success of Nixon's new economic policies:[17]

NIXON: Let me try to give you a little feel, Arthur, and I want to talk to you and John, and I don't want it to go beyond this [meeting] with what I feel, to Volcker, or anybody at the Fed, just talk as politicians and friends. Between now and the election in November [1972], there must be one paramount consideration. And that paramount consideration is not the responsibility of the U.S. in the world . . . it isn't the fact that in foreign [policy] we've done this, that, or the other thing. The main thing is that we have to create the impression that the president of the United States, finally, at long last, after twenty-five years with blood, sweat and tears, is . . . looking after its interests.

Applying the Nixon Doctrine came at a cost. Ending the gold standard was correct strategic thinking, and some degree of abruptness surrounding the announcement was probably unavoidable. The host of domestic complements to ending the gold standard – including a unilateral import surcharge and wage and price controls – were the more controversial aspects of Nixon's New Economic Policy. The import surcharge was clearly a tax, but the White House was careful not to call it a tax since new taxes have to be approved by Congress. These steps were taken to appease conservative and isolationist voters.

---

[16] RMN, Nixon Tapes, White House Telephone 008–042, September 7, 1971, 5:56 p.m.– 6:00 p.m.
[17] RMN, Nixon Tapes, Oval Office 570-004, September 11, 1971, 12:07 p.m.–12:53 p.m.

Meeting the demands of Europeans did not help Nixon politically and may have hurt him if it appeared that he put their concerns ahead of American concerns. Nixon was taking criticism from the right for withdrawing troops from Vietnam, unveiling secret talks with Communist China, and negotiating on arms controls with the Soviet Union; he was running out of time before the 1972 election to show conservatives and isolationists that he was doing something for them. If he was not reelected in 1972, then his other foreign policy breakthroughs would be negated if they were not continued by Nixon's successor. The import surcharge and wage and price controls were designed to stimulate manufacturing, control inflation, and boost American exports. In Nixon's view, it was those in the affected industries who would decide his fate in little over a year. In effect, Nixon believed he needed to shift rightward for the 1972 election in order to win. If his New Economic Policy damaged relations with Europe in the short run, he was confident in his ability and Henry Kissinger's diplomatic skills to smooth things over after the election.

Until then, Nixon believed, the United States must come first, just as he believed Europeans had already decided to put development of the EEC ahead of bilateral relations with the United States. Even the U.S.-UK "special relationship" no longer looked very special. Nixon knew that negotiations with Europe in the fall of 1971 would be difficult, but he believed that standing on the long-term American commitment to support Europe politically, economically, and military since 1945 would give the United States the superior negotiating position when asking for fairer terms vis-à-vis monetary policy from the British, German, and French governments:

NIXON: Now I have to tell you about the British. By God, [Prime Minister Edward] Heath has taken heat over there ... we do everything we can for the British, but the British ... they consulted their interests, and they stung us [when they decided to join the EEC]. ... Goddamn it, and I told Kissinger this, and Henry, we've got to bring him into this conversation at the proper time, because what I really say is, and you'll understand John, this is why it's so important this not go to any experts, all the experts, and you're an expert, too, will naturally be thinking as they should "what is the responsible statesmanlike thing to do." I want to do the responsible statesmanlike thing, but not now. Right now we've got to do what the people of the United States think their president is out fighting for.

... Now let's look at the Germans. [Chancellor] Willy Brandt. Arthur, the Berlin [Quadripartite] Agreement would never have been put through unless we had – I can tell you privately what really happened on that. And keep this to yourself, because some of the State Department people would not be happy. Kissinger sits down, for four months, meeting with [Soviet Ambassador to Washington Anatoly] Dobrynin, worked out the odds and ends of that damned agreement. And finally, [Kenneth] Rush, our ambassador, a hell of an ambassador, with great skill, got it through. But I'll tell you what I did. I got in the opposition leader [Rainer Barzel], you know, the leader of the Christian Democratic Party in here, and he was going to pull this on the ground. And I told him "two months," I said, "I would not bring Brandt down on the issue of foreign policy." I told him "it means everything." I mean, if they don't have the Berlin Agreement, then they don't have the treaty with the Russians, and if they don't have the Berlin Agreement, they don't have access to Berlin, and also some degree of lessened tension between East and West Germany. The Berlin Agreement was as important or even more important to Brandt and his political future as [repatriating] Okinawa was to [Japanese Prime Minister Eisaku] Sato. At this point, with them, they owe us one, and they owe us a hell of a big one, and I don't know how the terms are going to end.

... Now, let's take the French. The French are selfish bastards. You know, they're experts. [President Georges] Pompidou himself knows about this. Of all the foreign leaders, he's the one, that you know, John, who's the real expert, and I would hope that either or both of you have a private talk with him. Sometime I want you to do it, because he's very proud of his expertise in this area. Believe me, we've played their game on several things, and I've been extremely courteous to him. We say to France, where would you be without the United States? Down. Nothing. And, when you think of the damn Netherlands, and the Belgians, and the rest, all those people, Arthur, would be nothing without us.

... Now we come down to the United States. It's time for America to look after its own interests. What I'm getting at is, we face here a political problem, very basic. What I want you and John to do is, talk this over between yourselves. We have got to work out something that, sure, be as responsible we can be, but between now and next year, we have go to take a position which we can sell the American people that "thank God, the President of the United States might be as strong as the Europeans and the Japanese, and we're looking after Uncle Sam." We've got to do that. And if it raises a little hell for a while in international monetary fund markets, so be it. We'll take care of that at a later time. But it's very important that we do that. Now, in order to play that game, we can perhaps ... split them up, don't let them get together. Don't let them get together. But I take it they have got to know that I supported the Marshall Plan, I was on the Herter Committee, I supported reciprocal trade, I've been supporting the damn foreign aid. I believe in world responsibility, and I've taken all these risks, the China trip, and all the rest, and there are going to be others to follow, other things of very great significance for them. Darn it, they must not think that they now have a soft touch here. We have got to play a very hard game.

... Now, what I'm really trying to do is, I'm just trying to give you my feeling and guidance, so that you can have in mind ... you're both politicians, and you're both friends. Arthur, the stakes are too high here. We cannot elect, we cannot elect, and I'm going to say quite candidly, some of those irresponsible people that are running around the country now. We inherited a hell of a lot of hard problems and we're trying to handle it as well as we can. And, that means, frankly, playing this international thing to the hilt politically. Now if we give up too soon, we back down, and we decide we're going to revalue the dollar, and we're going to do this, and we're going to be responsible, and we're going to be good neighbors, and we're going to grin and bear it, believe me, the American people are going to say what the hell, we thought we had a president finally who was going to stand up for us. Now that's where it's at.

... My point is, that right now, we are in a period, where the United States, the people of this country, could very well turn isolationist unless their president was looking after their interests. And we must not let this happen.

Burns was speechless. Neither he nor Connally could say anything to rebut Nixon's points, and the conversation was effectively over following Nixon's long soliloquy. Burns's diary indicates that he thought Nixon's tactics were overly harsh, but he could not agree more that the American president had a duty to address the needs of the American public before any foreign country. From that point forward, Burns ceased to be a public critic of the administration's monetary policy. Maintaining a stance of opposition would only erode his ability to affect the outcome. Instead,

Burns increasingly confided to his diary his concerns that the domestic economy and the coming 1972 election would impede a proper solution to the international crisis. "This communication confirmed my fears that considerations of domestic politics would delay and distract serious efforts to rebuild international monetary order."[18]

The Group of Ten (G-10) finance ministers met in London on September 15–16, 1971, to discuss a response to Nixon's New Economic Policy. Hosted by British Chancellor of the Exchequer Anthony Barber, references to "the outrageous demands of the Americans" could not be avoided.[19] German Economics Minister Karl Schiller was the least critical among the group. "We were happy to come to London and we hope that the city's spirit, famed for its cool judgment and the global view it takes, will guide our councils."[20] Unlike the rest of Europe, the Germans actually supported Nixon's decision to end convertibility and believed that the more undesirable aspects of Nixon's policy would be defeated easily in the General Agreement on Tariffs and Trade (GATT).[21] In their view, therefore, there was nothing to panic about. Instead, they believed, Europeans should seize the opportunity to devise a monetary settlement that met European needs.

Representing the United States at the G-10 was Treasury Secretary John Connally, who maintained his familiar tough line.[22] He noted that the United States devoted 8.9 percent of its gross national product – 36 percent of its annual budget – to defense and that no other nation came close to that level of commitment to the Atlantic alliance. Connally stated that the American goal of the New Economic Policy was a US$13 billion turnaround in the balance of payments and that he expected American allies to make the bulk of the concessions.[23] The US$13 billion would come from additional revenue generated primarily by the unilateral import surcharge. Schiller argued on behalf of the Europeans. "We should

---

[18] GRF, Papers of Arthur Burns, Handwritten Journals, 1969–1974, Box 1, September 10, 1971.

[19] Volcker and Gyohten, 82.

[20] PAAA, B52/III/A1, "Statement by Minister Professor Dr. Karl Schiller at the Group of Ten Conference, London, September 15 and 16, 1971."

[21] PAAA, B31/337, Report by Foreign Office, "German-American Relations," September 6, 1971.

[22] Many of Nixon's aides noted how the president preferred aides to be "tough," like Connally. In a letter to the author on April 8, 2009, George H. W. Bush noted, "I worry a little bit about what Nixon really thought of me. I know he didn't think I was tough enough in the mold of John Connally."

[23] *FRUS*, 1969–1976, Volume III, Editorial Note 78.

at least reach an understanding on an adequate flexibility. Without rules for the interim period of floating we might become further entangled in escalating controls and interventions. Nor would this be the way to achieve a decisive improvement in the U.S. balance of payments," he said.[24]

Schiller argued that without a settlement, European nations would enact their own import tariffs in response to the American actions, which would disrupt currencies and the EEC. Paul Volcker, also in attendance at the G-10 meeting, agreed with European finance ministers that Connally's goal was too ambitious in such a short time period. It was a rare public betrayal of Connally. In addition, Volcker conceded that the price of the dollar in terms of gold had to change – an effective devaluation – and the U.S. import surcharge should be removed. Europeans also argued forcefully that an effort to return to fixed parities should occur as soon as possible.[25]

On September 17, Pete Peterson called Henry Kissinger. Peterson said that Connally's rigid approach to negotiating with the Europeans on monetary relations was producing ill will likely to spill over into other areas of foreign policy. "I think this is a serious problem for us. We have some international political problems." One other American challenge, Peterson added, was Connally himself. Nixon seemed unaware of how brutal Connally was to the Europeans. "Let's not only think about the president but Connally ... do you think the president has any perception of this problem at the moment?" he asked. "No," Kissinger replied.[26]

On September 20, Connally reported to Nixon on the G-10 meeting in London:[27]

CONNALLY: They want the United States to lift the import surcharge, and agree to change the price of gold, and they said the United States has to make a contribution. The United States and its trading partners around the world, has been very unfair with the imposition of the surcharge, that we're asking them to make up in effect for our mistakes and that the United States has to make a contribution toward the settlement of this problem.

NIXON: How did you respond?

[24] PAAA, B52/III/A1, "Statement by Minister Professor Dr. Karl Schiller at the Group of Ten Conference, London, September 15 and 16, 1971."

[25] *FRUS*, 1969–1976, Volume III, 175.

[26] RMN, HAK Telcons, Box 11, September 17, 1971, 6:15 p.m.

[27] RMN, Nixon Tapes, Oval Office 576-008, September 20, 1971, 9:52 a.m.–11:27 a.m.

CONNALLY: I responded finally on the last afternoon ... [that] the
surcharge had not been done for domestic political reasons. The
surcharge was imposed for reasons of improving our domestic
balance of payments. Those who severely criticized it were those who
had the most experience with it by having imposed it themselves in the
past. This was Great Britain who was raising hell, and they imposed it
in 1964. They had an import surcharge for eighteen months, and
nobody said a damn thing. And I said at no time in any discussion did I
hear anyone here suggest the border taxes, the import taxes, or the
export rebates that are prevalent around the world, that they be
moved. It's all directed toward the United States ... I have gathered,
from the various speeches made here, that the solution to this problem
is a problem for the United States, and for the United States
unilaterally, one, to remove the surcharge, and two, to change the
price of gold. I simply say to you gentlemen, if indeed it is a matter of
unilateral action by the United States, the United States has already
acted ... that we're quite happy with where we are. I said, may I
humbly say, without being immodest, that over the past quarter of a
century, we have indeed made a contribution.

The conversation was a test for Connally. Nixon did not dislike what
he heard. Nixon resented that some Europeans wanted to have it both
ways: they wanted American foreign aid, military support, and help
with establishing a new monetary system. At the same time, however,
Europeans wanted the United States to stay out of European affairs.
During the Nixon era, the president was criticized both for meddling
too much on some issues and neglecting Europe on others. Both Europe
and the United States had changed dramatically since 1945. A new
understanding of transatlantic relations, one that reflected the 1970s,
was needed. Europeans did not have the needs that they did a quarter
century before, nor did Americans any longer have the ability to meet
those needs.

Even while Connally had the support of President Nixon, silent oppo-
sition to Connally's tactics grew. Among Nixon's advisors, few had the
courage to stand up to Connally, a dominating figure with strong views.
On September 20, Arthur Burns gently tried to inform Nixon of what the
Europeans thought of Connally, based on a meeting he attended with
European central bankers.[28]

---

[28] RMN, Nixon Tapes, Oval Office 577-003, September 20, 1971, 12:45 p.m.–1:30 p.m.

BURNS: The Europeans recognize that they must realign currency parities, everyone recognizes that. Basically they realize that we can't go back to convertibility. That's quite an advance. I don't know what to think about the French. I explained that if we tried to restore convertibility, the whole thing could blow up in a few days. They're not going to cause any trouble on that issue. They are very stubborn on the price of gold issue. And we're very stubborn, too. Our stubbornness, on both these issues, I've talked to John Connally thoroughly, our stubbornness is tactical. There is no reason in the world why we shouldn't help them deal with their problems by raising the price of gold, from thirty-five to thirty-seven [dollars] ... The British no longer have any political dependents, because they are entering the Common Market, and they have got to play with the Europeans. The Germans are, well, privately they tell me they are with the United States, and for a while I think that's true. Whether that will be their permanent policy or not I don't know. ... You know what really makes no sense is the British.

NIXON: Connally has implied that they will do anything to be sure they get into the Market, so they're going to play us against the others.

BURNS: They are, well this has implications that I think you would understand a lot better than I, but the British are going to play with the Common Market, to what degree they will be your partners in foreign policy, I don't know.

NIXON: That's the point. It's what we talked about before you left. What is involved here are great political forces and movements, and we've got to try link economics with the politics. It's got to be linked. ... The question is how do you rationalize these things? ... We don't want to move too quickly. We have a terrible problem. I met with the members of Congress. The people of this country are pretty damn isolationist economically. They like the surcharge, they'd like to keep it permanently, they like cuts in foreign aid, they'd like to cut it all, now they're wrong. You and I know we have to live in the world, and I don't believe that kind of thing. On the other hand, I do realize that it is necessary that the United States have a better deal abroad to sell at home. ... We must publicly say that we will be responsible in the world, we've always been good neighbors and competitors, and we want to build international stability, perhaps, but on the other hand, some way we've got to find some ways Arthur, and you've got to see if you will, could you help us find a way to serve this domestic political interest at the same time.

These views were consistent with the Nixon Doctrine and were the real purposes behind the New Economic Policy. Even before his announcement on August 15, Nixon consistently made these points to his top advisors. Burns's disagreement came not with Nixon's objectives but with Connally's tactics, which he felt were unnecessarily provocative. As the conversation progressed, Burns became more forceful in his views about Connally, saying that he was out of touch with the Europeans. "I told the President that Connally . . . did not show enough understanding of the position of other countries."[29] He took some risk by offering his unsolicited view on Connally, someone Nixon saw as his successor and believed could win the Republican Party's presidential nomination in 1976.

Knowing Nixon's preference for secret diplomacy, Burns volunteered himself for the job of conducting secret negotiations with European central bankers, parallel to Connally's public negotiations with European finance ministers. He must have known that such a proposal would appeal to Nixon:

BURNS: Now Connally was both a success and a failure. I'm being very candid to you, I'm not useful to you unless I am. He was very successful in indicating that they are going to have to give, and that our position is going to be a firm one, and they understand that better than they did. What he was not successful in indicating to them, is that we have some understanding of their problems . . . on this gold price question, what we ought to say to them is, not that our position is inflexible, [that] we'll never even talk about that, we'll say this is a technical problem that we will be ready to discuss with you after some fundamental economic issues have been approximately worked out. That would make a tremendous impression on them, and in my book, we'd be giving up nothing. If something is important to the other fellow, and it costs you little or nothing, why not indicate to him that your mind does not have to be closed, at a certain stage. The next thing that I would do I think is to say to them that we don't like this import surcharge any more than you do. We explained time and again this is a temporary expedient. And if you will indicate to us what realignment of currency you're willing to agree to, and if that comes anywhere near the warrant, as far as our needs are concerned, we will gladly give up the surcharge, and you're not losing anything by this.

[29] GRF, Papers of Arthur Burns, Handwritten Journals, 1969–1974, Box 1, September 20, 1971.

Because they're going to give up very little on this, and this will be a negotiation that will take a year, or two, or three.

NIXON: Really?

BURNS: I think so, yeah ... psychologically and politically. Look, let me tell why this is important to some of the Europeans. The purpose of central banks, if we don't raise the price of gold in terms of U.S. dollars, and there is an appreciation of foreign currencies in terms of the U.S. dollar, then the price of gold in terms of the currencies of European countries and Japan will have to go down. And the central banks say, hell, we're a lot poorer than we were, they don't like that. Now next they say, that international reserves, as measured in terms of gold, will be reduced. Now in the world of SDRs, that doesn't matter any longer. So there's nothing here of economic substance, but politically, politically I think they have to go to their parliaments, not all of them, but some of them do, and justify an appreciation of their currency against the U.S. dollar, and they feel since they have to make this concession they can argue the case with their own people in government that the U.S. has this rigid position on the price of gold. And in a sense, you know, when everybody has a political problem –

NIXON: Misery loves company.

BURNS: That's right ... I can take the same position as Connally. If I do that, I'm not going to learn a thing. I can take another position, indicating, well, I am a central banker, and an economist. I don't really represent my government at these negotiations, but I am interested in resolving a U.S. problem, an international problem, I can say it in that fashion. I won't do it unless you want me to.

NIXON: The problem with that is a domestic one. It might be all right with them, but the problem is that I would hate to see a paper get out that Arthur Burns splits with Connally.

BURNS: Oh no, this I would do first with your explicit permission, and second only with the central bankers, and with two finance ministers.

NIXON: ... As a matter of fact, that sort of thing appeals to me.

BURNS: I've done a little of this, but not very much.

NIXON: You may go out on a sort of fishing mission, and say "what do you fellows risk?"

BURNS: This is exactly my point.

NIXON: But say, "look, I can't speak for the administration and you're not going to hurt [yourselves] when you indicate to me what we have to do." Maybe that's the way to approach it ... It appeals to me.

BURNS: See, Connally isn't going to find out a thing. His technique is not one designed to elicit any information from the others. I know this much: let me tell you what I found out without Connally ... I've been able to draw them out by indicating one thing, that this gold problem is a political problem rather than an economic problem. That's quite a concession. Because the position of the U.S. government has been that this is a terribly important economic problem, and it isn't. Let Connally take that position, let him take the position that he can't discuss it because he is under instructions from his president. It's a very good bargaining position for him. But it's not a position that enables him to extract anything from the other fellow. There is also a tradition among central bankers who talk rather frankly, more frankly than political people.

NIXON: I have every confidence in your ability to negotiate and talk and so forth. I just have, the only concern I have is that I don't want to have the feeling there's is a hell of a split about the thing, because they'd really eat us alive.

BURNS: Well, I'm going to play this, as far as the press is concerned. I'm going to be with Connally 100 percent, completely. As far as these other fellows are concerned, the economists, and exploring questions with them, not representing the government.

NIXON: Good.

BURNS: ... There's something else, Mr. President. I'm not sure Connally is your best negotiator here. He doesn't understand foreigners sufficiently, and now there's a certain opinion that Europeans have formed of him, and the opinion I think has two dimensions. First, he's very tough, that's good. Second, he doesn't understand us, and that's not good.

NIXON: The fact that he's tough is good. We haven't had much of that in recent years.

BURNS: ... Now, whether you want Kissinger in on the act, or not, I don't know. He should be informed, because he's so close to you on questions [of foreign policy].

NIXON: He'll know all the political questions. Kissinger's got awfully good judgment on a thing like this. What I mean is that he's smart enough to stay out of things he doesn't know anything about. On the other hand, he'll say he doesn't know anything about it, but he'll put in a heavy word and say, look, you can't do this to the Germans, or you shouldn't do that to the French, or Pompidou owes us one, or the British had better not talk that way, or particularly the Japanese, he knows. This is very important. Kissinger ought to sit in on a meeting when we get further down the road.

As a result of this conversation, Nixon authorized Burns to open a back-channel with European central bankers, much like Henry Kissinger had been doing with China and the Soviet Union. Coincidentally, just as Burns exited the Oval Office, Kissinger walked in.

Although having little expertise on monetary policy, Kissinger offered advice on the best way to negotiate with the Europeans. His entry could not have been timed any better with Burns's departure. This conversation was the beginning of Kissinger's rise in influence on monetary relations, which set him on a path to supplant Connally as lead negotiator with the Europeans by the end of the year.

KISSINGER: One thing you might consider, Mr. President, I've talked to Connally about it ... We could say that we are ending the surcharge but we are insisting that the currencies continue to float until we have a system that is satisfactory, because they're all united against the surcharge.

NIXON: The difficulty is the surcharge, Henry, is so popular domestically that we just can't end it until we get something for it. Hell, the surcharge is supported by 85 percent of the people. Good God, you just can't give it away. ... There is much more involved here than simply a currency revaluation, non-tariff barriers, etc., that there is a question here of burden-sharing, and political questions. And since with some of these nations we have some political stroke, and others we don't, I'm inclined to think, and Arthur Burns and Connally both share this, that you should be in on it.

KISSINGER: ... But our handicap right now is that we don't know exactly what we want, and what to put our weight behind.

This was a concern similar to one Kissinger expressed to Nixon earlier, when he was previously troubled about the lack of a clear policy toward NATO. Connally was very effective at telling the Europeans what the United States would not accept, but he offered very little in the way of what he would accept. The United States was also not offering any realistic, concrete proposals. In Kissinger's view, the longer the United States remained on the sidelines, the more damaging it could be.

Another obstacle Nixon faced was whether any aspects of his New Economic Policy required Congressional approval. John Connally said no, and sent his deputy Paul Volcker to testify before the Subcommittee on

Foreign Economic Policy of the House Foreign Affairs Committee on September 21. Volcker downplayed the need for Congressional approval, stating that what was needed instead was "temporary support to our external financial and trading position while durable arrangements to cope with the difficult process of international payments are developed and put into place."[30] For Connally, yielding to Congress meant losing control of a portion of the negotiations with the Europeans. That was why ending gold convertibility was far superior to devaluing the dollar from US$35 an ounce to US$37 or US$38. "To change the price of gold we'll have to go to Congress, and to go to Congress with an issue of this kind, we're opening up a Pandora's Box," he said to Nixon on September 24. "They're going to hold extensive hearings on our trade with every country in the world."[31]

Nixon was concerned. "I will not allow this decision to be made without weighing in the international political situation and also without weighing very heavily, until the elections of November '72, the domestic political repercussions, because boy is it true. Domestically in this country, there is a strong attitude which is not healthy, and we've got to be just a little bit ahead of them, or somebody can seize that, you know what I mean?" Nixon lost in 1960, in part, due to the economy. He narrowly won in 1968 after a last-minute effort by President Johnson to boost Hubert Humphrey. Nixon was not about the concede control of his electoral chances in 1972.

President Nixon invited Milton Friedman to the Oval Office to get his view on the impasse in negotiations with the Europeans. Friedman served as an advisor to Nixon's 1968 campaign, and if he was seen supporting Nixon's New Economic Policy it would help to convert other conservative critics. Friedman, like Shultz, was supportive of the international aspects of the policy but less supportive – even harshly critical – of the domestic protectionist aspects. He helped Nixon to understand, for political reasons, why some Europeans emphasized the importance of gold playing a part in Nixon's new policy. Friedman argued:

It's very simple, purely political. [Say] you're a central banker in France, and you stand up in Parliament ... one of the [parliamentarians] says to you, "are you on the dollar system," "are you a satellite of the U.S.?" The central banker likes to say, "no, we're on a gold standard." That's a hundred percent of the whole reason. It's to provide a political achievement at home, because in fact, changing the price

[30] RMN, WHCF, SMOF, Papers of Paul W. McCracken, Box 10, Statement of Paul A. Volcker before Subcommittee on Foreign Economic Policy of the House Foreign Affairs Committee, September 21, 1971.
[31] RMN, Nixon Tapes, Oval Office 578-004, September 24, 1971, 9:52 a.m.–10:29 a.m.

of gold or leaving the window closed has no effect. It makes no differences whether we don't sell gold at 35 dollars an ounce, or we don't sell it at 38 dollars an ounce. From their point of view, they can maintain the fixed rate, that gold has a role to play, and they can say to their politicians [that] the U.S. contributed to this change. In a way, it's very tempting to do it, because it costs us nothing.[32]

Friedman argued that it made sense to come around to the European view on gold, even if it meant going to Congress for approval to officially devaluate. For some Europeans, if gold were no longer convertible, it would mean an increased reliance on the dollar. Europeans resented a currency regime that allowed the United States to extend American influence in Europe both economically and militarily.[33]

The EEC continued to have difficulty formulating a response as long as national interests took priority over multilateral concerns. The French concluded that Nixon's actions were "contrary to the International Monetary Fund, to GATT, and to the norms of trade."[34] On the other end of the spectrum, the Germans nominally supported at least some aspects of the American actions. The split between the French and Germans left the British without a viable policy. "We are particularly badly placed to complain about the import surcharge: because we put one on ourselves [in 1964] ... it is in these circumstances that a US import surcharge and a float are probably about as good a deal as we are likely to get," noted an internal FCO report.[35] Prime Minister Heath had little interest in establishing any type of personal relationship with President Nixon at that point, so negotiations at that level would not help. Heath admitted privately that he had few options when it came to "how the United States could best be persuaded to revert to saner and more acceptable policies."[36]

On the American side of the negotiations, resistance continued to build against John Connally. In an Oval Office meeting on September 30, Nixon and Kissinger agreed for the first time that Connally was a liability. "I have to meet more regularly with Connally, because the Texans really don't have the diplomatic touch. [But] I think he's by far the best man in your

---

[32] RMN, Nixon Tapes, Oval Office 578-005, September 24, 1971, 10:33 a.m.–11:44 a.m.
[33] Michael D. Bordo, et al., "France and the Bretton Woods International Monetary System, 1960 to 1968," in Jaime Reis, ed., *International Monetary Systems in Historical Perspective* (New York: St. Martin's Press, 1995), 153.
[34] AN, 5 AG 2/660, "Conférence de presse de Pompidou, Palais de l'Elysée, 23 septembre 1971. Transcription de la sténotypie," September 23, 1971.
[35] PRO, FCO 49–337, "Implications of President Nixon's Measures," September 23, 1971.
[36] PRO, PREM 15–310, "Note of a Meeting Held at 10 Downing Street on Wednesday 3 November 1971 at 4:30 p.m.," November 3, 1971.

cabinet," Kissinger said.[37] George Shultz emphasized to Kissinger the problem that Connally's tough negotiations were causing in other areas of foreign policy. "The President doesn't have a feel for it at all, do you think?" Shultz asked. "Absolutely not at all ... he just doesn't know," Kissinger responded. "Connally has seized all power but doesn't know how to exercise it," Shultz added.[38] However, no one was willing to approach Connally as long as he had Nixon's obvious support. "Did anyone ever tell you, you are a mean negotiator?"[39] Kissinger teased Connally.

Negotiations with the Europeans faltered during October and November, in part because the United States lacked a single spokesperson for international monetary policy.[40] Connally was closest to the president, but numerous others were also involved, including Kissinger, Burns, Volcker, Shultz, and Secretary of State William Rogers. Nixon was conspicuously absent from a direct role. "President Nixon has not thought it necessary to intervene, despite his interest in international questions. The preoccupations of domestic politics are ever-present in his mood," summed up a European view.[41] Connally continued to take a tough line, which proved less and less effective. In a major address to the American Bankers Association Annual Meeting on October 20, he stated that the import surcharge "is going to stay on for a while because it frankly is to our advantage to keep it on for a while."[42]

The situation became so dire that Nixon considered returning to a system of convertibility. But, as often happened, Connally provoked Nixon to return to a hard line a few days later. On October 26, in a meeting with Connally and George Shultz, Nixon said he wanted to "screw the French and the British, all the way" and that "the only country worth a damn in Europe are the Germans." Ostensibly this was because the Germans nominally supported the American policy, which caused a split with France and Britain within Europe.[43] "In my view, knowing as

[37] RMN, Nixon Tapes, Oval Office 582-009, September 30, 1971, 4:10 p.m.–5:31 p.m.
[38] RMN, HAK Telcons, Box 11, September 29, 1971, 7:25 p.m.
[39] RMN, HAK Telcons, Box 11, October 1, 1971, p.m. [no time given].
[40] AN, 5 AG 2/117, Note de M. Bellard (Directeur des Services d'Information et de Presse du Ministère des Affaires Etrangères), October 14, 1971.
[41] AN, 5 AG 2/117, Note du Ministère des Affaires Etrangères (Direction des Affaires Politiques, Amérique), undated.
[42] *FRUS*, 1969–1976, Volume III, 188.
[43] RMN, Nixon Tapes, Executive Office Building 303-009, October 26, 1971, 2:49 p.m.–5:55 p.m. The disagreement with Germany is expanded upon in Ambassade de France, *Address Delivered by Maurice Schumann, French Minister of Foreign Affairs, Before the National Assembly on November 3, 1971* (New York: Service de presse et d'information, 1971), 3, and technical details over which they disagreed are succinctly summarized in

little it as I do, I lean to the proposition that is basically Shultz's, which is float. Let the goddamn thing float," Nixon said. The unilateral tariff on European imports was even more controversial. Connally and Shultz warned that the longer the surcharge was maintained, the more likely it would "probably drive Europe to coalesce even tighter and maybe get fixed exchange rates between their respective countries." On the other hand, the longer Germany supported the United States over France and Britain, Connally triumphantly noted, "we would break the European Common Market, the Community!"[44]

Up until this point, John Connally had exclusive authority to negotiate on behalf of President Nixon with the Europeans on monetary affairs. Connally was the president's most trusted cabinet member, and while Connally travelled for the purpose of negotiations his subordinates in the Treasury were forbidden from speaking to any foreign finance ministers or central bankers in his absence. On November 4, Paul Volcker told Henry Kissinger that Connally's hardball tactics were too aggressive and jeopardized the chances for multilateral reform.[45] "I had a talk with Arthur Burns this morning, who is weeping all over me about your refusal to see the Dutch central banker [Jelle Zijlstra]," Kissinger said. "It's not my decision," Volcker responded. Kissinger, understanding that he was interfering with Connally's orders, was hesitant. "I know Connally's views. If you could see him for twenty minutes until Connally gets back so we can have peace here." Volcker refused: "It's not my decision. I am under orders."[46] Burns, who instead met with Zijlstra, was later critical of Volcker. "Volcker's part in all this was not manly ... but he is an indecisive man, full of flaws, and anxieties."[47]

Alfred Grosser, *The Western Alliance: European-American Relations since 1945* (New York: Continuum, 1980), 257–258.

[44] RMN, HAK Telcons, Box 11, September 7, 1971, 11:47 a.m. At the time, Connally represented the extreme view within the administration. However, following British accession to the European Community, by early 1973, Nixon's views hardened: "I have come completely around to the view that Connally so eloquently expressed a year ago and which we rejected for what then appeared to be good reasons. The way the Europeans are talking today, European unity will not be in our interest, certainly not from a political viewpoint or from an economic viewpoint. ... What matters now is what we do and we must act effectively and soon or we will create in Europe, a Frankenstein monster, which could prove to be highly detrimental to our interests in the years ahead." See *FRUS*, 1969–1976, Volume E-15, Part 2, 9.

[45] Volcker and Gyohten, 83.

[46] RMN, HAK Telcons, Box 12, November 4, 1971, 10:32 a.m.

[47] GRF, Papers of Arthur Burns, Handwritten Journals, 1969–1974, Box 1, November 3, 1971.

Throughout the negotiations with Europe during the fall of 1971, Nixon remained focused on the domestic consequences of international monetary policy. On November 5, John Ehrlichman reminded him of his loss to John F. Kennedy in 1960, a loss that Nixon partially blamed on Federal Reserve policy that was too restrictive on the money supply.[48] Ehrlichman spoke to Milton Friedman on the subject. "Milton, interestingly enough, when I talked to him on the phone a couple of days ago, he said, 'the parallels to 1960 just scare the daylights out of me.' Those were Milton's words." That was sure to get a stir out of Nixon. "Would you tell Milton that he ought to call Arthur, or would it do any good?" Ehrlichman did not think it would do any good. "He's on the outs with Arthur, but if he writes an article, that has its impact on Arthur," he said. "Well, I want a program of people putting the heat on Arthur, calling him. You and Colson and Flanigan sit down and think, who are the people that Arthur respects the most?"[49] Burns knew that he was in Nixon's crosshairs, and he confided to his diary regularly. "The President's preoccupation with the election frightens me. Is there anything that he would not do to further his reelection?"[50]

Henry Kissinger evolved quickly from the role of an outsider to becoming the central figure in an unfamiliar area of policy making.[51] After the departure of Fred Bergsten a few months earlier, Kissinger's staff was left without depth in international monetary policy. However, Kissinger had to act in order to prevent further damage to foreign policy. "Connally ... appears to be determined to sweat everyone out and to ultimately jury rig some kind of an economic union built around U.S. cooperation with Germany in Europe and Japan in the Pacific," Alexander Haig said to Kissinger.[52] Nixon increasingly utilized Kissinger to rescue Connally's negotiations and prevent permanent damage with European allies. Although Kissinger disapproved of Connally's negotiating style, he was careful not to appear disloyal to the president. Other Nixon aides were less cautious in confronting Connally. On November 5, Pete Peterson told

---

[48] In a 1961 speech at the University of Chicago, Burns argued that the 1960 recession was prolonged due to tight Federal Reserve monetary policy. Although he agreed with Nixon then, when at the helm of the Fed, he took a more independent position. See Hobart Rowen, "Changes Ahead for the Fed?" *Washington Post*, August 5, 1976.

[49] RMN, Nixon Tapes, Oval Office 615-008, November 5, 1971, 9:27 a.m.–10:04 a.m.

[50] GRF, Papers of Arthur Burns, Handwritten Journals, 1969–1974, Box 1, November 5, 1971.

[51] *FRUS*, 1969–1976, Volume III, 167.

[52] RMN, NSC, Box 473, Memorandum from Alexander Haig to Henry Kissinger, "Presidential Travel Plans," November 5, 1971.

Kissinger that he was going to stand up to Connally, no matter the consequences. "I will be goddamned for whatever small place I have in history. We have to raise hell, and to be willing to take risks and confront the president with it." Kissinger calmed him down and agreed to talk to Connally. "I love my job – what are the girls going to do if I don't have this job? I will do anything that doesn't take on the president. I will take on Connally."[53]

Meeting with Nixon on November 11, Kissinger offered his assessment of the negotiating situation, which included open criticism of Connally for the first time. He again raised the problem that the United States was saying to the Europeans what it would not accept, but not declaring its position or offering any proposals. Kissinger had no more training than Connally in international finance, but he understood the damage that such an attitude could cause with Europe. They were supposed to be American allies, but they were not being treated like allies.

KISSINGER: Connally's present strategy, as I understand it, Mr.
    President . . . is to undo all the grievances that we have piled up over
    the fifteen years of discriminatory treatment . . . we have to do all of
    it in one big negotiation, and therefore we have to squeeze them by
    the balls, and not tell them what we want until they get so desperate
    that they have to come to us and yield . . .
        We're uniting all of these countries against us by not telling them
    what we want. My feeling is that we ought to say what we want . . . if
    we screw everybody in this free world, and force them to surrender,
    we are going to give them an incentive to organize . . . we will then
    undermine the whole structure of free world cooperation. . . .
        The danger is that at the precise moment that a new generation is
    coming to power in Europe, we are putting it to them in such an
    abrupt way, and, my judgment is, you know how much I admire
    conflict, but I think Texans hate foreigners. I've seen LBJ operate, and
    Texans think that the way to make a deal is to get the other guy by the
    balls and squeeze them. . . .[54]
        You can still drive a very hard bargain. But give them the sense that
    they are participating in the decision.[55]

---

[53] RMN, HAK Telcons, Box 12, November 5, 1971, 7:00 p.m.

[54] Kissinger's reference is to the fact that Connally cut his teeth in Washington politics as a young aide to newly elected Congressman Lyndon B. Johnson in the late 1930s.

[55] RMN, Nixon Tapes, Executive Office Building 298-005, November 11, 1971, 11:29 p.m.–1:16 p.m.

Nixon was starting to understand that Connally was a problem, but who else could take his place? "You cannot separate economics from politics, and this is something that George [Shultz] would never understand. ... Peterson doesn't understand either. The key to the game is Connally. Peterson is not Connally's type of man ... Peterson basically is an internationalist, you know, sort of a liberal type, and Connally's conservative." More than anything else, Nixon valued Connally for his political experience, which the others did not have. Kissinger called John McCloy and begged him to join the National Security Council staff. McCloy was respected by Nixon and was the type of senior figure who could act as a counterweight to Connally. "We need a strong man who can sit on the National Security Council on European matters. I tell you this as a friend – we need a counter to Connally. We can't throw away twenty-five years of what has been built up for Treasury reasons."[56]

On the one hand, Nixon and Kissinger admired Connally because of his charisma and stature, which had only grown since the assassination of President Kennedy. On that day, Texas Governor John Connally was seated directly in front of President Kennedy, and Connally survived five gunshot-related injuries of his own. Nixon and Kissinger shielded Connally from public criticism, but they undermined him privately. "You'll find Connally, as I said, be very careful because I imagine he's sensitive. He's been reading the papers and he knows he's taking a kick in the ass and so forth, and just be terribly sympathetic," Nixon advised Kissinger. "When I talked to him yesterday, I just called him to welcome him home, and he chatted along for half an hour. ... I thought to myself, 'God, what a man,' " Kissinger said. "I went over, and I told him, I was not coming as the president's emissary, I'm coming as his friend," he said. "You've now smashed the system. No one would have had the guts to do it except you ... now I figure it's my judgment, if you want to emerge as a statesman out of this, you have to move into the constructive phase," Kissinger reported.[57]

On November 16, in a meeting with Pete Peterson, George Shultz, and Henry Kissinger, Nixon emphasized the importance of Kissinger being more involved in the ongoing negotiations.[58] The absence of John Connally from this meeting was conspicuous. Earlier in the day, the

---

[56] RMN, HAK Telcons, Box 12, November 11, 1971, 7:30 p.m.
[57] RMN, Nixon Tapes, Oval Office 618-011, November 15, 1971, 8:54 a.m.–10:20 a.m.
[58] RMN, Nixon Tapes, Executive Office Building 295-014, November 16, 1971, Unknown; between 5:05 p.m. and 6:39 p.m.

president met with him in the Oval Office and conveniently sent him out of
town on a public relations campaign to speak to leaders in the business
community.[59] Nixon was forced to take action. American Ambassador to
Paris Arthur Watson reported that "key French officials have begun to
warn us that, if we do not soon indicate clearly what our terms for a
settlement are, opinion will turn decisively against us, with incalculable
consequences for our political interests in Europe ... a major effort on our
part to break the present stalemate is needed."[60] Kissinger discussed with
White House Chief of Staff Bob Haldeman how to break the news to
Connally about Kissinger's new assignment. "He can be really rough if he
gets the impression that something is being done behind his back,"
Haldeman warned. "I've been lucky enough to not have had that experience yet," Kissinger replied.[61]

Nixon also ordered that the American negotiating position should be
worked out before negotiations advanced any further. "We may have
meetings with the European heads of state in the month of December
and we can't go into those meetings without something to say on this
problem," he said. "One thing, Henry, that I want you to get across to
John [Connally] is quit haggling around about the goddamn offset. Now,
with the Germans, you can haggle around for 50 million dollars more or
less on the offset, whereas you might be haggling about 500 million
dollars or more on something else."[62] That was the same point that
Bundesbank deputy Otmar Emminger made to American Ambassador
to Bonn Kenneth Rush. Rush explained to Kissinger that Emminger was
concerned that the deadlock in negotiations could result in the collapse of
the German government. A collapse would force a cabinet reshuffle that
could produce cabinet ministers not as friendly to American interests, as it
did when the government of Ludwig Erhard collapsed in 1966.
"Emminger reiterated that for all of these reasons, the United States
would not be able to get a better deal next spring than it could now."[63]
German Ambassador to Washington Rolf Pauls came to a similar conclusion. "The present crisis exposes the difficulties that American foreign
policy leaders have had recognizing the insoluble connection between
foreign policy and external economic policy," he reported to the Foreign

[59] RMN, Nixon Tapes, Oval Office 619-007, November 16, 1971, 9:53 a.m.–10:13 a.m.
[60] *FRUS*, 1969–1976, Volume III, 197.
[61] RMN, HAK Telcons, Box 12, November 15, 1971, 1:30 p.m.
[62] RMN, Nixon Tapes, Oval Office 619-007, November 16, 1971, 9:53 a.m.–10:13 a.m.
[63] *FRUS*, 1969–1976, Volume III, 199.

Office.[64] The Germans accepted the de facto links among political, economic, and military issues more than other Europeans.

To make his New Economic Policy function as planned, Nixon needed to keep the pressure on Arthur Burns for a loose money supply. Burns, meanwhile, was more distracted by the administration's lack of action on gold. "We're going to have to bring Arthur in and be ready to roll," Nixon said to Kissinger. "Because Arthur is playing, without question, the game here working all over town and all over the international community to go back to convertibility, is he not? Well, he says no, but he is – 'raise the price of gold' in some form, a limited form of convertibility." Kissinger admitted his own limited competence on the subject and instead focused on politics. "I'm really very concerned about the way that things are shaping up politically in every one of these countries," he said. "Italy has a recession … Germany has a recession … we're going to Moscow, but Japan is a mess. Western Europe is in a mess. We've given up our friends to our enemies."[65] Since Kissinger was not going to be much help, Nixon recruited Paul McCracken to pressure Burns. "You see Paul," Nixon said, "we've got to keep Arthur's feet to the fire on the money supply. By God, we have got to put his feet to the fire on this thing. Connally's going to start working on him incidentally, and I've got [Washington Redskins owner] George Allen … he's going to work on him from the private side."[66] Nixon pressured Burns from every conceivable public and private angle.

Nixon announced an interest in holding bilateral summits with the leaders of France, Germany, and the United Kingdom. He accepted that a certain portion of the negotiations could only be resolved at that level, meeting one-on-one. In a backchannel message to Arthur Watson intended for George Pompidou, Kissinger said "the President's main interest is in having exploratory talk with Pompidou before he sees [the] other leaders."[67] Nixon knew that getting an agreement with Pompidou would in effect solve the crisis, given Pompidou's expertise on the topic and his position as the main obstacle in Europe to a settlement. The French were skeptical that the Americans would adhere to any agreement determined at the Azores, the site planned for the summit.[68] Edward Heath

[64] *AAPD* 1971, Botschafter Pauls, Washington, an das Auswärtige Amt, 406.
[65] RMN, Nixon Tapes, Oval Office 619-007, November 16, 1971, 9:53 a.m.–10:13 a.m.
[66] RMN, Nixon Tapes, Oval Office 619-012, November 16, 1971, 11:13 a.m.–11:38 a.m.
[67] RMN, NSC, Box 55, Backchannel telegram from White House to American Embassy Paris, November 11, 1971.
[68] AN, 5 AG 2/660, Note du Secrétariat général de la Présidence de la République (J.R. Bernard) pour Monsieur Jobert, 9 décembre 1971: "récapitulation de quelques

expressed a similar concern to Pompidou. Since the Americans had already shown an inclination for unilateral action, what would stop them from doing so again?[69]

The planning for Nixon's upcoming visits to China and the Soviet Union soon eclipsed the importance of the European summits. The agendas for the European summits, originally designed to solve the remaining details of the international monetary crisis, became filled with other discussion items, including China, the Soviet Union, Vietnam, and NATO.[70] Secretary of Defense Melvin Laird had just returned from Europe and, in a report to Nixon, noted that his counterparts were far more concerned with the "rhetoric emanating from the Congress" and a general "mistrust in U.S. future actions," especially with the American summits to China and the Soviet Union in the near future.[71] In a phone conversation between Nixon and Connally on October 21, Nixon said "prior to our trips abroad [to China and the Soviet Union], I've got to meet with our allies. I've got to meet with the French, the Germans, and maybe the British. That will be in the month of December and early January."[72] "I think if I'll pick 'em off one by one, it's better ... because you see, they're whining that I, apart from the monetary thing, they're complaining 'you're not telling us, consulting with us about Russia, you're not consulting with us about China, you're not consulting with us about NATO,' and so forth."

As China and the Soviet Union became the major items for discussion with the Europeans, remaining areas of monetary disagreement gradually dissipated. Connally reported to Nixon on November 24 that the major outstanding issue in the negotiations impasse was gold. The French were expected to be the most vocal. "France has a phobia about gold. Pompidou has it. Everybody has it, because they have told their people over a long period to buy gold, to hoard gold," Connally reported. "There's probably 3 billion dollars held by French citizens in gold. They just squirrel it away. So it's a major issue with France, no question about it."[73] Connally remained unwilling to settle with the Europeans

problèmes monétaires avant les conversations entre le Président de la République et le Président des Etats-Unis aux Açores," December 9, 1971.

[69] AN, 5 AG 2/660, "Lettre de E. Heath to G. Pompidou," undated.

[70] Willy Brandt, *People and Politics: The Years 1960–1975* (London: Collins, 1978), 296.

[71] GRF, Papers of Melvin Laird, Box C18, Memorandum from Melvin Laird to Richard Nixon, "Report on My Trip to Europe," November 9, 1971.

[72] RMN, Nixon Tapes, White House Telephone 012–053, October 21, 1971, 6:08 p.m.–6:24 p.m.

[73] RMN, Nixon Tapes, Oval Office 623-003, November 23, 1971, 10:01 a.m.–11:40 a.m.

simply for the sake of rebuilding international harmony. "I did not take this apart to put it back at a cheap price," Arthur Burns heard Connally say more than once.[74]

While Nixon planned for the summits, he asked Connally to put more pressure on Arthur Burns. "I'm going to heat him up again tomorrow," Nixon said. "You can tell him that. Why don't you just say this, that 'Arthur,' tell him, 'in fairness, you should know the president has ... had some very, very heavy pressures ... the money supply thing is just not on a good track. It's got to go up.' "[75] Nixon knew few limits in his pursuit of Arthur Burns. He met with Herb Stein later the same day to discuss his coming promotion to Chairman of the Council of Economic Advisors. Nixon reminded Stein that the most important qualification for the job was influence with Burns. "The main thing is, we've got to be damned insistent on, stand up to Arthur and kick him in the nuts on the money supply," Nixon said.[76]

As a precursor to Nixon's summits with the Europeans, the G-10 finance ministers, chaired by John Connally, met in Rome from November 30 to December 1. Connally focused on maximizing Nixon's chances for success in the 1972 election. "We are going to start negotiating here at the end of this month," he told Henry Kissinger. "What we need domestically at least for the Midwest, if we could crack agriculture and help get the Midwest, which the president will have to carry. It would be a tremendous help it seems to me."[77] Connally was confident that the monetary crisis could be solved with a minimum of effort. "The international matter could be settled and it was only a question of how much to give."[78]

The newfound American optimism that settlement was imminent was exceeded only by French optimism. Paul McCracken reported to President Nixon that the French mood had changed from pessimism to a pro-American position as soon as Nixon had agreed to meet with Pompidou. McCracken returned from the Economic Policy Committee of the Organization for Economic Cooperation and Development (OECD) and reported that "traditionally in these Economic Policy Committee meetings the French delegation could be expected to flay the American

---

[74] GRF, Papers of Arthur Burns, Handwritten Journals, 1969–1974, Box 1, November 26, 1971.
[75] RMN, Nixon Tapes, Oval Office 623-003, November 23, 1971, 10:01 a.m.–11:40 a.m.
[76] RMN, Nixon Tapes, Oval Office 623-024, November 23, 1971, 4:57 p.m.–6:07 p.m.
[77] RMN, HAK Telcons, Box 12, November 22, 1971, 6:30 p.m.
[78] *FRUS*, 1969–1976, Volume III, Editorial Note 203.

position at some point in the deliberations." However, according to Jean René Bernard, economic advisor to President Pompidou, the French were optimistic that "the G-10 meetings November 30–December 1 should at least start the process for an orderly solution" to the monetary problem. The price of failure was simply too high. "In his [Bernard's] judgment, it might be difficult for European unity to survive."[79]

Behind the scenes, Arthur Burns continued his attempts to undermine John Connally, while also resenting George Shultz's rising influence with Nixon. "Shultz's performance was an astounding exercise on the part of a man who should know that he has not the slightest understanding of international economics or finance!" Burns confided to his diary.[80] Henry Kissinger stayed out of the feud but, at the same time, hedged his bets. "I can't associate with you at these meetings but I agree with you," Kissinger said to Burns on November 26. He assured Burns that he (Kissinger) was calling the shots now, not Connally. "I will solve it . . . and it will be close to your proposal . . . you are the only sane person . . . it will be 98 percent your proposal. Don't tell Connally I told you this," Kissinger added, who was not only going around Connally but also Nixon.[81] Burns's aggravation was not with Connally and Shultz alone, but with Nixon's entire team of economic advisors:

Here we are – Kissinger, a brilliant political analyst, but admittedly ignorant of economics; Connally, a thoroughly confused politician, suppressing his desire to punish foreigners in view of the President's moving away from narrow domestic political considerations; Shultz, a no less confused amateur economist; I, the only one there with any knowledge of the subject, but even I not a real expert on some aspects of the intricate international problem! What a way to reach decisions! No one from the State Department there, no technical expert to aid us![82]

At the G-10 meeting, Connally presented a coherent American negotiating position for the first time:

1. "The U.S. will eliminate its 10 percent surcharge and the related provision of the proposed investment tax credit.
2. To assure better a successful adjustment process consistent with freer and fairer trade, tangible progress is required in dealing with artificial restraints on the competitive opportunities of U.S. exporters. Early

[79] *FRUS*, 1969–1976, Volume III, 204.
[80] GRF, Papers of Arthur Burns, Handwritten Journals, 1969–1974, Box 1, November 26, 1971.
[81] RMN, HAK Telcons, Box 12, November 26, 1971, 2:15 p.m.
[82] GRF, Papers of Arthur Burns, Handwritten Journals, 1969–1974, Box 1, November 26, 1971.

decisions on some matters of immediate consequences should be made, particularly with respect to agriculture, and commitments are necessary with regard to ensuing negotiations. These matters have been under intensive bilateral review with Canada and Japan. We have sought a similar review with the EC and its members. The U.S. is prepared to continue to negotiate intensively in coming weeks.

3. Progress in needed toward achieving a better sharing of mutual defense expenditures. To this end, certain bilateral matters are near decision, and multilateral efforts should be intensified at the forthcoming NATO meeting.

4. A pattern of exchanges rates should be established providing, at the minimum, a weighted average appreciation of currencies of all other OECD countries of 11 percent, measured in U.S. cents per unit of foreign currencies, with a base point of May 1, 1971. (The appreciation is calculated on the basis of weighted shred of U.S. trade with these countries.) Based on an appraisal of individual country positions, depreciation of foreign currencies in terms of its own trading partners should not be contemplated.

5. The new exchange rates should be accompanied by margins of 3 percent, plus and minus. IMF [International Monetary Fund] surveillance should be directed to assure that there be no heavy market intervention in exchange markets within the band for the purpose of keeping market rates artificially low. There should be no manipulation or arrangements of exchange markets designed to maintain undervaluation of exchange rates for current accounts or trade purposes."[83]

The proposal contained the first substantive American concession: removal of the unilateral import surcharge. In private sessions, Connally even exceeded Nixon's negotiating position. According to a summary of the G-10 by prepared by George Shultz, he reported: "Problem. Connally offered devaluation of the dollar and it now appears Arthur [Burns] is winning on convertibility. These are both firmly opposite to the President's direction."[84] Connally withdrew his previous insistence that both monetary reforms and trade be negotiated in a single package.[85] Syndicated columnist Joe Kraft called Henry Kissinger to get "some sense

---

[83] *FRUS*, 1969–1976, Volume III, 211.

[84] *FRUS*, 1969–1976, Volume III, Editorial Note 212.

[85] HAEC, BAC 3-1978 556, Telex from European Commission Liaison Office Washington D.C. to European Commission, "echos de la reunion du groupe des dix," December 7, 1971.

to what degree Secretary Connally has been turned around." In a conversation that he insisted be off the record, Kissinger stated "I don't like to use the word 'retreat,' " but that a meeting between Kissinger, Connally, Burns, and the president the previous Wednesday "was important." When Kraft tried to get Kissinger to go a bit further, he replied "keep me out of it."[86]

As President Nixon prepared to meet with British Prime Minister Edward Heath, he called American Ambassador to London Walter Annenberg to discuss the agenda. Annenberg noted that when Nixon met with Heath, he "will find the Prime Minister in a cordial frame of mind. I think he was unhappy for a period. I think he's getting over it." John Connally, sitting next to the president in the Oval Office, did not miss an opportunity to criticize the British government. "Walter, without belaboring this, in the paper the day before yesterday, we saw where Great Britain was going to run a *3 billion dollar surplus* in her balance of payments this year, the largest surplus in her history." Annenberg changed the subject. "The reaction around Europe is that you're pretty close to a deal. It's just a question of the president and some of the leaders putting the finishing touches on it, at least that's the reaction I get out of all the countries over here," he added. "Well, Walter, that's right," Connally said. "The president's options are entirely open to him. We've tried to structure it in such a way that we're fairly close, but those countries over there have to be forthcoming a bit ... if Pompidou, Heath, and the rest of them are halfway reasonable, I think it can be settled in the next month."[87] Connally wanted to keep the Europeans off balance, even though, as the summits neared, he became less important since it was Kissinger who was setting the summit agendas.

A few minutes later, Arthur Burns called Nixon to let him know that he had cooperated with the president's demand for an expansionary money supply. Burns announced his surrender to the White House. The Federal Reserve Board Open Market Committee reduced the discount rate to 4 ½ percent, which helped to set the economy on an expansionary footing in 1972.[88] "We've made the change in order to bring the discount rate in line with market conditions ... but also to further economic expansion." He did not want to be blamed for a Nixon loss in 1972. "There is no doubt

[86] RMN, HAK Telcons, Box 12, November 29, 1971, 9:30 a.m.
[87] RMN, Nixon Tapes, White House Telephone 016–080, December 10, 1971, 4:20 p.m.–4:27 p.m.
[88] RMN, Nixon Tapes, White House Telephone 016–082, December 10, 1971, 4:36 p.m.–4:42 p.m.

in my mind whatever that if the Fed continues to keep the lid on with regard to increases in the money supply and if the economy does not expand as you, along with most other respected economists, have predicted in 1972 the blame will be put squarely on the Fed for holding the lid on too long – just as, in my opinion, it was very properly put on the Fed in 1960."[89] Burns's about-face was no spontaneous matter. Milton Friedman had been writing Burns a series of blistering letters during early December. "What in God's name is happening?" Friedman demanded to know in just one example. "In 1971, you are at the head of the Fed, and *a far sharper slowdown has occurred in monetary growth than in 1959* ... try as I may, I find it hard to see any excuse for such an irresponsible policy."[90] Just as Nixon desired, Friedman pressured Burns for an expansionary money supply and at just the right time.

The following week was spent drawing up an interim solution that would act as a bridge between August 1971 and the final end of the gold standard, which came in March 1973. Henry Kissinger had a secret meeting with French Ambassador to Washington Charles Lucet, where both men agreed that the forthcoming summit between Nixon and Pompidou should be used to symbolically settle the monetary impasse.[91] It was to be a public relations opportunity for both men since there were no major issues to settle. None of the summits was to be held in any country's capital; in this way, the meetings could take place with a minimum of protocol and press. Willy Brandt and French President Georges Pompidou met in advance in Paris on December 3 to arrange their positions before Pompidou met with Nixon. Pompidou, the expert on this issue, instructed Brandt on the best position to take. "The American proposal, which includes a rather high devaluation, raises problems. While the proposal does not cause problems for Germany or Japan, it would for France, Italy, and Great Britain," Pompidou said.[92]

Nixon was eager to have all remaining monetary issues settled before his summits with Brandt, Heath, and Pompidou. In this way, the agendas could instead focus on issues that Nixon was eager to talk about, namely, his forthcoming visits to China and the Soviet Union. Nixon got what he

[89] GRF, Papers of Arthur Burns, Box N1, Memorandum from President Nixon to Arthur Burns, November 4, 1971.

[90] GRF, Papers of Arthur Burns, Box K12, Letter from Milton Friedman to Arthur Burns, December 13, 1971.

[91] AN, 5 AG 2/117, Telegram N. 7248/57 from French Embassy in Washington (Lucet), "Entretien avec M. Kissinger, December 1, 1971 (Très secret)," December 1, 1971.

[92] AAPD 1971, Gespräch des Bundeskanzlers Brandt mit Staatspräsident Pompidou in Paris, 427.

wanted. At a G-10 finance ministers meeting held in Washington over December 17–18, the impasse was at last broken. Named the Smithsonian Agreement after the location of the meetings, Connally called Nixon from the Smithsonian Castle to report the breakthrough. "They've had cabinet meetings all over the world" because once the agreement goes into effect, "they have to affirmatively act to devalue."[93] "The Japanese ... have offered [a] sixteen-point nine [revaluation]," the Germans "about [a] five [percent revaluation]," the Italians, "I think we've just kind of run over 'em." Nixon congratulated Connally for his work on "not only the most historic, the most difficult, [but] the most far-reaching [agreement]."[94] He referred to the Smithsonian Agreement as "the most significant monetary agreement in the history of the world" and the "most difficult in history."[95] In reality, it was little more than a bridge between Nixon's August 15 announcement and a longer phase of negotiations that did not conclude until 1973.

Nixon could proceed to the bilateral heads of state summits in late December 1971 without having to prepare for difficult technical discussions about exchange rates or gold. With the Smithsonian Agreement accomplished, neither Americans nor Europeans had an appetite to discuss monetary affairs.[96] Privately, there was skepticism that monetary problems would be solved for very long. Paul Volcker called the Smithsonian Agreement "Bretton Woods without the gold ... I hope it lasts three months."[97] French Foreign Minister Maurice Schumann was also skeptical. "The solution finally adopted by Washington is close to the suggestions which were studied by both presidents ... but it must be stated that President Nixon and his advisors have been vague about the means necessary to attain these results."[98]

---

[93] RMN, Nixon Tapes, White House Telephone 016–111, December 18, 1971, 1:40 p.m.–1:46 p.m. and White House Telephone 016–114, December 18, 1971, 3:05 p.m.–3:09 p.m.

[94] RMN, Nixon Tapes, White House Telephone 016–126, December 19, 1971, 7:55 p.m.–8:01 p.m.

[95] Eichengreen, 245, and RMN, White House Special Files, President's Personal File, Box 70, handwritten notes.

[96] PAAA, B31/332, Memorandum from Per Fischer, Bundeskanzleramt an das Auswärtige Amt, "Gerspräche des Herrn Bundeskanzlers mit Präsident Nixon Ende Dezember 1971," December 7, 1971.

[97] Volcker and Gyohten, 90.

[98] AN, 5 AG 2/117, Circular telegram n. 449 from Paris (Maurice Schumann) to the main diplomatic posts, "Conférences des Açores," December 22, 1971 (Strictement réservé), December 22, 1971.

In the Azores, over breakfast on December 14, Nixon and Kissinger endured what Paul Volcker termed "a Gaullist lecture on gold and the evils of the dollar standard."[99] Pompidou was pleased that Nixon was willing to remove the import surcharge and the job development credit "without delay."[100] These had been the two most disagreeable protectionist policies of August 15 in the eyes of the Europeans. After breakfast, Kissinger drafted a communiqué to be agreed upon by Nixon and Pompidou in order to symbolically affirm the end of the monetary crisis.[101] The major points included the American lifting of the 10 percent import surcharge, raising the price of gold to US$38 an ounce, a revalue of the German mark by approximately 5–6 percent, and a U.S. guarantee that it would defend these new parities within the agreed upon 2.25 percent bands.[102] The communiqué was a way for Pompidou to document that the Americans understood what they were agreeing to. If the Americans did not uphold their side of the agreement, Pompidou privately concluded that France would have no choice but to switch from a dollar standard to a mark standard.[103] "In the Azores agreement, we got Pompidou to go higher not with an economic argument but with a political argument," Kissinger remembered later. "We didn't want to settle the economics matters without the French, but we made him aware that if he didn't cooperate France would be isolated."[104]

After his return from the Azores, a relieved Kissinger told Joe Kraft, "the meeting achieved the best we could hope for ... there were no winners or losers and we've stopped playing confrontation with our allies."[105] An obvious criticism of Connally, Kissinger also told Arthur Burns that he had kept his earlier promise to "fix" the monetary impasse. "We settled on your scheme, but Connally got the credit. As I recall, I convinced Pompidou to agree to your scheme," Kissinger said.[106] Connally was not happy with the Azores agreement and suggested that

---

[99] Volcker and Gyohten, 88.
[100] AN, 5 AG 2/1022, Entretien de M. Pompidou avec M. Kissinger, aux Açores le 13 décembre 1971, 8h45, December 13, 1971.
[101] RMN, White House Special Files, President's Personal File, Box 70, "Framework for Monetary and Trade Settlement."
[102] *FRUS*, 1969–1976, Volume III, 220.
[103] AN, 5 AG 2/1022, "Extrait du compte-rendu de l'entretien du 13 décembre 1971 dans l'après-midi, relatif aux questions monétaires. (Nixon, Pompidou, Kissinger)," December 13, 1971.
[104] *FRUS*, 1969–1976, Volume E-15, Part 2, 5.
[105] RMN, HAK Telcons, Box 12, December 15, 1971, 8:45 a.m.
[106] *FRUS*, 1969–1976, Volume III, 236.

the new parities would not be defended.[107] He resigned his position and left the government within a matter of months. Some Europeans openly doubted whether the Americans would uphold their end of the deal. Jean Monnet wrote to Robert Triffin, "What do you think of all that is happening? I personally am somewhat puzzled ... I don't know what is the likely future."[108] Triffin's response emphasized that any modification to international monetary relations "gravely menaced the preservation of commerce between the countries of the [European Economic] Community."[109]

The Smithsonian Agreement was signed on December 18 and represented a realignment of exchange rates, as had been agreed on by Nixon and Pompidou at the Azores.[110] The press communiqué stated simply that "The Ministers and [Central Bank] Governors agreed on an inter-related set of measures designed to restore stability to international monetary arrangements and to provide for expanding international trade."[111] Nixon was happy he remained loyal to Connally throughout even the most difficult moments of negotiation. "It's really a massive achievement ... what Connally did with the Group of Ten, you know. He shoved that thing ... he just beat 'em, and cajoled 'em, and finally got an agreement," he bragged to Chuck Colson. "You see, we spent with Heath, and also Pompidou, eight, ten, twelve hours, you know, tough negotiating."[112]

The exchange rate realignments of December 1971 negotiated at the Smithsonian, in which American allies offered the majority of the concessions, strengthened the short-term prospects for maintaining the dollar standard and sharply improved the competitive position of the United States. The realignment lasted barely more than a year, until the entire exchange rate structure collapsed in the first months of 1973.[113] Memoir

---

[107] AN, 5 AG 2/1022, "Entretien de M. Pompidou avec M. Kissinger aux Açores, le 14 décembre 1971 à 8 heures du matin," December 14, 1971.

[108] HAEU, RT 24–25, Letter from Jean Monnet to Robert Triffin, December 16, 1971.

[109] HAEU, RT 24–25, Letter from Robert Triffin to Jean Monnet, December 23, 1971.

[110] The key tenets of the Smithsonian Agreement were made official by Congress in March 1972. See the Par Value Modification Act, 86 Stat. 116, March 1972.

[111] GRF, Papers of Arthur Burns, Box B54, "Press Communiqué of the Ministerial Meeting of the Group of Ten on 17th–18th December, 1971 in Washington, D.C.," December 18, 1971.

[112] RMN, Nixon Tapes, White House Telephone 016–131, December 21, 1971, 10:11 p.m.–10:35 p.m.

[113] Fred C. Bergsten, "Reforming the Dollar: An International Monetary Policy for the United States" (New York: Council Papers on International Affairs, 1972), 5; Otmar Emminger, "The D-Mark in the Conflict Between Internal and External Equilibrium,

accounts of policy makers and others influential in the Nixon administration have since admitted that the reforms, especially the more far-reaching protectionist aspects such as wage and price controls, were mistakes.[114] The strong unilateral action taken by the United States in the summer and fall of 1971 demonstrated how disruptive an American turn to economic nationalism could be. The Nixon administration clearly subordinated relations with allies to domestic political concerns. This new attitude was epitomized by John Connally's notorious observations that "the dollar may be our currency, but it's your problem" and that "foreigners are out to screw us . . . our job is to screw them first."[115]

However, the United States should not receive all of the blame for worldwide monetary troubles. Even without the drastic American action of August 15, the Bretton Woods system was clearly unsustainable. Over the years, exchange rates had hardened, discussions of major reforms to the system seemed increasingly unlikely in the absence of a serious crisis, the monetary expansion that the United States underwent during the Great Society and Vietnam War was not reversible, and the different national policy stances seemed more incompatible than ever.[116] The United States was entitled to be released from the special burden of acting as the fulcrum of the world's monetary system. President Nixon's monetary crisis was essentially a continuation of his predecessors' crises.[117] He was merely the first American leader to pursue the comprehensive reforms that some say was the birth of the modern age of globalization.[118]

The reforms were a short-term domestic success. In 1972, the United States enjoyed the largest real growth (5.7 percent) and the lowest rise in consumer prices (3.3 percent) in years. Unemployment declined to 5.1 percent, and the American balance of payments deficit shrunk drastically from US$29.8 billion in 1971 to US$10.4 billion in 1972.[119] Most importantly for Nixon, his New Economic Policy visibly reestablished

---

1948–1975" (Princeton: Essays in International Finance, 1977), 23; Yves-Henri Nouailhat, *Les Etats-Unis et le monde au 20e siècle* (Paris: Armand Colin, 2000), 247.

[114] Connally, 241; Ebenstein, 185; Milton and Rose D. Friedman, *Two Lucky People: Memoirs* (Chicago: University of Chicago Press, 1998), 376.

[115] Eichengreen, 243–244; Gavin, 194.

[116] James, 205.

[117] Dominique Carreau, *Le Système Monétaire Internationale: Aspects Juridiques* (Paris: Librairie Armand Colin, 1972), 15.

[118] Those who have written recently about the collapse of Bretton Woods as the birth of the modern era of globalization include Niall Ferguson, Francis Gavin, and Thomas Zeiler.

[119] Calleo, 64.

presidential economic leadership just in time for the final drive to his 1972 reelection victory.[120] Nixon touted his economic and monetary policies as a centerpiece of his 1972 campaign, as depicted in his campaign literature in advance of the Republican National Convention in Miami. A full four pages were devoted to John Connally, Arthur Burns, and the group that met at Camp David over August 15.[121]

Nixon compared the impact of his August 15 announcement with his surprise, a month before on July 15, that he would be the first American president to visit the People's Republic of China. Nixon clung to the praise he received for the dramatic China announcement, and he wanted an encore performance a month later on monetary policy. As with China, he wanted people to think that the situation had been under consideration for some time. With the monetary reforms, Nixon felt his way into a policy area that was foreign to him, he assembled a kitchen cabinet, and then he figured out how to get the rest of his administration on board.

Nixon realized that he had a chance to remove the United States from the burden of being the pivot for the Bretton Woods system and that doing so could help to prepare the economy for the 1972 election. He did not intend to defend the new parities created during the Smithsonian process, and he avoided any real structural reforms until after the 1972 election. The longer that settlement was delayed, the more it imposed on other Nixon priorities, such as the summits with China and the Soviet Union. The Smithsonian Agreement was doomed to fail, but Nixon's attention was focused elsewhere.

---

[120] Jean Denizet, *Le Dollar: Histoire du Système Monétaire Internationale Depuis 1945* (Paris: Fayard, 1985), 109.
[121] USAF Archives, Papers of Stanley Goodwin, AR.2002.175 Box 3, Trips 3, "Republican National Convention, Miami Beach, August 1972."

4

The Year of Europe

Sipping on a cup of consommé in the Oval Office on the morning of September 16, 1972, Assistant to the President for National Security Affairs Henry Kissinger described his press conference that had concluded a few moments before. "They were hanging from the rafters," he said to President Nixon. Kissinger announced that, following the upcoming election, "the European relationships had to be given a new vitality commensurate to the area. That no matter how much progress we make in our dealings with Moscow and Peking, Europe is the cornerstone of our foreign policy."[1] Nixon made his historic visit to China the previous February, signed the Strategic Arms Limitation Treaty (SALT I) at the Kremlin in May, and a ceasefire agreement in Vietnam was expected by the end of the year. These achievements, concentrated within a single calendar year and affirmed by the electorate in an overwhelming forty-nine-state reelection victory in November, remain without parallel in recent American foreign policy.

In the midst of these achievements with American adversaries, relations with European allies took a back seat. Henry Kissinger also recognized that the damage done to transatlantic relations by John Connally and the unilateral decision to end Bretton Woods the year before needed to be repaired. With Nixon grabbing headlines in Peking and Moscow, Europeans felt that they had been overlooked. As early as March 1972, German State Secretary Egon Bahr raised the need for improved relations

[1] RMN, Nixon Tapes, Oval Office 780-015, September 16, 1972, 10:55 a.m.–12:50 p.m.

between Europe and the United States.[2] Europeans also wanted an opportunity to provide greater input on Nixon's future foreign policy.[3]

Over time, the Nixon and Kissinger plan to rebuild relations during 1973 with European allies became known in the press as the "Year of Europe." It was intended to be just as significant a foreign policy achievement as China or the Soviet Union. "I gave a long philosophic disposition [of] how things have changed since the '60s. We're now in an era of totally new diplomacy," Kissinger said. Nixon agreed. "All the sophisticates will know that it's goddamn important."[4]

The Year of Europe was not a one-dimensional proposal. It was intended to be a reassessment of American relations with Europe, one that reflected the increased political and economic importance of the European Economic Community (EEC). The EEC anticipated its first expansion to include Denmark, Ireland, and the United Kingdom, effective January 1, 1973. Richard Nixon had been a supporter of the European integration movement since its establishment by the Treaty of Rome in 1957. As president, he publicly applauded the 1973 expansion in his official response. "The closest cooperation between the U.S. and the emerging Europe is a cornerstone of our foreign policy," he remarked.[5] However, in the years since the Treaty of Rome, Europe had steadily become less dependent on the United States and had, in fact, become a commercial competitor by the 1960s.

The Year of Europe was also intended to address a backlog of transatlantic issues, including disagreements over trade, NATO, East-West relations, and monetary affairs. *Ostpolitik* had advanced, American relations with the Soviet Union and China had become more complex, and the last American combat troops had departed from Vietnam.[6] The expansion of the EEC was more than symbolic, and the region required a new assessment by the United States. The Year of Europe was also a recognition that the Nixon Doctrine had been applied too abruptly during 1971 by removing the U.S. dollar as the pivot of the global monetary system. Following John Connally's departure from the Department of Treasury

[2] RMN, NSC, Box 686, Memoranda of Conversation between Egon Bahr and Henry Kissinger, March 28, 1972.

[3] PAAA, ZA 101383, Memorandum from Rolf Pauls, Germany Ambassador to Washington, to the Foreign Office, "Anmerkungen zur amerikanischen Politik 1972," January 15, 1973.

[4] RMN, Nixon Tapes, Oval Office 780-015, September 16, 1972, 10:55 a.m.–12:50 p.m.

[5] Woolley and Peters, http://www.presidency.ucsb.edu/ws?pid=3441.

[6] Jussi M. Hanhimäki, "Kissinger et l'Europe: entre intégration et autonomie." *Relations Internationales* 119 (2004): 325.

in 1972, his replacement, George Shultz, prioritized a more accommodating phase of American diplomacy.

What Richard Nixon had in mind in 1973 was a new "Atlantic Charter."[7] The original Atlantic Charter was signed in 1941 by President Franklin D. Roosevelt and Prime Minister Winston Churchill. It articulated an early vision of the postwar world that committed the United States and Europe to cooperate on issues related to trade, economic and monetary policy, and freeing the world of aggressors. In 1973, work was needed on all of these fronts. There were numerous trade disputes between Europe and the United States, there was a need for better monetary cooperation following the collapse of Bretton Woods, and there was a need to address the future role of NATO. For Nixon, having achieved reduced Cold War tensions with China and the Soviet Union in his first term, he believed future initiatives carried out with adversaries needed to be first backed by fresh, meaningful commitments with American allies.

The Year of Europe never happened as envisioned. After the launching of the initiative in September 1972, it suffered from fits and starts, delays, and interference from competing policy priorities on both sides of the Atlantic. Nixon's long planning sessions for his second term at Camp David prevented any immediate progress. The "Christmas Bombing" in Vietnam during December 1972 caused more delays. Following the formal resolution of the war, the Year of Europe was relaunched but torpedoed again in January 1973, revived in April, dead again in July, resuscitated in the fall, strained by the Yom Kippur War, and then, as 1973 became 1974, what was left fell apart for good. In February 1974, the British government under Conservative Prime Minister Edward Heath flipped to a minority Labor government under Harold Wilson after taking two elections in a single year to determine the new government. In April, French Presidential Georges Pompidou died after secretly suffering for eighteen months from a rare bone cancer. That same month, German Chancellor Willy Brandt resigned following a scandal.

President Nixon lost all of his key European collaborators in the span of three months, and, being immersed himself in the intensifying Watergate investigation, the task of redressing relations with the European Community (EC) was left to Henry Kissinger and Nixon's successor, Gerald Ford. The other side of the Atlantic seemed just as distracted: the EC went through major internal changes following

---

[7] *FRUS*, 1969–1976, Volume E-15, Part 2, 14.

enlargement. Such dramatic change – occurring so quickly – left a lack of agreement, some distrust, competing visions for the future of the supranational organization, and visions yet to be fully articulated.[8] The most disappointing aspect of the Year of Europe was that although Nixon achieved more difficult breakthroughs with China, the Soviet Union, and Vietnam, he was not able to renew and strengthen existing ties with European allies.[9]

* * *

In the fall of 1972, public opinion polls consistently showed Nixon ahead by double digits over Senator George McGovern, his Democratic rival for the presidency. Although Nixon never got too comfortable, he did begin to think about the post-election period. Early in his second term, Nixon wanted an even grander replay of his well-received 1969 European tour that launched his first term. However, the 1973 trip could not simply be a goodwill trip, like that of 1969, as important as that was for the new president. Four years later, he had to show critics that something was accomplished on his next trip. Since 1969, relations with Europe, based on associations much different from those with China or the Soviet Union, had been inevitably altered when the whole of the American foreign policy apparatus was overhauled to prioritize secret negotiations with enemies. The greater use of the National Security Council (NSC) as the sole decision-making forum meant that although parts of the State and Defense Departments were privy to what was going on in the minds of Nixon and Kissinger, large parts were not.[10] Transatlantic relations had been traditionally marked by protocol, cultural exchanges, and a commitment to Europe that had been sustained since the end of World War II. By 1973, those Europeanists left in the State Department, as well as the department itself, had lost considerable influence in the Nixon foreign policy-making process, a situation that would be only remedied after Henry Kissinger became Secretary of State.

Initially, the Nixon plan for a focus on transatlantic relations during 1973 drew support from European leaders who were consulted long before the phrase "Year of Europe" became popular in

---

[8] *FRUS*, 1969–1976, Volume E-15, Part 2, 4.

[9] James O. Goldsborough, "France, The European Crisis and the Alliance." *Foreign Affairs* 52 (April 1974): 538.

[10] Alastair Buchan, "Europe and America: From Alliance to Coalition." Paris: The Atlantic Institute for International Affairs, 1973, 9–10, 12–13.

the press.[11] German Economics Minister Helmut Schmidt approved of the concept but made it clear that the American government should avoid a replay of the "political effects in Europe of Secretary Connally's actions" the previous year on international monetary affairs, which caused much strain.[12] Throughout the summer and fall of 1972, Nixon and Kissinger had numerous discussions about how to shift the focus of their attention from adversaries to allies and were clearly hopeful about Nixon's chances for a second term. "As we look back over the last year, this year has been a year of enormous change in the relations between great powers," Nixon said. Kissinger emphasized that relations with Europe should be put "on a new basis ... now we need a new framework."[13] The favorable polls in the run-up to the election in 1972 gave Nixon a prolonged period of time in which to plan the major initiatives of his second term. "I think one of your first moves ought to be toward the Europeans," Kissinger said. The goal should be "a new European Charter of some sort."[14]

Memoir accounts confirm that Europe was a major initiative of Nixon's second term, but they do not explain why the Year of Europe failed. Decades later, Henry Kissinger considered it a lost opportunity, one that to some degree continues to mystify him.[15] "As President, I sought to make 1973 the Year of Europe in order to focus the energies of my administration on resolving the problems which had had arisen from changing times," Nixon wrote.[16] The impetus for the initiative was rooted in the Cold War struggle with the Soviet Union. "It is vital that we strengthen, not weaken, the alliance. Europe is still the geopolitical target of the Kremlin." Kissinger took a similar tone in his memoirs. "With the end of the Vietnam War, Nixon and I thought the time had come to revitalize the Atlantic Alliance. On behalf of the President, I put forward an initiative."[17] Kissinger raised the issue repeatedly with Nixon, who soon started talking about it himself.

[11] William C. Cromwell, *The United States and the European Pillar: The Strained Alliance* (New York: St. Martin's Press, 1992), 80.
[12] RMN, NSC, Box 687, Memorandum of Conversations between Helmut Schmidt and Henry Kissinger, July 20, 1972.
[13] RMN, Nixon Tapes, Oval Office 780-007, September 16, 1972, 9:26 a.m.–10:20 a.m.
[14] RMN, Nixon Tapes, Oval Office 784-007, September 21, 1972, 10:15 a.m.–10:50 a.m.
[15] Conversation with the author, June 23, 2008.
[16] Richard Nixon, *1999*, 207.
[17] Henry A. Kissinger, *Years of Renewal: The Concluding Volume of His Memoirs* (New York: Simon and Schuster, 1999), 600.

Nixon told French Ambassador Jacques Koscuisko-Morizet and former Foreign Minister Maurice Schumann on September 29 that "in the next year, I want to devote more time to the European Community ... the bedrock of everything is the European-American alliance."[18] Nixon also briefed British Foreign Secretary Alec Douglas-Home on the proposal. "Once we get past the election ... I think it's very important ... now that everybody is discovering China and moving with the Russians and the rest, I think it's very important to establish a strong line of communication within the alliance." Nixon returned to this theme before the meeting was concluded. "Once we get past the election, I would say quite early, after that maybe around the first of the year, or Christmas, depending on how it works out, I would like to devote some attention to that," he said. Douglas-Home understood the importance of the proposal. "We'll be ready for you whenever you want to ... there are very big questions [to discuss]."[19] Kissinger also briefed West German Chancellor Willy Brandt on the proposal. "The Chancellor ... suggest[s] that after the elections here and in Germany (which are on November 19) he wishes to discuss with you the medium of long-term prospects for the U.S.-European relationship."[20] It was clear that a major American initiative was on the horizon. Seeking input from Europeans was intended to demonstrate that the United States prioritized its allies over adversaries. However, advance notice also inadvertently raised European expectations higher than Nixon or Kissinger were prepared for.

On November 7, Nixon sequestered himself away at Camp David for an extended second-term planning session.[21] On November 18, he emerged to issue National Security Study Memorandum (NSSM) 164, which "direct[ed] the preparation of a basic study of our relations with Europe, with particular focus on Western Europe."[22] Europeans predicted what might emerge. According to the British, President Nixon "would undertake some striking new initiative towards Europe, probably in the form of another tour of the European capitals," similar to his 1969 tour.[23] However, some Europeans were skeptical that Europe would

---

[18] RMN, Nixon Tapes, Oval Office 788-001, September 29, 1972, 9:45 a.m.–10:45 a.m.

[19] RMN, Nixon Tapes, Oval Office 788-015, September 29, 1972, 4:04 p.m.–5:15 p.m.

[20] RMN, NSC, Box 754, Memorandum from Henry Kissinger to President Nixon, "Brandt Letter to the President on EC Summit," October 27, 1972.

[21] Lundestad, 9.

[22] RMN, NSC, Box 1027, NSSM 164, "United States Relations with Europe," November 18, 1972.

[23] PRO, PREM 15–2089, "East-West relations: 'The Year of Europe': part 8," undated study by FCO Policy Planning Staff on Year of Europe.

come before ongoing initiatives with China or the Soviet Union. Others simply did not trust Nixon or Kissinger after the way they had been handled by Connally the previous year.[24] Already, the Year of Europe was met with disbelief and confusion.[25] There was even a fear that the United States might have reached a secret agreement with the Soviet Union that would undermine NATO, following the lack of consultation that led to the SALT I agreement.[26]

On December 8, Secretary of State William Rogers spoke to the NATO North Atlantic Council for the first time about the Year of Europe. Rogers downplayed the European mistreatment by John Connally, who left the administration in 1972. "Because of the complexities of the economic issues, there has been a tendency to lose sight of the broader political goals," Rogers said to the NATO allies.[27] German Foreign Minister Walter Scheel spoke in favor of the American proposal. "In the twenty-three years since it came into existence, the North Atlantic Alliance has undergone an amazing development ... from my Government's point of view, we have without doubt reached a new point where it is necessary to give again special attention to the further development and stimulation of the Atlantic partnership." Rogers affirmed that Scheel's remarks accurately summarized the American intentions. "We in the United States know that the progress already made in East-West relations could not have been achieved if the Allies had not held together. This will continue to be a guiding principle of President Nixon's policy toward Europe during the next four years."[28]

The British government was more cautious due to the lack of specifics about the Year of Europe.[29] Robert Hormats of Kissinger's NSC staff told his counterparts at the British Foreign and Commonwealth

---

[24] Helmut Schmidt. *Men and Powers: A Political Perspective* (New York: Random House, 1989), 150.

[25] Hubert Zimmerman, "Western Europe and the American Challenge: Conflict and Cooperation in Technology and Monetary Policy, 1965–1973," in M. Trachtenberg, ed., *Empire and Alliance: America and Europe during the Cold War.* (Lanham, Md.: Rowman & Littlefield Publishers, 2003), 127.

[26] PRO, PREM 15–1279, "Deterioration in Confidence between U.S. and Europe in defense field," memorandum from Minister of Defense Peter Carrington to Prime Minister Heath, November 29, 1972.

[27] RMN, NSC, Box 669, Telegram from the U.S. Mission to the European Community to the Secretary of State, "Secretary's Meeting with Commission of the European Communities," December 4, 1972, EC Brussels 4715.

[28] NATO, C-VR(72)60, Verbatim Record of the Meeting of the Council held on Thursday, 7th December, 1972 at 9:30 a.m. at NATO Headquarters, Brussels.

[29] PRO, PREM 15–2089, undated study by FCO Policy Planning Staff on Year of Europe.

Office (FCO) that "as they [the U.S.] saw it, there were three elements in a single picture – the trade negotiations, the monetary negotiations and security – and the United States was looking for the means of dialogue across the board." FCO officials were concerned that "the Americans wish to establish the maximum linkage between all these various problems so as to exploit those issues on which their position is strong in order to obtain advantage in those issues where their position is weak." The British preferred to keep the different negotiations separate. "The Nine are agreed that there can be no globalization of international negotiations on trade, money, and defense, let alone on the other issues of interest to the Americans."[30]

On December 18, President Nixon ordered the resumption of bombing in Vietnam even though "peace was at hand" had been announced just before the election in November. He hoped that the "Christmas Bombing" would force the North Vietnamese back to the negotiating table, a unilateral decision that caught Europeans by surprise and was harshly criticized by a number of European governments, in particular the Germans. West German Ambassador to Washington Rolf Pauls blasted the bombing as a "crisis of morals that has shaken the foundation of the Western alliance."[31] Although some European nations downplayed the American bombing, including France, Great Britain, Greece, Portugal, and Turkey, others were openly critical, including Canada, Denmark, Iceland, Italy, the Netherlands, Norway, and the Vatican.[32] Nixon appeared to lose his composure in an area where it had been assumed final withdrawal had already been settled. Taking advantage of the situation to open a wider rift between the United States and Europe, on December 21, 1972, Soviet Communist Party General Secretary Leonid Brezhnev said it was possible "to discover the elements of certain forms of relationship between the Common Market and [the Council for Mutual Economic Assistance]," the communist counterpart to the EC.[33] The Soviets had long desired to host a European Security Conference, which

---

[30] PRO, FCO 30–1744, "Meeting of Edward Heath, UK Prime Minister, with Richard Nixon, US President, at Washington, 1–2 February 1973," memorandum from Robert Armstrong, Downing Street to Antony Acland, FCO, December 12, 1972.

[31] PAAA, ZA 101393, Telegram from German Embassy Washington to the Foreign Office, "bemerkungen zur amerikanischen aussenpolitik 1973," January 2, 1973.

[32] PAAA, ZA 101374, "Haltung der Bundesregierung zu den amerikanischen Bombenangriffen auf Nordvietnam," January 15, 1973.

[33] *Myth and Reality: A Reference Manual on US-European Community Relations*, 4th ed. (Washington, D.C.: European Community Information Service, 1974), 58.

would reduce or eliminate the need for NATO if Europeans could come to an agreement on security needs on their own.

* * *

The Christmas Bombing did achieve the intended result but at a substantial cost to the United States generally and to Nixon personally. He then returned his attention to Europe, which still appeared to hold promise in 1973. The German government under Willy Brandt was retained with a strong majority, the French and British governments appeared to be stable, and the EC was both enlarged and committed to take firm steps toward initiatives such as monetary union.[34] On January 11, 1973, White House spokesman Ron Ziegler, when asked during a press briefing whether the failure to reach a Vietnam settlement as planned had led to the suspension of the Nixon's plans for visiting Europe, said that the president had no such plans.[35] In the three months since President Nixon pledged to make Europe a centerpiece of 1973, he demonstrated few results in advancing the idea.

The British were especially taken aback by Ziegler's announcement. Having joined the EC on January 1, British foreign policy received a setback at a time when it should otherwise have had every occasion to be triumphant.[36] The American mishandling of European matters was brought to the attention of Secretary of State William Rogers by Jean Monnet. Known as the "founding father" of the European integration movement, he expressed concern over the recent deterioration in U.S.–European relations, especially with regard to economic matters. Rogers wrote President Nixon directly on the matter, on January 22, 1973, but the letter was intercepted by Henry Kissinger's staff before it got to the president. In the midst of Vietnam-related work, Kissinger did not authorize transmission of Rogers's concerns to Nixon until a month later, on February 22.[37]

Henry Kissinger was busy tending to other matters. Much of January was devoted to finalizing the details of the Vietnam ceasefire. On January

---

[34] Buchan, 3.

[35] Robert Dallek. *Nixon and Kissinger: Partners in Power* (New York: HarperCollins, 2007), 473.

[36] Grosser, 267.

[37] RMN, NSC, Box 322, "European Common Market Vol I 1969–1970 to EC Vol IV Aug 73," memorandum from William Rogers to President Nixon, Subject: "Monnet Proposal on U.S.-Western European Dialogue," January 22, 1973.

23, President Nixon announced on nationwide television that "peace with honor" had finally been attained. American troops were to be withdrawn and prisoners of war returned within sixty days, an act for which Kissinger would earn the Nobel Peace Prize later in the year.[38] Former President Lyndon Johnson, who had spent so much energy during his presidency on Vietnam, did not live to see the signing of the agreement. He was briefed on the imminent ceasefire in his final hours of life, but died on January 22, 1973. Nixon, whose decades-long relationship with Johnson was complicated, insisted that Air Force One return Johnson's body to Texas after lying in state in Washington, D.C. Less than a decade earlier, the same aircraft was used to transport Kennedy's slain body from Texas.[39]

Following the Vietnam ceasefire and Johnson's funeral, European leaders hoped that progress would be made toward the Year of Europe. German Chancellor Willy Brandt and French President Georges Pompidou met in Paris on January 22–23, 1973. The two leaders expressed concern over unresolved disagreements between the United States and Europe, including the need for a new offset agreement with Germany, East-West relations, and trade.[40] German Foreign Minister Walter Scheel put these concerns in writing to Secretary of State William Rogers. "I hope the signing of the [Vietnam] truces will lead to a new era of international understanding. I am hopeful that on both sides of the Atlantic there will be a further strengthening of our cooperation."[41]

Rather than focus on cooperation, some Americans planned to extract the greatest concessions possible from the Europeans. Kissinger's National Security Council Senior Review Group (SRG) met on January 31 to discuss NSSM 164, "U.S. Relations with Western Europe." Helmut Sonnenfeldt laid out the basic alternatives with regard to proceeding with the Year of Europe:

(a) Scale down our maximum program of economic objectives as required to preserve a long-term political-strategic relationship, but define an irreducible minimum of economic concessions that we must

---

[38] John J. Maresca, *To Helsinki: The Conference on Security and Cooperation in Europe, 1973–1975* (Durham: Duke University Press, 1987), 31–32.
[39] USAF Archives, Papers of Stanley Goodwin, Box SAM [Special Airlift Mission] 26000.
[40] *AAPD* 1973, Gespräch des Bundeskanzlers Brandt mit Staatspräsident Pompidou in Paris, January 22, 1973, 15.
[41] PAAA, ZA 101374, "Schreiben des Herrn Ministers an Außenminister Rogers," January 26, 1973.

achieve in order to generate sufficient domestic support to preserve that relationship.

(b) Pursue our maximum economic program, envisaging only minimal U.S. concessions, and keeping the Europeans on notice that if we fail to attain near to our maximum, we will find it difficult to maintain an undiminished political-strategic relationship along current lines.

(c) Make no explicit or implicit strategic linkage between what the Europeans do on economic issues or what we will do on long-term political/security relations (except to define an irreducible minimum necessary to preserve the present political-security relationship). Pursue our economic objectives for maximum results, but settle for less as each issue may dictate.[42]

The U.S. planned to use its strategy of linkage in negotiations with the Europeans, just as had been done with China and the Soviet Union. However, unlike China and the Soviet Union, Europe was not a single entity. The EC had nine members, whereas NATO had fifteen. Membership did not overlap, and the latter included non-Europeans like the United States and Canada. A European country could be a member of one alliance, both, or neither, and each organization had a different history of bilateral relations with the United States. How could American policy treat Europe as a single entity? If the strategy failed, American policy makers were prepared to have "a more distant relationship" with Europe.[43]

Not all Americans agreed with Sonnenfeldt's proposals. Fellow NSC staff member Robert Hormats argued that the EC conducted negotiations differently than the American Cold War adversaries. The major problem with applying linkage to transatlantic relations, he said, was that "Europe is organized differently to deal with different problems ... Europe is in a period of change and uncertainty. It fears that we will attempt (à la Connally) to extract non-reciprocal economic concessions and play one country off against another."[44] American policy makers seemed to have little understanding of European integration or of the difficulty overcome in just a quarter century since World War II. One cynical view was that the

---

[42] RMN, NSC, Box 1027, Memorandum from Helmut Sonnenfeldt to Henry Kissinger, "SRG Meeting, January 31, 1973, NSSM 164: U.S. Relations with Western Europe," January 30, 1973.

[43] *FRUS, 1969–1976,* Volume E-15, Part 2, 4.

[44] RMN, NSC, Box 322, Memorandum from Robert Hormats to Henry Kissinger, "Report on My Discussions in Europe and Recommended Strategy for Dealing with Economic Issues," December 18, 1972.

only reason why the United States supported European integration was because the greater the number of nations in the EC, the harder it would be to speak with one voice.[45] Some Americans believed Europe had "grown fat, greedy, and flabby on an excess of good living, health care, and so forth, and [were] eventually no longer fearful of the Polar Bear to the east."[46] According to some in the Nixon White House, it was time to shake Europe up.

President Nixon revived the Year of Europe during a press conference on February 1. "We must now turn to the problem of Europe. We have been to the People's Republic of China. We have been to the Soviet Union. We have been paying attention to the problems of Europe, but those problems will be put on the front burner."[47] However, he downplayed the phrase "the Year of Europe," which he said was a creation of the press that distracted people from the important issues involved. Europeans hoped that Nixon would use the press conference to announce his intentions for a high-level visit to Europe at some point during the coming year. An announcement would have communicated that the United States was serious about making Europe a priority in American foreign policy during 1973. That did not happen. "I will not be making any trips to Europe certainly in the first half of this year. Whether I can make any trips later on remains to be seen."[48]

The British were given advance warning that Nixon would not announce plans for a visit during a meeting between Henry Kissinger and British Ambassador to Washington Sir Burke Trend. "The President's tour of Europe was in jeopardy because the President was 'coldly furious' with all of the European Governments (apart from Her Majesty's Government) for their statements about Vietnam," Kissinger said, referring to the Christmas Bombing. "The president might abandon his tour entirely or make it later in the year."[49] The British government believed Nixon's press conference was another lost opportunity to improve transatlantic relations, even symbolically. "The White House tends to see the Europeans nations as weak, selfish, indecisive, and suspicious of U.S. motives, and hence a pretty unrewarding lot to try to

---

[45] Egon Bahr, "Willy Brandt et l'Europe," in Andreas Wilkens, ed., 32–33.
[46] Alistair Horne. *Kissinger: 1973, The Crucial Year* (New York: Simon and Schuster, 2009), 107.
[47] William R. Kintner and Richard B. Foster, *National Strategy in a Decade of Change: An Emerging U.S. Policy* (Lexington, Mass.: D. C. Heath and Company, 1973), 198.
[48] *Nixon: The Fifth Year of His Presidency* (Washington, D.C.: Congressional Quarterly, Inc., 1974), 151.
[49] PRO, PREM 15–2089, undated study by FCO Policy Planning Staff on Year of Europe.

manage," noted Hugh Overton, the head of the FCO North American division.[50] Although appropriately critical of the United States, the statement betrays how helpless Europeans saw themselves. It was as though transatlantic relations could not be addressed without American leadership, a U.S. proposal, or a personal visit by President Nixon.

Prime Minister Edward Heath visited Nixon on February 1–2, hoping to get the Year of Europe back on track and to address a significant backlog of other issues, including nuclear weapons, Vietnam, trade, China, the Soviet Union, the Middle East, and many others, according to records of their meetings.[51] "Everyone is saying we should tell Prime Minister Heath that he has to be a leader," Kissinger said privately to his staff the day before Heath's arrival, "if he says 'what do you want me to do?' " thus revealing how uncoordinated American policy was at the time.[52] The visit had already been rescheduled twice following conflicts with Nixon's second-term planning at Camp David and the Christmas Bombing, the latter a major focus of European criticism toward Nixon. But that was in the past. The FCO advised Heath that "one of the best ways of making an impression upon the president might be to appeal to his desire to be remembered in history as a great president."[53]

Nixon, an avid admirer of Winston Churchill and someone naturally responsive to such a suggestion, suggested to Heath that "we must try to recreate the wartime habit of getting together for really intimate and deep discussions in a relaxed atmosphere – discussions which should range over the whole field of problems, political, military and economic."[54] On another occasion, Nixon said, "They're no longer a world power, but the British are bright and they think strategically ... Goddamn it, without the British, Hitler would have Europe today."[55] However, Nixon's statements did not reflect an appreciation for the position of the United Kingdom in Europe. As a new member of the EC, the British government had new responsibilities, and other European countries made it clear that they resented the idea of a "special relationship" between the United Kingdom and the United States. Nixon took no notice, even though

[50] PRO, FCO 30–1744, "Prime Minister Meeting with President Nixon: 1–2 February 1973," February 1, 1973.

[51] RMN, Nixon Tapes, Oval Office 846-004, February 1, 1973, 10:35 a.m.–12:35 p.m.

[52] *FRUS*, 1969–1976, Volume E-15, Part 2, 5.

[53] PRO, FCO 30–1744, Telegram from United Kingdom Representative to Brussels Michael Palliser to FCO, February 5, 1973, 051830Z.

[54] PRO, PREM 15–2089, undated study by FCO Policy Planning Staff on Year of Europe.

[55] RMN, Nixon Tapes, Oval Office 840-012, February 3, 1973, 12:12 p.m.–1:20 p.m.

advisors such as Secretary of State William Rogers, NSC staffer Robert Hormats, and Kissinger realized that dealing with an enlarged EC that included the United Kingdom required new strategies.

Nixon also used his meeting with Heath to explain why the Year of Europe was delayed, namely, due to the Christmas Bombing and the prolonged Vietnam settlement. Although Heath did not publicly criticize the United States because of the bombing in the way that other Europeans did, Nixon recognized the difficult position Heath was in. "I am aware of the fact that you are under considerable bombardment. It certainly meant a great deal to me personally," Nixon said. "It did not go unnoticed, and also what the others said did not go unnoticed." Nixon suggested to Heath that both nations should "do some really hard thinking together – without necessarily telling the rest of the alliance at any particular stage but keeping privately in step and moving publicly, if not together, at least in parallel."

In fact, virtually the entire four hours of meetings between Nixon and Heath focused on bilateral relations. Nixon carefully avoided issues that could cause embarrassment to Heath, including Northern Ireland and Rhodesia. Neither leader mentioned the importance of the Year of Europe or the importance of the United States talking to Europe as a bloc. Privately, Nixon indicated to his advisors that he had no desire to visit Europe and deal with the Europeans as a unit, a situation in which the United States would be outnumbered. In addition, he doubted whether continuing negotiations with Europe were even in U.S. interests at all.[56] "I am so glad that we got Heath over here," Nixon said to Kissinger following Heath's departure. "We've got to have a friend in Europe, and he's the only solid one we've got. And, by golly, let's play them." Nixon's private notes referred to Heath as "one of the prime architects of the New Europe ... a man of courage."[57] After a hiatus during Britain's accession to the EC, the "special relationship" seemed to have returned following Heath's 1973 visit. "By letting the British in on these things ... you're really doing them a favor by enabling them to continue to think in big terms," Kissinger responded. Nixon agreed. "Heath has changed enormously since 1970."[58]

***

[56] RMN, NSC, Box 322, Memorandum from Henry Kissinger to President Nixon, Subject: "Jean Monnet's Ideas on U.S.-West European Relations," February 21, 1973.
[57] RMN, White House Special Files, President's Personal File, Box 84, handwritten notes.
[58] RMN, Nixon Tapes, Oval Office 840-012, February 3, 1973, 12:12 p.m.–1:20 p.m.

As Watergate began to occupy more of Nixon's time, beginning in the early spring, the Year of Europe was delayed again until late April.[59] On April 23, Henry Kissinger gave a major foreign policy speech to the Associated Press Annual Luncheon in New York City that called for the creation of a new Atlantic Charter rooted in greater Atlantic cohesion. He said that President Nixon planned to visit Europe in the fall of 1973.[60] Kissinger referred to the "world responsibilities" of the United States and the "regional responsibilities" of Europe.[61] That statement further provoked Europeans at the very time that the United States hoped to improve relations. Assistant Secretary of State for European Affairs Martin Hillenbrand noted, "most of the gaffes and miscalculations of our diplomacy, in my view, derived from this combination of factors and the inability of many of our leaders psychologically to rise above them. A classic case in point was the speech of national security adviser Henry Kissinger on April 23, 1973." The timing was not accidental. The need to resume discussions with Europe on economic matters became acute, as articulated in Nixon's speech on the growing energy crisis on April 18.[62]

Many in the American press covered only Kissinger's brief comments about Watergate, the real news story of the day, during the question-and-answer session. *The Washington Post*'s coverage of the speech would have led readers to believe it was a speech about Watergate, or perhaps Vietnam, but not Europe. "That's a strange way of reporting," Joe Alsop said to Henry Kissinger. "I say we are now like a house with the roof on fire and the cellar flooding, and the housewife constantly talks about the immorality of the chambermaid."[63] However, influential journalist James Reston had a very different take. In a four-column headline, he compared Kissinger's speech to Secretary of State George C. Marshall's Marshall Plan address of 1947.[64] It was so favorable to Kissinger than Rowland Evans joked that he thought Kissinger must have ghostwritten Reston's article.[65]

[59] Hillenbrand, 330.
[60] Gérard Bossuat, "Jean Monnet et le partenariat atlantique des années soixante." *Relations Internationales* 119 (2004): 296.
[61] Jussi Hanhimäki, *The Flawed Architect: Henry Kissinger and American Foreign Policy* (New York: Oxford University Press, 2004), 275–276.
[62] Franz Schurmann, *The Foreign Politics of Richard Nixon: The Grand Design* (Berkeley, Calif.: Institute of International Studies, 1987), 314.
[63] RMN, HAK Telcons, Box 19, April 25, 1973, 9:20 a.m.
[64] Dallek, 474.
[65] RMN, HAK Telcons, Box 19, April 24, 1973, 9:30 a.m.

The judgment of history has generally been that the speech did more harm than good and did not present a good answer to why such an apparently important proposal had been delayed so frequently. Kissinger told Joe Kraft later in the day that nothing he said in his speech could not have been said six months earlier. The Year of Europe was "pushed back a bit by Vietnam. We've always wanted to begin that dialogue after Vietnam was finished."[66] The speech was "not Kissinger's finest hour," Alistair Horne summarized.[67] A major policy address about a presidential initiative should have been delivered by President Nixon. The Europeans ignored Kissinger's call that trade, money, and defense should be linked in a common perspective. The EC insisted that before it could even begin to negotiate with the Americans on trade or monetary topics, Europeans themselves had to work out a common position.[68]

The speech was received very coolly by every European capital except London.[69] The Germans interpreted the speech as an ultimatum: "the options for Europe are clearly stated – either an agreement with the USA over a common objective or a slow decline of the alliance by neglect, distrust, and indifference."[70] Chancellor Brandt himself commented that while the concept of a Year of Europe was welcome, his preference was for bilateral negotiations. For the United States to deal with the Europeans as if they were already major American partners was incorrect.[71] The French government condemned the speech as an "imperial text," designed to emphasize the power of the United States while not even mentioning past American failures such as Vietnam and international monetary relations.[72] The cool reception to the Year of Europe became icy as Europeans fumed into the summer of 1973.[73] The phrase itself became taboo. During a meeting of the EC Foreign Ministers in Copenhagen in July, Europeans claimed that the content of Kissinger's speech was a

[66] RMN, HAK Telcons, Box 19, April 24, 1973, 4:37 p.m.

[67] Horne, 107.

[68] Henri Simonet, "Energy and the Future of Europe." *Foreign Affairs* 53 (1975): 450.

[69] PRO, PREM 15-2089, undated study by FCO Policy Planning Staff on Year of Europe.

[70] PAAA, ZA 101383, Memorandum from the Foreign Office to the Chancellor's Office, "Zusammenfassung und Bewertung der Rede Kissingers vom 23. April 1973," April 27, 1973.

[71] PAAA, ZA 101393, Telegram from the Foreign Office to German Embassy NATO, "Rede Kissingers vom 23.4.1973," May 8, 1973, 2685,

[72] AN, 5AG2/1021, Note de J. B. Raimond, Secrétariat General de la Présidence de la République, pour monsieur le Président de la République, "Discours de M. Kissinger," May 3, 1973.

[73] Buchan, 3–4.

complete surprise to them, they were not consulted on the specifics in advance, and to be treated in such a way was to be "treated like a non-person" and "humiliated."[74] The French called the speech "another Yalta" and "unnecessarily crude."[75]

Kissinger's memoirs record his reaction to the European criticism of his speech. "Naming it the 'Year of Europe' was perhaps too grandiloquent but, in retrospect, I would not alter the analysis with which, in a speech in New York on April 23, 1973, I defined its objectives, many of which remain to be fulfilled," he recalled.[76] Defending his speech to *Washington Post* reporter Marilyn Berger, Kissinger stated that the impetus behind his major policy address on Europe was "because the president is meeting Brandt next week, he's meeting Pompidou later, because he's been talking about the Year of Europe." When Berger suggested that calling for a new Atlantic Charter was a significant change of American policy, Kissinger responded "no, I wrote a book about it once."[77] Kissinger also defended his speech to journalist George Sherman, noting that it was meant to be nothing more than a catalyst for transatlantic dialogue that was to be capped with a summit. "I think initially it will start as a series of bilateral talks but eventually they'll have to merge," he said.[78]

Absorbed in Watergate at the time, in the days leading up to the firing of Chief of Staff Bob Haldeman, top domestic advisor John Ehrlichman, and Counsel to the President John Dean, Nixon's memoirs made no attempt to defend the April 23 speech. However, Kissinger reflected on the failure of the Year of Europe to date:

The Year of Europe initiative immediately ran up against the reality that, in the early 1970s, our European allies were far more preoccupied with European integration than with Atlantic cohesion. And Europe – especially the old established nations such as Britain and France – found the transition to supranationalism traumatic. The more complicated the process of European integration became, the less its supporters were willing to brook any interruption or dilution of it by American schemes promoting broader Atlantic cooperation, however well intentioned. In this context, our initiative for enhanced consultations between the European Community and the United States came to be viewed – mostly in

---

[74] RMN, NSC, Box 679, Telegram from American Embassy Paris to Secretary of State, "The French View of U.S.-Soviet Détente," November 29, 1973, Paris 30644.

[75] Michel Jobert, *L'Autre Regard* (Paris: Bernard Grasset, 1976), 289.

[76] Kissinger, *Years of Renewal*, 600.

[77] RMN, HAK Telcons, Box 19, April 24, 1973, 4:15 p.m.

[78] RMN, HAK Telcons, Box 19, April 25, 1973, 5:29 p.m.

France, but not only there – as an American stratagem to thwart the reemergence of a specifically European identity and institutions.[79]

Another complicating factor was the complete lack of any "special" relationship between Nixon and Heath. American policy makers seriously underestimated the extent to which Prime Minister Heath was committed to the EC, more so than any of his predecessors at 10 Downing Street.[80] Nixon had rejoiced when Wilson's Labor Party was defeated in the general election of 1970 that brought Heath to power. Yet, once in office, Heath proved very difficult to work with. In his memoirs, Kissinger noted that with Heath, "charm would alternate with icy aloofness, and the change in his moods could be perilously unpredictable. After talking with Heath, Nixon always felt somehow rejected and came to consider the Prime Minister's attitude toward him as verging on condescension."[81] Heath staked his legacy on being the one to take the United Kingdom into the EC once and for all, and that meant being closer to Europe than to the United States. "He was the only British leader I encountered who not only failed to cultivate the 'special relationship' with the United States but actively sought to downgrade it and to give Europe pride of place of British policy. All of this made for an unprecedented period of strain in Anglo-American relations," Kissinger commented.[82]

Nixon and Kissinger also had little luck in appealing to French President Georges Pompidou. "In the short time that I have been here ... we, the British, and others have heard more extravagant rumors that the president is suffering from cancer or from another unnamed but terminal disease," American Ambassador to Paris John Irwin reported.[83] A new French cabinet was appointed that worked well with the United Kingdom but not with the United States.[84] These new cabinet members, including Robert Galley at Defense, Michel Jobert at Foreign Affairs (to whom Pompidou referred as *mon Kissinger à moi*), and Pierre Messmer as premier, marked a recognition that Georges Pompidou's imprimatur on foreign policy was on the decline.[85] Jobert's appointment came as a complete surprise beyond *La Hexagone*. Perhaps Pompidou

[79] RMN, HAK Telcons, Box 19, April 25, 1973, 5:29 p.m.
[80] Lundestad, 103.
[81] Kissinger, *Years of Renewal*, 602–603.
[82] Kissinger, *Years of Renewal*, 602–603.
[83] RMN, NSC, Box 679, Telegram from American Embassy Paris to Secretary of State, "President Pompidou's Health," March 18, 1973, Paris 8698.
[84] Buchan, 6.
[85] Goldsborough, 545.

concluded that he could retain some control over foreign policy by appointing his former Élysée Secretary General.[86] Kissinger later summarized Jobert's ambitions as "the old Gaullist dream of building Europe on an anti-American basis."[87] Alistair Horne referred to Jobert as a "Gaullist of the Left."[88] By the spring of 1973, the chance for improving relations with France became dim, for reasons just as significant in France as in the United States: Pompidou was dying, and Nixon's presidency was on the road to unraveling.

The greatest European criticism of the United States following Henry Kissinger's April speech was that the European governments were not consulted on it in advance, nor were they informed of the high-level importance that the United States planned to attribute to the proposal. Kissinger delivered his speech on a European holiday (Easter Monday), which meant European governments had to catch up after the fact.[89] Europeans have continued to refer to the American "spontaneous call for a Year of Europe," even decades later.[90] Although it is true that the United States did not consult with Europeans as often as the latter preferred, a significant archival record documents the planning and communication that went into the launch of the initiative.

The suggestion perpetuated by many scholars that the United States did not consult with Europeans in advance of Kissinger's April speech is false. There was a flurry of diplomatic activity that led up to the speech, as well as in its aftermath. Nixon and Kissinger participated in meetings with nearly all American diplomatic and military representatives in Europe, as well as with numerous European ambassadors to the United States and representatives of various European governments. Kissinger told President Pompidou and Michel Jobert about the Year of Europe himself on two different occasions, September 15 and December 8, 1972, and both were supportive of the initiative.[91] Jean Monnet was consulted in January.[92] Kissinger discussed the initiative

---

[86] NARA, RG 59, CFPF, Telegram from American Embassy Paris to Secretary of State, "Michel Jobert, New French Foreign Minister," April 6, 1973, Paris 9775.

[87] Henry Kissinger, *Years of Upheaval* (Boston: Little, Brown, and Company), 1982, 165.

[88] Horne, 115.

[89] Donald Rumsfeld, *The Rumsfeld Papers* [online]. "The Declaration of Atlantic Relations: An Interpretive History," June 26, 1974. Available from http://www.rumsfeld.com/.

[90] Egon Bahr, "Willy Brandt et l'Europe," in Andreas Wilkens, ed., 32.

[91] RMN, NSC, Box 679, Telegram from Secretary of State to American Embassy Paris, "U.S.-French Consultations," November 30, 1973, State 235704.

[92] Horne, 110.

at length with Edward Heath and Willy Brandt, and he also provided a summary of the April 23 speech in advance to Michel Jobert. Nixon met with Heath and Burke Trend for four hours on February 1–2. In the Oval Office on February 15, Nixon briefed Supreme Allied Commander, Europe (SACEUR) Andrew Goodpaster.[93] On February 16, Nixon explained the rationale for the Year of Europe to his cabinet. "If the U.S. turns inward, the world will be a mess, because the Soviets and Chinese will turn outward."[94]

In March, Henry Kissinger had a thorough discussion with British senior FCO official Sir Thomas Brimelow. Kissinger explained that, with the 1972 election in the past, President Nixon could afford to be unconventional and that he was eager "to do the right thing." Brimelow explained the difficulty of finding a solution that was fully acceptable to all the European members of both NATO and the EC, but agreed to give the problem further study over the next month. Brimelow commissioned an extensive internal FCO study entitled "The Next Ten Years in East/West and Transatlantic Relations," which was handed to Kissinger on April 16. The study considered many factors, including economic, monetary, and military relations, and involved over 2,000 pages of research and collaboration of various reports from every major department of the British government.[95]

Brimelow met again with Kissinger on April 19, along with British Ambassador Burke Trend. Kissinger said that Nixon still planned to visit Europe in the fall in order to demonstrate transatlantic progress, but the visit would be planned to coincide with the time the Congress resumed consideration on the latest and presumably most potent reincarnation of the Mansfield Amendment, which proposed a withdrawal of a majority of American troops from Europe.[96] Kissinger said that he planned to give a major speech on April 23 to move the discussion of U.S.–European relations forward and that he planned to also brief the French and the Germans. In fact, Kissinger had already been talking with them. On March 9, Nixon met with U.S. Ambassador to France John Irwin and explained the Year of Europe.

[93] GRF, NSA, Memcons, Box 1, Memorandum of conversation between President Nixon and Andrew Goodpaster, Oval Office, February 15, 1973.
[94] GRF, NSA, Memcons, Box 1, Memorandum of conversation, Cabinet meeting, Cabinet Room, February 16, 1973.
[95] PRO, PREM 15-2089, undated study by FCO Policy Planning Staff on Year of Europe.
[96] PRO, PREM 15-1359, "Personal Record of a Discussion in the British Embassy, Washington D.C. on 19th April 1973."

"Having made a breakthrough with the Chinese and the Soviet Union, we want to focus on Europe," he said. Although Kissinger had been telling the Europeans that Nixon planned for a fall visit to Europe, Nixon said to Irwin "I have no plans for a visit now ... please indicate that I wish to come, but I must stick around – Congress, the Soviet summit."[97]

Nixon sought the views of John McCloy on the Year of Europe. McCloy was legendary in Europe for his past service as U.S. High Commissioner for Germany, in which he was responsible for the rebuilding of the de-Nazified state following World War II.[98] McCloy agreed with the need for a Year of Europe, but he believed the administration should have done a better job of articulating the principles it was based on and what it specifically hoped would be achieved. McCloy was also critical that Kissinger insisted on running everything himself rather than letting the Year of Europe grow out of a NATO effort. McCloy also believed that Nixon had shifted American foreign policy too abruptly with the end of Vietnam, advancing U.S. relations with China and the Soviet Union, and the ending of Bretton Woods. These had all occurred within two years. The White House had not adequately considered the impact of these policies on Europeans.[99]

Nixon and McCloy did agree on one thing: from an American point of view, additional European unity was no longer desirable.[100] Kissinger made a similar statement to Arthur Burns, Chairman of the Federal Reserve. "Kissinger ... spoke without any doubt: what we had to do adroitly is to throw a monkey wrench into the Common Market machinery, for European unity in economic areas would definitely work against U.S. interests," Burns recorded in his diary.[101] Kissinger and Nixon agreed long before that "one of the worst mistakes we made was to push Britain into the Common Market."[102] The old generation of

[97] GRF, NSA, Memcons, Box 1, Memorandum of conversation between President Nixon and John Irwin, Oval Office, March 9, 1973.
[98] Thomas A. Schwartz, *America's Germany: John McCloy and the Federal Republic of Germany* (Cambridge: Harvard University Press, 1991), 29.
[99] Donald Rumsfeld, *The Rumsfeld Papers* [online]. "Memorandum for Rumsfeld Files: Meeting with John McCloy, February 6, 1973." Available from http://www.rumsfeld.com/.
[100] RMN, NSC, Box 1025, Memorandum of conversation between President Nixon and John McCloy, Oval Office, March 13, 1973.
[101] GRF, Papers of Arthur Burns, Handwritten Journals, 1969–1974, Box 1, April 3, 1973.
[102] RMN, HAK Telcons, Box 12, December 2, 1971, no time indicated.

Americans who believed in European integration simply for integration's sake was over.[103]

Richard Nixon liked bold initiatives that kept critics off balance and surprised allies and adversaries alike. This was the motivation behind so many of his initiatives: his announcement on July 15, 1971, that he would visit China; the August 15 decision to end the gold standard; the May 8, 1972, decision to bomb and mine Hanoi and Haiphong, which put the Soviet Summit in jeopardy even while Nixon's advance team was in Moscow; and, finally, Nixon's approval of the shocking Christmas Bombing in December. He loved to read news summaries in which his critics asked: what will he do next?

This style of decision making was especially damaging to U.S.–European relations. Perhaps Americans are from Mars, and Europeans are from Venus, as Robert Kagan once suggested.[104] Europeans had a reasonable expectation of being treated better than the North Vietnamese, the Chinese, or the Soviets. As Nixon once said, sometimes the challenge in diplomacy is not that you do not know a country well enough, but that you know each other too well.[105] Over time, Nixon's preferred style of diplomacy seemed increasingly incompatible with transatlantic relations, which were based on traditional diplomacy, consultation, and a greater degree of transparency. In the summer of 1973, a tipping point was reached for many Europeans. They realized that, in the future, they had to depend less on the United States, which now placed other areas of the world ahead of Europe. The reality of the Nixon Doctrine was beginning to set in, even in a year that was supposed to make transatlantic relations a priority.

---

[103] Weisbrode, 270.
[104] See Robert Kagan, *Of Paradise and Power: America and Europe in the New World Order* (New York: Knopf, 2003).
[105] RMN, Nixon Tapes, Oval Office 662-004, February 1, 1972, 10:03 a.m.–11:37 a.m.

PHOTO I. Nixon and British Prime Minister Harold Wilson. Despite the fact that Wilson was from the Labor Party, they were able to work together better than Nixon and Heath did.

PHOTO 2. Nixon receiving a tour of Buckingham Palace by Queen Elizabeth II and Prince Charles.

PHOTO 3. NATO headquarters in Brussels was the first stop on Nixon's European tour just a month into his presidency.

PHOTO 4. Nixon made it an early priority in his presidency to repair relations with French President Charles de Gaulle. Those accompanying them including White House Chief of Staff H.R. "Bob" Haldeman, Counsel to the President John Ehrlichman, Henry Kissinger, and Vernon Walters.

PHOTO 5. The "special relationship" between the U.S. and U.K. had its ups and downs in the early 1970s, as did the relationship between Nixon and Prime Minister Edward Heath. Here, Nixon and Heath and flanked by Secretary of State William Rogers.

PHOTO 6. Ford and Kissinger greet Wilson and Callaghan in the Oval Office. The Americans encouraged the British to remain in the European Community, which they felt was the only way to preserve the Anglo-American "special relationship."

PHOTO 7. In a presidency that involved so many international summits, time on Air Force One for Chief of Staff H.R. "Bob" Haldeman and National Security Advisor Henry Kissinger was an extension of their White House offices.

PHOTO 8. Nixon and French President Georges Pompidou meeting at the Azores to settle the international monetary dispute that ensued after Nixon's August 15, 1971 announcement of his New Economic Policy.

PHOTO 9. Nixon and Heath leaving dinner on the HMS Glamorgan during their summit at Bermuda.

PHOTO 10. Nixon meets with West German Chancellor Willy Brandt in Key Biscayne, Florida.

PHOTO 11. This image of Nixon and Heath at Camp David captures the fact that by 1973, relations between the U.S. and U.K., and transatlantic relations more generally, occasionally lost their way.

PHOTO 12. Nixon, West German Chancellor Helmut Schmidt, Foreign Minister Hans-Dietrich Genscher, and Henry Kissinger in Brussels.

PHOTO 13. President Nixon on the streets of Brussels.

PHOTO 14. President Nixon signing the Declaration on Atlantic Relations with NATO General Secretary Joseph Luns, while others – including Kissinger, U.S. Permanent Representative to NATO Donald Rumsfeld, and White House Chief of Staff Alexander Haig enjoy a lighter moment.

5

Europe coalesces

Despite its flawed launch, the summer of 1973 saw the Year of Europe move from proposal to action. The first NATO ministerial meeting following Kissinger's April 23 speech was productive. Secretary of State William Rogers spelled out the need for the Year of Europe:

President Nixon chose his first trip abroad as President to affirm the importance of the Atlantic Alliance. Addressing the NATO Council in 1969, President Nixon stated "I believe we must build an Alliance strong enough to deter those who might threaten war, realistic enough to deal with the world as it is, and flexible enough to explore new channels of constructive cooperation." This is still his strong view . . . this is why the President, Mr. Chairman, has referred in his statements to a "Year of Europe." He wants to make clear once again his fundamental policy about the Alliance.

There was no objection to Rogers's presentation, even from the French. Michel Jobert's comment was simply, "we have a good Alliance. Let's keep it."[1] The Americans expected that of the two bodies – NATO and the European Community (EC) – the reception to the Year of Europe would be warmer at NATO. NATO had a long history of transatlantic cooperation, and the United States had always played an active role. The reception in the EC – where there was no direct American involvement – was expected to be cooler.

The difficulty for Europeans in coming up with a common position in response to the Year of Europe was that the EC presented itself as the only

---

[1] NATO, C-VR(73)36, "Verbatim Record of the Meeting of the Council held on Thursday, 14th June, 1973, at 11:00 a.m. at The Bella Centre, Copenhagen," June 14, 1973.

legitimate European forum for transatlantic dialogue.[2] This feeling was driven by hesitancy lingering from the de Gaulle era over negotiating within "blocs." France preferred bilateral discussions with the United States, to the irritation of other EC members more loyal to the multinational framework of the EC. On May 17, Kissinger struck back at the Moroccan-born French foreign minister Michel Jobert for his attacks on Kissinger's speech of April 23.[3] Jobert "seemed to make a point of getting under Henry's skin; he studied his technique and set out to irritate him," Kissinger aide Helmut Sonnenfeldt reflected.[4] Jobert was not the only prominent Frenchman to attack Kissinger. Former de Gaulle deputy Alain Peyrefitte joined in. "Who other than a Gaullist could denounce the New Yalta contained within the Kissinger proposal, a proposal which overtly recognizes the subordination of Europe to American hegemony at the exact moment when the collective will of the Common Market countries can finally establish European independence."[5] The French challenged even the right of the United States to declare the Year of Europe, let alone to prompt a European response.

Kissinger defended himself to Jobert. "In our view the Atlantic relationship has for the last ten years been living off the capital of the '40s and '50s, and as a result there has been no new moral or political impetus. There will be a new generation of leaders that won't have the same commitment to the Atlantic relationship." Kissinger made his case more eloquently one-on-one with Jobert than he did in his April speech. "If we miss the opportunity ... Congress will undo it ... foreign policy will shift to measuring success only by adversaries. And it can't be a mistake to try to give content to relations among friends," he added. Jobert detected Kissinger's sense of urgency. "If you permit me a personal reproach, this did not come through in your New York speech. You are more convincing here than in your speech." Kissinger conceded, "I agree. There were certain technical mistakes. I could probably have prepared it better. We had our own preoccupations in America. This somewhat inhibited the amount of time that was available."[6]

---

[2] NARA, RG 59, CFPF, Telegram from U.S. Mission to the European Community to the Secretary of State, "Text of Soames Speech on US/European Relations," May 8, 1973, EC BRU 2545.

[3] RMN, NSC, Box 56, Memorandum of conversation between Henry Kissinger and Michel Jobert, Quai d'Orsay, May 17, 1973.

[4] Horne, 115.

[5] NARA, RG 59, CFPF, Telegram from American Embassy Paris to Secretary of State, "Gaullist Party Leader's Remarks on Kissinger Proposal," May 15, 1973, Paris 13404.

[6] RMN, NSC, Box 56, Memorandum of conversation between Henry Kissinger and Michel Jobert, Quai d'Orsay, May 17, 1973.

Kissinger continued this discussion the following day with French President Georges Pompidou. "When you speak, in your speech, of the regional position of Europe, I am not particularly shocked by what you say. In this sense I am not entirely in agreement with everyone else," Pompidou said. "Our position is that of strict United States-French bilateralism. We will not budge from this and we do not wish to include the United Kingdom in this business," he added. Kissinger appealed directly to French leadership. The EC lacked direction, and Kissinger believed the strongest, most responsible nation should lead. "We do not believe that Germany is sufficiently strong psychologically, and we believe it is too open to Soviet pressures to be able to contribute to develop a Europe in this sense," he said.[7]

Nixon and Kissinger hoped to get a secret Franco-American agreement on the Year of Europe, just as they had previously done at the Azores meeting on monetary policy.[8] Just as then, Nixon and Pompidou could personally break the transatlantic deadlock at a bilateral summit. "Pompidou is the key to getting Europe on board," Kissinger argued at a cabinet meeting on May 25.[9] A Franco-American summit was planned for May 31–June 2 at Reykjavik, Iceland. Jean Monnet condemned the planned bilateral meeting between Nixon and Pompidou as undermining European integration. He believed no single nation should pretend to speak for the rest of Europe.[10] Monnet's primary interest was in resolving outstanding economic and monetary issues that threatened European institutions such as the Common Market before deepening ties with the United States.[11] However, for Americans, the bilateral summit was essential. Pompidou also preferred bilateral summits, where France could have more influence with the United States one-on-one than in multilateral settings. "We have, to a certain extent, a privileged position ... European integration cannot happen without us, nor can changes occur without our consent," Pompidou said.[12]

[7] RMN, NSC, Box 56, Memorandum of conversation between Henry Kissinger and Georges Pompidou, Elysée Palace, May 18, 1973.

[8] Horne, 116.

[9] RMN, NSC, Box 1027, Memorandum of conversation between Henry Kissinger, President Nixon, and the Cabinet, Cabinet Room, May 25, 1973.

[10] Bossuat, 296.

[11] RMN, NSC, Box 679, Memorandum from Robert Hormats to Henry Kissinger, "Telephone Call from Jean Monnet," May 14, 1973.

[12] AN, 5 AG 2/1023, Memorandum prepared by the Ministère des Affaires Etrangères: "Entretiens de Reykjavik 31 mai-1er juin 1973: NOTE DE SYNTHESE," 18 mai 1973, June 16, 1973.

The United States was even more eager for the summit than Pompidou. "U.S. policies vis-à-vis France before 1969 were wrong and disastrous," Nixon said to Pompidou.[13] Nixon started a new relationship with de Gaulle, but solidifying that new relationship with Pompidou was just as important. "This first meeting now shapes up as *crucial* because the French clearly harbor the most deep-seated suspicions of our motives in launching our Atlantic initiative," Kissinger advised Nixon.[14] In Pompidou's briefing papers for the summit, Jobert argued that the reason transatlantic relations had deteriorated was because of the "interior malaise" of the United States. This malaise, Jobert argued, stemmed from the Vietnam War, financial difficulties, the emerging energy crisis, and, in a reference to Watergate, "the regrettable episodes which animate political life in Washington."[15]

At Reykjavik, Nixon asked Pompidou to identify ways in which to expedite European consideration of the Year of Europe. The goal was to get French buy-in on the principles behind the Declaration on Atlantic Relations before other nations became involved.[16] Pompidou, referring to the internal gridlock following expansion of the EC on January 1, cautioned him: "Conception is more fun than giving birth."[17] But Nixon did not back down. Reimagining transatlantic relations was essential for the Nixon Doctrine to have application in U.S.–European relations. He explained his policy of pragmatic internationalism to Pompidou:

Let me say, at the outset, of the Nixon Doctrine, that the Doctrine is certainly not based on the idea that the U.S. will play a maternalistic or dominating role in Europe, Asia, or South America. The Nixon Doctrine is based on the principle that each country seeks its own interests and develops its own defense. This precept applies to the French and to the world.[18]

In relation to international monetary policy, that meant a recognition that the United States must no longer be the dominant economy in the world, even if that had implications for the dollar as the world's reserve currency.[19]

---

[13] *FRUS, 1969–1976*, Volume E-15, Part 2, 311.

[14] RMN, NSC, Box 949, Memorandum from Henry Kissinger to President Nixon, "Points for Your First Meeting with Pompidou," May 30, 1973.

[15] AN, 5 AG 2/1023, Memorandum prepared by the Ministère des Affaires Etrangères: "Entretiens de Reykjavik 31 mai-1er juin 1973: NOTE DE SYNTHESE," 18 mai 1973, June 16, 1973.

[16] *FRUS, 1969–1976*, Volume E-15, Part 2, 19.

[17] Kissinger, *Years of Renewal*, 605.

[18] *FRUS, 1969–1976*, Volume E-15, Part 2, 20.

[19] RMN, White House Special Files, President's Personal File, Box 86, "Talking Points on Monetary Issue."

Pompidou agreed to help, even though domestic political realignments in France meant that Pompidou had less direct influence over foreign policy than he did at the Azores summit in December 1971. The rest of the EC was even more complicated. "If I were the U.S. President, I would be exasperated by Europe," Pompidou said.[20] In exchange for his help with European matters, Nixon offered expanded bilateral nuclear cooperation with France. He even suggested that it could be possible for France to obtain a level of military cooperation similar to that between Britain and the United States, a long-standing desire of President Pompidou.[21] Arthur Burns, who continued to be influential on economic foreign policy, was more skeptical about Nixon's intentions. "The President has many shortcomings. He has few convictions, but now and then he gets into a euphoric mood where he wants to persuade himself that he's a statesman," he confided to his diary.[22]

"By early June the European response [to the Year of Europe] was still disparate," the British Foreign and Commonwealth Office (FCO) noted in an internal report. "We and the Germans had given general encouragement to the Americans, but ... [t]he French had blocked all attempts to achieve a collective European view" at the meeting of the European Community Foreign Ministers on June 5. American Ambassador to NATO Donald Rumsfeld traveled to France the first week of June. In a speech at the Atlantic Institute, Rumsfeld stated "the speech of Henry Kissinger entitled 'The Year of Europe' has been received with cool skepticism by some, with hopeful approval by others." Rumsfeld argued that the reason a Year of Europe was needed was because it marked the beginning of a new era. "The post-World War II era is over. A new era which has, as yet, no name and special defining characteristics, is beginning ... we are not free of problems, but the problems we have are not post-World War II problems."[23] The Year of Europe was designed to stimulate both American and European leaders to consider how the transatlantic relationship could shift its focus from postwar problems to the new challenges of the future. The impetus behind Rumsfeld's speech was John McCloy, who had advised the NATO Ambassador to clarify

[20] *FRUS*, 1969–1976, Volume E-15, Part 2, 20.
[21] Maurice Vaïsse, "Les 'relations spéciales' franco-américains au temps de Richard Nixon et Georges Pompidou." *Relations Internationales* 119 (2004): 359.
[22] GRF, Papers of Arthur Burns, Handwritten Journals, 1969–1974, Box 1, July 14, 1973.
[23] HAEU, Papers of Emanuele Gazzo, Box 207, "The Honorable Donald Rumsfeld, United States Permanent Representative on the North Atlantic Council, United States Ambassador to the North Atlantic Treaty Organizations, to the Board of Governors of the Atlantic Institute, Paris, June 2, 1973."

Kissinger's intentions as contained in his April speech. Rumsfeld was well aware of the long history of miscommunication between the United States and Europe.[24]

American leaders also undertook a program of education about the Year of Europe within NATO. With forthcoming NATO ministerial meetings on June 7 and June 14–15, the timing was ideal. Donald Rumsfeld explained the opportunity before him to the Department of State:

Against the background of the "Year of Europe" speech of April 23 and the president's foreign policy report of May 3, there are four interrelated subjects which could be addressed: a new declaration of principles; the development of or progress toward an allied substantive position on acceptable MBFR outcomes; the importance of improving conventional military forces and discussion of specific proposals; the need to achieve a more equitable sharing of the defense burden and discussion of specific proposals.[25]

During the ministerial meetings, Secretary of State William Rogers used his speech to address European criticism that the United States had ignored Europe since Nixon's 1969 tour. "Since that time, for reasons that are well known, the United States has been engaged in other activities in other parts of the world. But that fact has not changed our position," he stated. Rogers argued that it was only because of the strength of the transatlantic relationship that American initiatives with China and the Soviet Union were possible. "There can be no doubt about it that improved relations with the Soviet Union have come about because of the strength of the alliance. And I might say parenthetically that our relations with the PRC have been helped because of the alliance. Today with the transformation of U.S. relations with Moscow and Peking, and the Vietnam War coming to an end, we will devote much greater attention to the needs of the alliance itself."[26] The speech was as close as the United States came during the Year of Europe to officially acknowledging that Europe had been subordinated to too many other issues during Nixon's first term.

---

[24] Donald Rumsfeld, *The Rumsfeld Papers* [online]. Memorandum from Donald Rumsfeld to President George W. Bush, "Europe over the Decades," July 28, 2004. Available from http://www.rumsfeld.com/.

[25] NARA, RG 59, CFPF, Telegram from U.S. Mission NATO to Secretary of State, "The Forthcoming Ministerials," May 24, 1973, NATO 02561.

[26] NARA, RG 59, CFPF, Telegram from American Embassy Copenhagen to Secretary of State, "Secretary Rogers' Address to NAC, Thursday, June 14," June 14, 1973, Copenhagen 01337.

Henry Kissinger met again with French Foreign Affairs Minister Michel Jobert. In the briefing memo written to Kissinger by Helmut Sonnenfeldt, the importance of the Year of Europe was again linked to domestic affairs as opposed to foreign policy interests. The Watergate investigation led by Sam Ervin's Senate Select Committee was intensifying, as was Congressional scrutiny of the Nixon White House. "The objective is to have something in motion, so that this fall when Congress debates troops in Europe we can point to three reasons for standing firm: (1) the Year of Europe process of defining long terms goals is underway, (2) MBFR [Mutual and Balanced Force Reductions] is in train, and (3) the Alliance is analyzing burden sharing and force improvements," Sonnenfeldt wrote.[27] The White House needed to show Congress that progress was being made. The Year of Europe served more than one purpose.

Kissinger continued to be far more effective in bilateral meetings than multilateral settings, especially when he met with Jobert one on one. "Our design is really much simpler than what some French newspapers think," he said to Jobert. "We are very concerned at the erosion of the distinction between friends and enemies. And we wanted the Year of Europe to correct this to some extent." Following the recommendations in the Sonnenfeldt memorandum, Kissinger linked progress on the Year of Europe to domestic politics. "There is no public demand for the Year of Europe. The results of the Year of Europe will only bring us difficulties in the United States if we don't press our economic demands and if we try to keep our troops there – both of which are our intention. We foresaw this before Watergate. We are going into an isolationist period." The French and other Europeans were sympathetic to the American domestic situation, but they had heard this since the beginning of the Nixon administration.

Kissinger also addressed European fears that the Year of Europe would simply be another opportunity for someone like John Connally to take advantage of them, as had occurred following the collapse of Bretton Woods, a situation that would cause a breakdown not only in the postwar international monetary system, but also in transatlantic relations more generally. "We want to create an emotional commitment in America, not win a victory," he reassured Jobert. "So the manner in which we do it is important. I will be honest. Connally as Secretary of the Treasury

---

[27] RMN, NSC, Box 56, Memorandum from Helmut Sonnenfeldt to Henry Kissinger, "Your Meeting with Jobert," June 4, 1973.

recommended to the president that to be popular in America he should take on the Europeans. He was right." However, two years later, the United States had learned its lesson, and Connally left the Nixon administration. The United States now needed its European allies. "In eight years, if Europe becomes obsessed with a sense of impotence because of isolation from us, both sides will have lost. We raise strategic issues because if we don't raise them, they will be imposed on us [by the Congress] . . . but we need some cooperation. If we want to take our forces out [of Europe], we could let Congress do it," Kissinger said.[28]

If the Year of Europe was as unpopular domestically as Kissinger said, and if Europeans gave it a lukewarm reception at best so far, why pursue it? "I see two explanations," Jobert said to Kissinger. "That you wish to divide Europe to strengthen your mastery, or that you are doing it for internal or budgetary reasons. Then I think that after your contacts with the Russians you are returning a bit toward the Europeans to reassure them a bit, to reinforce your position vis-à-vis the Soviets." Kissinger did not disagree. "No, you are right. But I think it [the Year of Europe] reinforces everyone's position vis-à-vis the Soviets."[29]

On June 20, Prime Minister Edward Heath called a meeting of the EC foreign ministers to break the European stalemate over the Year of Europe. "At this meeting the Prime Minister pointed out that the American initiative could not be ignored," the FCO reported. However, it also would not proceed as the Americans intended. "The Prime Minister described Dr. Kissinger's proposal for a single declaration of principles as unrealistic." NATO and the EC did not share the same membership or basic objectives. Heath had a certain fascination with Henry Kissinger, and he asked the FCO to produce an extensive study of his life and career. "President Nixon has invested a philosopher with powers greater than those wielded by most of the princes of the world. Seldom has a theorist been given such opportunities to practice what he preached," the study found.[30] In an attempt to make progress, Heath proposed splitting the Year of Europe into two processes, one negotiated in NATO and one in the EC. Each would discuss only those portions of the Year of Europe related to the respective body. "The communiqué or declaration from NATO should be worked out in that

---

[28] AN, 5AG2/1023, Entretien du Ministre Jobert avec M. Kissinger à Paris le 8 juin 1973, de 9 h à 11h 30.
[29] RMN, NSC, Box 56, Memorandum of conversation between Henry Kissinger and Michel Jobert, Quai d'Orsay, June 8, 1973.
[30] PRO, PREM 15–1983, "Dr. Kissinger's Ideas," July 31, 1973.

forum ... [while] the Community should reach agreement among them-selves on the line to be taken with the Americans on other aspects of Atlantic relations."[31] It was this proposal that convinced the French to take part, overcoming their previous refusal to contribute to a solution negotiated within NATO.[32]

On June 22, Nixon and Leonid Brezhnev signed the Agreement on the Prevention of Nuclear War during his week-long visit to the United States on June 18–25. It was a landmark achievement that further reduced Cold War tensions only a year after Nixon's visit to Moscow for the signing of the Strategic Arms Limitation Treaty (SALT I). Europe was consulted very little in advance, just as they had feared they would not be.[33] President Pompidou and Chancellor Brandt met for eight hours over June 21–22 to discuss the impact of the latest U.S.-Soviet accord.[34] Kissinger also met with all ambassadors to NATO in an extraordinary session held at San Clemente on July 14 to calm them. There was a concern that the United States was now heading toward a "condominium" with Soviet Union. Joseph Luns had been telling American leaders for a month that Nixon and Kissinger needed to more fully consult with NATO members, other-wise distrust among them over U.S. actions would only increase.[35] Improved consultation was also supposed to have been a central theme of the Year of Europe. "What we need is a statement which will give an expression of our continued relations with Europe," Kissinger said. "If we cannot do that, the logic of events will mean that our contacts with Peking and Moscow will be the dramatic items and the contacts with Europe will become a backwater." As the meeting concluded, Kissinger set a goal to demonstrate progress on a new Atlantic Charter: "before December."[36] According to that timetable, the Year of Europe could still be salvaged by the end of 1973.

The Nixon-Brezhnev summit was the impetus the Europeans needed to get working. On July 23, the EC foreign ministers held an "extraordinary

[31] PRO, PREM 15-2089, undated study by FCO Policy Planning Staff on Year of Europe.
[32] Daniel Möckli, *European Foreign Policy during the Cold War: Heath Brandt, Pompidou and the Dream of Political Unity* (London: I.B. Tauris, 2009), 161.
[33] Grosser, 273.
[34] *AAPD* 1973, Gespräch des Bundeskanzlers Brandts mit Staatspräsident Pompidou auf Schloß Gymnich, June 21–22, 1973, 198–199.
[35] Donald Rumsfeld, *The Rumsfeld Papers* [online]. "Memorandum for Rumsfeld Files: Meeting with Joseph Luns, June 4, 1973, 10:45 a.m." Available from http://www.rumsfeld.com/.
[36] NARA, RG 59, CFPF, Telegram from Secretary of State to All NATO Capitals, "Dr. Kissinger's Meeting with NATO Permreps," July 14, 1973, State 138485.

meeting."[37] It was the first real opportunity to debate the Year of Europe since Kissinger's April 23 speech. Much of the discussion centered around the fact that the Soviets continued to have 1,500 rockets pointed toward the West even as the United States signed another agreement with Brezhnev on the renunciation of force.[38] Although EC members agreed on that much, they did not agree on the role of the EC in negotiations over the Year of Europe. Before the Europeans could come to any further agreement on the Year of Europe, they first insisted on articulating a statement of European identity.[39] The delays upset Henry Kissinger, but German Foreign Minister Scheel told him that "the Europeans were now focused on substantive discussions which the U.S. certainly did not want to disrupt."[40]

Some Europeans believed that they were being manhandled by Kissinger in a way similar to how they witnessed the Soviet Union had been played against the Chinese in the previous two years or as Connally had dealt with them in 1971. "Unless we shoot one across the bow to them brutally now ...," Kissinger trailed off. "Well, I think that you should do," Helmut Sonnenfeldt finished his sentence.[41] Speaking for the EC, Michel Jobert remarked that President Nixon "reminds them of a pyromaniac who sets fires and asks the victims to help."[42] Why should the EC respond to the American initiative on an American timetable, because of American domestic political difficulties? The EC foreign ministers agreed to meet again on September 10, 1973. The French believed it was more important to first focus on the problems of Europe before taking further steps to develop U.S.–European relations. The EC affirmed Prime Minister Heath's proposal that President Nixon, upon his forthcoming visit to Europe, would be asked to sign a NATO communiqué that addressed transatlantic defense issues at NATO, whereas an EC communiqué that addressed transatlantic economic relations would be issued at the conclusion of his meeting with the EC.

[37] RMN, NSC, Box 673, Telegram from American Embassy Copenhagen to Secretary of State, "Agree Press Statement on Foreign Ministers Meeting," July 24, 1973, Copenhagen 1685.

[38] *AAPD* 1973, Aufzeichnung des Ministerialdirigenten Brunner, July 16, 1973, 222.

[39] RMN, NSC, Box 673, Memorandum from Helmut Sonnenfeldt to Henry Kissinger, "First Reports on Copenhagen Meeting of the Nine," July 25, 1973.

[40] *AAPD* 1973, Bundesminister Scheel an den Sicherheitsberater des amerikanischen Präsidenten, Kissinger, July 25, 1973, 230.

[41] RMN, HAK Telcons, Box 21, July 26, 1973 [no time given].

[42] RMN, HAK Telcons, Box 21, July 30, 1973, 4:53 p.m.

Kissinger returned to the theme of the necessity of working more quickly on the Year of Europe so as to restrain isolationist American domestic political influences. In a meeting with Emile van Lennep, Secretary General of the Organization for Economic Cooperation and Development (OECD) – the Paris-based organization formed in 1961 to take over economic oversight duties that had originated with the Marshall Plan – Kissinger noted the importance of showing progress on the Year of Europe negotiations to an increasingly isolationist Congress that had plans for additional European troop cuts. "We can probably get through this session of Congress without cuts," he said. "But we won't be able to get through the next [session]." Kissinger argued that the cuts would mean that the White House would be much more constrained in its courses of action in foreign policy. "This will bring about a situation in which détente policies will so overwhelm relations with Europe that it will be difficult to get things going again. Then we will have to wait quite a while until we can pick things up."[43]

On July 30, Kissinger met with the British and informed them that he believed transatlantic relations had now evolved into an adversarial relationship and that the "so-called" Year of Europe was "over." "After three months, the Europeans have refused to give us a response or a comment on our drafts. And now the Europeans refused to talk to us except through the Danish Foreign Minister, and then they will present us a document. I am sure he is an estimable man. I don't even know who he is ... he is a messenger boy, not a negotiator."[44] For Kissinger, he was particularly insulted that the British would permit an arrangement that they would surely not accept themselves if they were in the position of the United States. "Having announced the trip, it is a big decision to announce that it is off," Burke Trend reminded Kissinger. "That's your problem as much as ours," Kissinger rebutted.[45]

In the prior four years, a wholly new American relationship had been achieved with China and the Soviet Union. As Kissinger was fond of recalling, he had done all of this "by highly personal and unconventional methods, including ... a degree of 'brutality' in negotiation."[46] European governments recognized when similar tactics had been used against them. The British believed that Nixon and Kissinger underestimated the

---

[43] RMN, NSC, Box 54, Memorandum of conversation between Henry Kissinger and Emile van Lennep, location unknown, July 27, 1973.

[44] *FRUS, 1969–1976*, Volume E-15, Part 2, 27.

[45] *FRUS, 1969–1976*, Volume E-15, Part 2, 27.

[46] PRO, PREM 15-2089, undated study by FCO Policy Planning Staff on Year of Europe.

difficulty of reforming relations within a Europe in the midst of significant changes. Writing Nixon on September 4, Heath reminded him that "Western Europe in general, and the United Kingdom in particular, are very heavily indebted to the United States for much generous aid, in many forms . . . it will surely be judged one of the greater ironies of history if, just at the moment when the purpose of that aid is being realized and nine of the countries of Western Europe are at last emerging as an entity, the United States themselves should be tempted to reject the concept of an equal partnership which all their effort for nearly thirty years have been designed to create."[47]

It was too sudden to now say that the Nixon Doctrine required Europeans to shoulder more of the burden in the transatlantic relationship. Change had come about too quickly during the Nixon administration for many Europeans. "Linking defense (where the European position was weak) with economics (where it was strong and, for the Community, entrenched in dogma) this strategy was unwelcome to the Europeans," an FCO study noted.[48] "Dr. Kissinger was trying to divide and rule by his insistence on secret, separate and bilateral talks, in which only he knew the full score . . . because of Dr. Kissinger's insistence on excluding the bureaucracy, no such exchanges ever took place and there was no opportunity to discover informally how thinking was developing on the two sides of the Atlantic." Following a period of intense negotiations with American adversaries, it was as though American diplomats had lost the ability to negotiate with allies.

The FCO placed the greatest blame for the decay in transatlantic relations not on the Americans, but rather on the British and the French. "The flames of American resentment were primarily stoked by Britain and France." On the one hand, "the French never regarded it as necessary or desirable to make substantial concessions to the United States in order to retain American support for Europe." On the other hand, "it is arguable that the British did not try hard enough. There were reasons for this. Nevertheless, the real embarrassment caused to the British by the prospect of discussing bilaterally with Dr. Kissinger a project he had rendered multilateral . . . did contribute to the prolonged absence of substantive Anglo-American consultation in June and July 1973. Moreover there was, after the Ministerial meeting of June 20, a definite

---

[47] *FRUS*, 1969–1976, Volume E-15, Part 2, 32.
[48] PRO, PREM 15–2089, undated study by FCO Policy Planning Staff on Year of Europe.

shift in the emphasis of British policy towards European unity as the precondition for transatlantic understanding."[49]

When the German government learned of Kissinger's statement that the Year of Europe was "over," Chancellor Willy Brandt sent a back-channel message to President Nixon that requested reconsideration. "I can understand your finding certain aspects of this learning process irksome, for instance the time it is taking. But I think it would be wrong for the United States, having for so long called upon the Europeans to speak with one voice, to feel left out when the Nine try to reach agreement among themselves." Brandt also made the suggestion that perhaps a less comprehensive agreement than the United States desired would still be better than no agreement at all. "I would prefer a more modest, common denominator to an ambitious, but controversial, project," Brandt said.[50] French Foreign Minister Michel Jobert stated his support for Brandt's position. "He [Jobert] recognized that we would prefer a paper with some substance in it but implied that he thought we would settle for the paper for its own sake," American Ambassador to France John Irwin wrote to Kissinger. "The Nine did not particularly like the draft declaration we had circulated, which he referred to as the 'Sonnenfeld[t] paper,' " named for Kissinger's assistant Helmut Sonnenfeldt.[51]

Following the EC foreign ministers meeting in Copenhagen on September 10, Kissinger updated President Nixon on the status of the Year of Europe. "They agreed on a draft declaration, which they submitted to us on September 19 together with a proposal that I meet with the Danish Foreign Minister in New York, who would act as the spokesman for the Nine and who would receive our comments."[52] That fact that one foreign minister delivered the European response but was not able to negotiate or even receive an official American response was "beastly" and unacceptable to the Americans.[53] "When I met with the Foreign Minister [Andersen of Denmark] I told him that the procedures followed by the Nine were totally unacceptable, that we could not accept a situation in which our views could not be made known to the EC while they were considering their position," Kissinger reported to Nixon. On the other

[49] PRO, PREM 15–2089, undated study by FCO Policy Planning Staff on Year of Europe.
[50] RMN, NSC, Box 61, backchannel telegram from Willy Brandt to President Nixon, August 4, 1973, Bravo Four 001 2171500.
[51] RMN, NSC, Box 56, backchannel telegram from John Irwin to Henry Kissinger, September 7, 1973, U.S. Embassy in Paris Hotline.
[52] RMN, NSC, Box 918, Memorandum from Henry Kissinger to President Nixon, "Meeting with Chancellor Brandt," September 29, 1973.
[53] RMN, HAK Telcons, Box 21, August 15, 1973, 10:30 a.m.

hand, Kissinger knew that an agreement that was less than perfect was better than no agreement at all, and he looked ahead to the president's eventual visit to Europe. "The Europeans, therefore, developed the proposal that you should be received by the President of the EC Council of Ministers (a rotating position) and by the President of the EC Commission (Mr. Ortoli) as well as by the Nine foreign Ministers. The two EC Presidents would represent the EC collectively. They are in effect your counterpart, and this arrangement would be acceptable in principle."[54] For purposes of diplomatic protocol, the EC considered the unelected and mostly powerless president of the Council of Ministers to be the equal of the president of the United States.

Despite the setbacks in the EC on its half of a Year of Europe declaration, NATO was making progress on its half. "There have been no major procedural problems in NATO; all of the Allies, save France, have been eager to begin work on a declaration on defense and East-West relations," Kissinger reported to Nixon on September 29.[55] Ongoing Congressional debate over the latest version of the Mansfield Amendment, as well as the proposed Jackson-Nunn Amendment, had been catalysts for NATO to take prompt action. Such threats were less effective in convincing the EC to act because American troop deployments were not a concern. The Mansfield Amendment, introduced in various forms since 1966, proposed up to a 50 percent withdrawal of American troops stationed in Europe. The Jackson-Nunn Amendment sought to compel Europeans to recoup the portion of the American balance of payments deficit created by the stationing of GIs in Europe. If Europeans did not comply with the program of reimbursements, the Jackson-Nunn Amendment prescribed that American forces would be reduced by the percentage of the balance of payments not covered by the Europeans. These were among the examples of the new isolationism in Congress about which Kissinger warned Europeans. "We are experiencing the greatest pressure yet from Congress to reduce troops in Europe," he reported. "It took a major effort to defeat Mansfield but we still face amendments for smaller cuts and the Jackson-Nunn Amendment linking force levels to offset."[56]

* * *

[54] RMN, NSC, Box 918, Memorandum from Henry Kissinger to President Nixon, "Meeting with Chancellor Brandt," September 29, 1973.

[55] RMN, NSC, Box 918, Memorandum from Henry Kissinger to President Nixon, "Meeting with Chancellor Brandt," September 29, 1973.

[56] RMN, NSC, Box 918, Memorandum from Henry Kissinger to President Nixon, "Meeting with Chancellor Brandt," September 29, 1973.

By the fall of 1973, remaining hope for a comprehensive Year of Europe before the end of the year looked bleak. "The Year of Europe ended as an almost unqualified failure, shipwrecked (not for the last time) on the rocks of European self-interest and American arrogance," said Alistair Horne.[57] Nonetheless, the drafting of the two separate communiqués in the EC and NATO chugged along. From the European perspective, rather than reassuring Europeans, the Year of Europe introduced new uneasiness as a result of Vietnam and "a new hostility in Congress toward executive branch commitments abroad, and a trend toward greater congressional involvement in foreign policy which may be dangerous."[58] Although some aspects of Nixon's foreign policy could be unpredictable, the tone coming out of Congress was undesirable. Europeans had no shortage of Congressional shots across the bow of the White House, each designed to reduce the ability of President Nixon to conduct foreign policy. These included the War Powers Act, the Trade Reform Act of 1974 and the Jackson-Vanik Amendment, the suspension of military aid to Turkey, and the refusal to grant military aid to Southeast Asia.

Meanwhile, Henry Kissinger was confirmed as Secretary of State on September 22, and he was planning another trip to China in the fall of 1973. Europe had won out; there would be two separate communiqués, one for defense issues within NATO, and one for political and economic issues drafted within the EC. In Kissinger's view, although the drafting continued, the Year of Europe became devoid of any vision or meaning for transatlantic relations. Kissinger blamed Michel Jobert for its failure.[59] In addition, the domestic political situation in the United States had become too hostile to the idea of expanding the nation's commitments to Europe. The intensification of the Watergate investigation caused a growing number of problems for the Nixon administration. Nixon had already lost his two most trusted aides – Bob Haldeman and John Ehrlichman – to the developing scandal, and a distracted Nixon appeared to be losing his once firm grip over American foreign policy to an isolationist Congress.

On August 3, Kissinger met with the President's Foreign Intelligence Advisory Board (PFIAB) aboard the presidential yacht *Sequoia* and lamented. "It's in this way that Watergate is a disaster. Everything is a

---

[57] Horne, 400.
[58] COE Archives, Box 889-031-1, Report from the Council of Europe, Parliamentary Assembly, "Contribution to the debate on relations between Western Europe and North America," September 29, 1975.
[59] Horne, 115.

little harder now and takes a little longer – Europe, China, etc. It is a national obligation to get Watergate behind us so we can be seen as an operating government."[60] The Watergate inquiry only accelerated further after the nation learned of the existence of Nixon's White House taping system during July 1973. Journalist Rowland Evans, one half of the Evans and Novak duo, stated to Kissinger that "to conceal these tapes is the most stupid single act this man [Nixon] has ever committed." Kissinger replied, "it is the second. Making the tapes was the first," even though he had also been taping his own telephone calls since 1969.[61] The tightening noose of the Watergate investigation increased all types of Congressional scrutiny of the Nixon White House. The U.S. Senate Committee on Foreign Relations referred to the confirmation hearings for Henry Kissinger as Secretary of State, held on September 7, 10, and 11, as "more extensive than those which have been held with respect to any nominee for this post since World War II, or before – indeed, according to the records available to the Committee, since the founding of the Republic."[62]

European governments distanced themselves from the United States as a result of Watergate and the increased Congressional scrutiny of the White House. Kissinger went on the defensive, meeting with Danish Foreign Minister Knud B. Andersen. He was chosen as the EC representative to deliver official messages from the EC to the United States, but he did not have any authority to negotiate or even to receive an American response. "We are going to try to bust the Europeans. The French can be useful in this. We will hit the British, ignore the French and deal with the Germans and Italians," Kissinger said to a meeting of his staff.[63]

Andersen stated that the French refused to accept several points that the Americans insisted on: inclusion of the word "globalization" (linkage) in any declaration; that President Nixon would only meet with Europeans at the summit level, which created a constitutional problem for France; and, finally, that an American representative should be present at the drafting of any European draft of a declaration.[64] Nonetheless, Andersen said that the EC completed its draft communiqué on the Year of Europe on

[60] GRF, NSA, Memcons, Box 2, memorandum of conversation, PFIAB, Sequoia, August 3, 1973.

[61] RMN, HAK Telcons, Box 21, July 25, 1973, 9:15 a.m.

[62] LOC, Manuscript Division, Papers of Elliot Richardson, Box 203.

[63] *FRUS*, 1969–1976, Volume E-15, Part 2, 312.

[64] *AAPD* 1973, Aufzeichnung des Staatssekretärs Frank, August 31, 1973, 267.

September 20.[65] Kissinger's immediate reaction was slight relief. "It is a positive thing that there is a European document."[66] Andersen read from a six-page statement, which represented the first attempt of the EC to speak with one voice on foreign policy issues in the history of the European integration movement. "In our deliberations among the Nine we have tried to put substance before procedure ... you must understand how difficult it is for the Nine to achieve what we have," Andersen said.[67]

Kissinger was not impressed. "Yes, it is a considerable achievement for Europe but not for Atlantic relations. ... Europe must decide if it intends to build Europe or also to build Atlantic relations. If the decision is to build Europe when the Atlantic relationship is collapsing then the European achievement will be at the expense of Atlantic relations," he said.[68] "Our problem is that from July 23 to September 19 there has been no consultation at all." Acting Secretary of State Kenneth Rush reiterated this point to German Ambassador to Washington, Berndt von Staden. "We cannot accept that Europe acts as if we are on one side of the fence and they are on the other," Rush stated.[69] German Foreign Minister Walter Scheel summed up the European problem. "The hardest question is to take a policy decision in the EC when unity doesn't exist," he said.[70] "This is hardly surprising in view of what we know of the negotiating difficulties and the resistance of the French," U.S. Ambassador to the European Community Robert Strausz-Hupe commented.[71] "We seem to be talking to those who can't negotiate and those who can negotiate won't talk to us," Kissinger summarized. "Frankly, I must tell you that this is not a procedure we can accept as a permanent arrangement."[72]

---

[65] RMN, NSC, Box 669, Telegram from U.S. Mission to the European Community to Secretary of State, "Copenhagen Draft Outline on US-EC Relations," September 20, 1973, EC Brussels 5357.

[66] RMN, NSC, Box 1027, Memorandum of Conversation between Walter Scheel and Henry Kissinger, September 25, 1973.

[67] RMN, NSC, Box 673, Udenrigsministerens indlæg under samtalen med Dr. Kissinger tirsdag den 25. September 1973, kl. 10.30.

[68] RMN, NSC, Box 1027, memorandum of conversation between Henry Kissinger and K. B. Andersen, United States Mission to the United Nations, September 25, 1973.

[69] *AAPD* 1973, Botschafter von Staden, Washington, an Bundesminister Scheel, September 7, 1973, 277.

[70] RMN, NSC, Box 1027, Memorandum of Conversation between Walter Scheel and Henry Kissinger, September 25, 1973.

[71] RMN, NSC, Box 669, Telegram from U.S. Mission to the European Community to Secretary of State, "Atlantic Relations-US/EC Declaration," September 21, 1973, Brussels 5407.

[72] *FRUS*, 1969–1976, Volume E-15, Part 2, 34.

The following day, on September 26, Henry Kissinger met Michel Jobert at Kissinger's Waldorf Towers apartment. "I think you have conducted a very clever campaign this past six months," Kissinger said. "I am like a leaf in the wind. I am passive. First, I am blown to the West, then to the East," Jobert responded.[73] Regarding Knud B. Andersen, the Danish Foreign Minister who was not permitted to negotiate, Kissinger said "this will create an adversary relationship in the long run which could be very bad." Meanwhile, Europeans were not happy that Nixon's visit depended on an American timetable for European progress.[74] Chancellor Willy Brandt told Kissinger that if he was looking to speed the pace of European progress, Kissinger should announce that President Nixon still intended to visit Europe by the end of 1973.[75]

On October 1, Nixon met with the President of European Commission, François-Xavier Ortoli. "First, it is fair to say that the position I take about continued U.S. participation in the NATO alliance is not helpful in this country politically," Nixon said. "The position I take regarding trade matters is also a political loser here ... you will note in the weeks ahead some tough struggle with our Congress." Nixon emphasized the importance of strengthening the Atlantic alliance, especially given the strains placed on it by the Yom Kippur War. "If Europe and the U.S. come apart, the Soviets can pick us off one by one, not through military conquest, but through other methods. Their goals have not changed, only their techniques have changed. The purpose of the Year of Europe initiative is for all of us to reevaluate the world in which we live, to see what is obsolete and what still speaks to the times, and then to come forth at the end with economic and military principles that we can work to implement."[76]

Brandt unsuccessfully tried to break the impasse between the United States and Europe.[77] "The Federal Government contributed, among other things, three high level bilateral visits to the United States in a period of only five months," the German Foreign Office noted.[78] At a White House

[73] RMN, NSC Box 679, Memorandum of Conversation between Henry Kissinger and Michel Jobert, September 26, 1973.

[74] NARA, RG 59, CFPF, telegram from Secretary of State to All NATO Capitals, "Secretary's Call on FRG Chancellor Brandt," October 1, 1973, State 194714.

[75] *AAPD* 1973, Aufzeichnung des Botshaftters von Staden, Washington, September 26, 1973, 297.

[76] RMN, NSC Box 322, Memorandum of conversation between President Nixon, Henry Kissinger, and Franois-Xavier Ortoli, Oval Office, October 1, 1973.

[77] *AAPD* 1973, Gespräch des Bundeskanzlers Brandt mit Präsident Nixon in Washington, September 29, 1973, 298.

[78] PAAA, ZA 101383, "Europäisch-Amerikanische Beziehungen; Beitrag der Bundesregierung zur Förderung des transatlantischen Dialogs," October 2, 1973.

press conference on October 3, Nixon updated the press corps on the status of his trip to Europe. "[I]t is difficult to pinpoint the timing of a trip to Europe, but in order that all of you can make your plans a little better, the trip to Europe will be made within the next few months and the timing will be based on these factors: First, the progress which is made on the discussions now going on with regard to a declaration of principles with regard to the Alliance, and with regard to economic matters as well," he said. Nixon also noted the severe effect that Congress was having upon his foreign policy. "I cannot take a trip to Europe or any place else at a time when there are matters before the Congress of very great significance."[79] The rest of the month took a turn for the worse for President Nixon. On October 10, Vice President Spiro Agnew resigned due to a scandal unrelated to Watergate. The next week, Nixon negotiated the release of his White House tapes to the Watergate Special Prosecutor. This led to the resignation on October 20 of Attorney General Elliot Richardson and the dismissal of Watergate Special Prosecutor Archibald Cox, known as the "Saturday Night Massacre." Henry Kissinger was in Moscow negotiating a Middle East ceasefire to the Yom Kippur War at a time when Nixon could have used his advice.[80] Europe was again subordinated to other events.

The British government sought to understand how things had going so terribly wrong in transatlantic relations during a year that was intended to do the opposite. Foreign Secretary Douglas-Home placed some blame on the change in British foreign policy since accession to the EC. Following accession, the EC took a privileged position in British foreign policy normally occupied by the United States alone. "We must necessarily try to get the best of both worlds: to combine our European policy with the preservation of a fruitful Anglo-American and Transatlantic relationship," he reported to Prime Minister Heath.[81] However, the Americans were not blameless. "To my mind one of the main causes of the trouble we have all experienced lay essentially in the fact that Dr. Kissinger insisted on himself running everything that was crucial in the foreign and defense policy in the U.S. ... most of his diplomatic experience, after all, has been gained comparatively recently in successful negotiations with the adversaries of the U.S. and he had perhaps made insufficient allowance for the different approach demanded by allies with whom he had little

---

[79] *Nixon: The Fifth Year*, 174.
[80] Henry Kissinger, *Crisis: The Anatomy of Two Major Foreign Policy Crises* (New York: Simon and Schuster, 2003), 2.
[81] PRO, PREM 15–2089, Memorandum from Alec Douglas-Home to Prime Minister Heath, October 17, 1973.

contact."[82] This was the most accurate assessment to date on the failure of the Year of Europe.

Going against France, Prime Minister Heath and Chancellor Brandt met at Chequers over October 6–7, 1973. They agreed that at least between their respective governments, they could come to agreement on a Year of Europe communiqué.[83] They hoped to use the document to secure approval with the rest of Europe, with or without France. "[The] Brandt-Heath summit at Chequers conveys [the] impression of two good friends either agreeing or avoiding discord on nearly all issues," an American report of the meeting stated.[84] Henry Kissinger called a meeting in London of all American ambassadors to European posts on October 15. More than just a meeting, it was an all-day conference during which Kissinger had all of his representatives to Europe in one place where he could issue their marching orders.[85] The stated purpose of the gathering was "to examine the totality, as well as the individual parts, of U.S. policy in the period ahead towards Europe, including Western Europe, Canada, the USSR, and Eastern Europe."[86] Kissinger made it clear that with him in charge of the State Department, he planned to be tougher on the Europeans. They "are always interested in tying us in with them if it is something related to the defense of Europe, but they try to dissociate from us the moment there is trouble anywhere else in the world. Now that I am here, nothing will be free. We will no longer be available to kick around."[87] Kissinger aide Helmut Sonnenfeldt was more direct. "Bilaterally we are partners, collectively we are not."[88] To his ambassadors, Kissinger reminded them, "on April 23 I offered a partnership to the Europeans. This is something there is no demand for in this country, no pressure from the Congress or from the public. The president and I already believed in partnership with Europe. We don't have to be persuaded. Our idea was that it would be good to build a structure while we are both still

[82] PRO, PREM 15-2089, Memorandum from Alec Douglas-Home to Prime Minister Heath, October 17, 1973.

[83] *AAPD* 1973, Botschafter von Hase, London, an das Auswärtige Amt, October 7, 1973, 312.

[84] NARA, RG 59, CFPF, Telegram from American Embassy Bonn to Secretary of State, "Brandt-Heath Summit at Chequers: Focus on Europe," October 11, 1973, Bonn 14764.

[85] NARA, RG 59, CFPF, Telegram from Secretary of State to all European posts, "European Chiefs of Mission Meeting," October 8, 1973, State 199737.

[86] NARA, RG 59, CFPF, Telegram from Secretary of State to all European posts, "European Chiefs of Mission Meeting," October 10, 1973, State 200520.

[87] RMN, NSC, Box 688, Memorandum of conversation between Henry Kissinger and Franz Josef Strauss, October 18, 1973.

[88] HAEU, Papers of Klaus Meyer, Box 70, handwritten notes of U.S.-EC meeting by Klaus Meyer, October 18, 1973.

here, something for our successors. So what did the Europeans do? Nothing but legalism and pettifogging."[89]

On October 18, a joint U.S.–European conference was held in Copenhagen. Both sides wondered how things had been so misplayed up to that point.[90] The American representative, Walter Stoessel, stated privately, "personally, I doubt that we can get much more from an EC draft ... my own conclusion is that we should continue with the exercise and, depending on the outcome of the NATO draft, eventually [we] should accept a US-EC draft of the type indicated."[91] French President Georges Pompidou suggested that EC member states hold regular summit meetings for the first time, in order to prevent future crises.[92] Prime Minister Heath privately expressed to Egon Bahr his "bitterness" over Nixon and Kissinger, that "everything they say is said in self-interest." Heath expected Kissinger to have demonstrated a better understanding of his difficult political position. "England has lost not only the Empire, but also its military and economic supremacy," he said to Bahr.[93]

The United States and the EC met again in mid-November to work out remaining differences on the two communiqués. Little was achieved. "There was modest give in EC positions, but still strong resistance. ... France clearly remained principal stumbling block on main issues," Walter Stoessel summarized.[94] British Foreign Secretary Alec Douglas-Home wrote to Kissinger that "our European response to the initiative which you launched with your speech in April may, it is true, have seemed almost culpably slow. But, frankly, it caught us on the hop." France received Kissinger's speech very coolly, and in Germany both Chancellor Brandt and SPD Bundestag leader Herbert Wehner were both traveling. "Our Community machinery for rapid response simply wasn't there," Douglas-Home said, blaming the internal difficulties of the EC.[95]

---

[89] NARA, RG 59, CFPF, Telegram from Secretary of State to all European posts, "European Chiefs of Mission Meeting," October 10, 1973, State 200520.

[90] RMN, NSC, Box 673, Telegram from American Embassy Copenhagen to Secretary of State, "US-EC Nine Meeting, October 18," October 18, 1973, Copenhagen 2605.

[91] RMN, NSC, Box 679, Telegram from American Embassy Paris to Secretary of State, "Our Discussions with EC Nine," October 20, 1973, Paris 27407.

[92] NARA, RG 59, CFPF, Telegram from American Embassy Paris to Secretary of State, "Pompidou Calls for Regular EC Summit Meetings," October 31, 1973, Paris 28215.

[93] *AAPD* 1973, Botschafter von Hase, London, an das Auswärtige Amt, October 31, 1973, 348.

[94] RMN, NSC, Box 673, Telegram from American Embassy Copenhagen to Secretary of State, "U.S.-EC Nine Meetings: Summary," November 14, 1973, Copenhagen 2864.

[95] PRO, PREM 15–2089, Telegram from Alec Douglas Home to Henry Kissinger, via Lord Cromer, November 23, 1973, FCO 281705Z.

Kissinger refused to accept any blame for himself. "Entry into the European Community should have raised Europe to the level of Britain. Instead it reduced Britain to the level of Europe," he said to British Ambassador Lord Cromer.[96] "Heath is the first Prime Minister who has no special American ties. He is a Gaullist. I think the British have decided to be wholly European," Kissinger said to Secretary of Defense James Schlesinger.[97]

Often, when Henry Kissinger faced a tough decision, he invited in a bipartisan group of foreign policy experts to brainstorm and commiserate with him. He did this in 1971 before the defeat of the Mansfield Amendment, and he did it again on November 28, 1973, to discuss the Year of Europe. Kissinger laid out his grievances to the group. "There is no real negotiation, since the Europeans state their position, then we state ours, and then the Europeans go away to work out their response, after which the whole process is repeated."[98] Kissinger expressed his frustration again to the EC foreign ministers on December 9. "We deeply regret that the European response has drained the Year of Europe initiative of much of its symbolic value. And we believe it will be difficult to sustain U.S. public support for our military commitments in Europe, unless we can restore a positive emotional content to the Atlantic relationship."[99]

The tenor of Kissinger's comments put Prime Minister Heath on the defensive at a time when Heath was already suffering through miserable domestic public approval ratings. There was talk within the opposition Labor Party of "renegotiating" the terms of British EC membership. "He [Heath] had high hopes of convincing the British public that entry into the Common Market would give Britain a new and glorious role to play on the world stage. But his wishes have turned to ashes," Lord Cromer said. "The latest opinion poll here shows that only 29 percent think membership helps the country, 44 percent think it hurts and the rest don't know or can't decide." Heath blamed the United States for his demise. "It was wrong to imagine that the Americans could have 'The Year of Europe' without any consultation and yet it had been launched without a single

---

[96] PRO, PREM 15–2089, Telegram from Lord Cromer to Alec Douglas-Home, November 24, 1973, Washington 242000Z.

[97] GRF, NSA, Memcons, Box 2, Memorandum of conversation between Henry Kissinger and James Schlesinger, Pentagon, November 23, 1973.

[98] RMN, NSC, Box 1027, Memorandum of conversation among Henry Kissinger, Dean Rusk, Douglas Dillon, Nelson Rockefeller, McGeorge Bundy, Cyrus Vance, and John McCloy, Secretary's Office, November 28, 1973.

[99] NARA, RG 59, CFPF, Telegram from Secretary of State to U.S. Mission to NATO, "Secretary's Meeting with EC-Nine Foreign Minister," December 9, 1973, State 240949.

word," he said. The United States would never "ask for 'A Year of China' without consulting the Chinese but they had done that in the case of Europe." Another FCO official commented that, "Mintoffs do not only grow in Malta," referring to the Maltese leader who at times gave the British fits.[100] Heath did take credit for his two communiqués compromise and suggested that a secret Franco-British agreement was what kept the Year of Europe together. "It was a British initiative which had achieved that and it had been the British who had dealt with the French and brought them along: it had all been agreed in the garden of No. 10 with the French foreign minister," Michel Jobert said.[101]

At the December NATO ministerial meeting, British Foreign Secretary Douglas-Home continued the run of the bad news. "Our Alliance is in a very bad shape. Its body is afflicted with all the ills of old age and its limbs are no longer coordinated." Secretary General Luns tried to move the group forward. "*This time,* let us resolve to translate some of our words into action." German Foreign Minister Scheel noted one positive development as a result of the recent turbulence in transatlantic relations. "Work on the Atlantic Declaration has moved more into the spotlight as a result of the Middle East crisis." Douglas-Home agreed. "I take it it was the recognition of this that caused Dr. Kissinger to ask for a fresh act of creation within the Alliance, necessary in relation to public opinion when détente is in the air, and, what is more, necessary to match the postwar generation of leaders in Western Europe and in the United States and the initiatives that they have taken."[102]

In attendance at the NATO gathering, Kissinger defended himself. "Let me be frank," he said. "The Europeans really did to us what we did to them in 1956," he noted, in a reference to the Suez crisis during which the Eisenhower White House harshly undermined the British and French in Egypt. "What we did then was wrong, and I feel I have a moral right to say this, since I felt and said this at the time."[103] Later in the gathering, Kissinger also provided a closing statement. "For a quarter of a century, the United States has regularly renewed its commitment to our closest and

---

[100] PRO, PREM 15–1989, Telegram from Number 10 Downing Street to Chequers, December 2, 1973.

[101] PRO, PREM 15–1989, "Dr Kissinger complained that Prime Minister had made personal attack on him at dinner with US correspondents, 28 November 1973," telegram from Lord Cromer to Foreign Office, December 1, 1973.

[102] NATO, C-VR(73)74, "Verbatim Record of the Meeting of the Council held on Monday, 10th December, 1973, at 9:30 a.m. at NATO Headquarters, Brussels," December 10, 1973.

[103] *FRUS*, 1969–1976, Volume E-15, Part 2, 40.

oldest ally ... three decades after Bretton Woods we lack an agreed view or cooperative mechanism ... this has strained our unity," he said. "For several months preceding the April speech, President Nixon and I discussed our approach with many European leaders and received their encouragement. There was broad consensus that we faced urgent problems and on the need for a new common effort."[104] Kissinger learned that making progress with allies was even more difficult than with adversaries. Europe was the closest American ally, but Kissinger found foreign policy rejection nowhere like he did in Europe.

Kissinger delivered the keynote address at the Pilgrim's Society in London on December 12, where he said that dealing with the EC was almost impossible since it was so difficult for the EC to renegotiate its position once it had arrived at a compromise.[105] "Who do I call if I want to call Europe?" Kissinger asked. "We require another act of will, a determination to surmount squabbles and legalistic preoccupations and to become the master of our destinies. We in this room are heirs to a rich heritage and friendship. If we are true to ourselves, we have it in our power to extend it to a united Europe and to pass it on, further enriched and ennobled, to succeeding generations."[106] He had not given up yet, and he was determined to press ahead.

On December 14, the EC completed a draft European identity paper. "The Nine members of the European Communities have decided that the time has come to draw up a document on the European identity. This will enable them to achieve a better definition of their relations with other countries and of their responsibilities and the place which they occupy in world affairs," an official press release stated.[107] On December 19, Kissinger met with French Foreign Minister Michel Jobert. "I think the NATO declaration is coming along quite well and we should leave further negotiations to our Ambassadors," Kissinger said. Both men recognized the damage that had been done to the Atlantic alliance over the course of the previous year. "I feel like paraphrasing Churchill and saying that never did a man do so much for so little reward," Jobert said. "Or perhaps we should say that there was never so much effort for so little purpose,"

[104] NATO, C-VR(73)74, "Verbatim Record of the Meeting of the Council held on Monday, 10th December, 1973, at 9:30 a.m. at NATO Headquarters, Brussels," December 10, 1973.
[105] Karl Kaiser, "Europe and America: A Critical Phase." *Foreign Affairs* 52 (1974): 727.
[106] NARA, RG 59, CFPF, Telegram from American Embassy London to Secretary of State, "Secretary's Address to Pilgrims Society," December 12, 1973, London 14609.
[107] NARA, RG 59, CFPF, Telegram from American embassy Copenhagen to Secretary of State, "European Identity Paper," December 14, 1973, Copenhagen 3173.

Kissinger added.[108] On December 20, Kissinger also met with President Pompidou, who was now being attended full-time by his personal physician almost everywhere he went. He even started to miss diplomatic events that he had attended for years.[109] Only months later was the full extent of his bone cancer revealed.

The Nixon administration stewed in frustration over the Year of Europe negotiations with the EC after the latter agreed on a position of neutrality in the Yom Kippur War, a position that the United States considered to be pro-Arab and anti-Israel.[110] On February 9, 1974, Kissinger lamented, "our forces give Europe the security to bitch at us ... the last thing we want is a rupture. But now we are putting a Band-Aid on a cancer. We have tried and they have kicked us."[111] The Germans were so tired of Michel Jobert that they suggested that France should move toward a "half in/half out" position in the EC, as in NATO.[112] Although transatlantic relations were a mess, Kissinger comforted himself with the knowledge that the EC was in an even bigger mess. "We have broken the Community, just as I always thought I wanted to," he said to Brent Scowcroft.[113] Nixon felt the same way. "The point is the European Community, instead of having that silly unanimity rule, learned they can't gang up against us ... people will see it later, Henry. By God it was a hell of thing."[114]

Then, everything changed. On February 28, 1974, British Prime Minister Edward Heath was defeated, and a more American-friendly Labor party under Harold Wilson came to power. What a difference a political shake-up made. New Foreign Secretary James Callaghan echoed complaints about the EC that sounded as if they could have been written by Henry Kissinger himself. The new British government immediately accelerated progress on the NATO agreement, "The Declaration on Atlantic Relations," which previously had been known only as the

---

[108] RMN, NSC, Box 56, Memorandum of conversation between Henry Kissinger and Michel Jobert, Quai d'Orsay, December 19, 1973.

[109] PRO, FCO 30–2401, "President Pompidou's Health," undated [December 1973].

[110] Buchan, 4.

[111] RMN, NSC, Box 1028, "Presidential/HAK Memcons," memorandum of conversation among President Nixon, Henry Kissinger, George Shultz, William Simon, and Brent Scowcroft, San Clemente, February 9, 1974.

[112] NARA, RG 59, CFPF. Telegram from American Embassy Bonn to Secretary of State, "FRG, France and Europe: German Bitterness Intensifies," February 14, 1974, Bonn 2461.

[113] RMN, HAK Telcons, Box 24, February 12, 1974, 7:45 p.m.

[114] RMN, HAK Telcons, Box 24, February 14, 1974, 6:15 p.m.

nameless "EXS/74/70." Ambassador to NATO Donald Rumsfeld emphasized the importance of moving forward with the NATO document. "The
main point in so far as the public was concerned was not the different
assessments allied countries might make of changes in the world situation
but the joint action they proposed to take for their defense, bearing in
mind these changes and the continuing ties between them."[115] After
further progress has been made by the March North Atlantic Council
meeting, Secretary General Luns noted, "a critical point had been reached
not only in East-West relations but also within the Alliance itself."[116]
Surprisingly, Michel Jobert agreed. "Although the discussions had been
protracted, the Communiqué was very succinct," he said. Belgian
Ambassador to NATO André de Staercke affirmed Jobert's view and
"expressed the conviction that within the next few weeks the Council
would be able to agree on a version which, although not perfect, would
reaffirm the solidarity of the fifteen member countries." The meeting
ended on a high note. "The Alliance remained as necessary as ever: it
was the starting point for détente and for the collective defense. It was also
the focus of the Atlantic dialogue on changes in inter-Allied relations – a
difficult process, but one which could strengthen the cohesion and solidarity of the Alliance," Danish Ambassador Ole Bierrign concluded.

Following the arrival of a British government more friendly to the
United States, changes in France and Germany were next. On April 2,
Georges Pompidou died, and a more conciliatory French government
under newly elected President Valéry Giscard d'Estaing was formed.
New Foreign Minister Jean Sauvagnargues stated, "c'est la fin de la
dispute la plus inutile du monde."[117] Henry Kissinger monitored the
situation closely. "The trend in France is toward the left and left is anti-
American," he said to his staff. "I would rather break the European
Community than have it organized against the U.S. Only the French
have a strategy and it is anti-American."[118]

German Chancellor Willy Brandt resigned on May 6, bringing pro-
American Helmut Schmidt to power. These new leaders stated that they
were concerned with correcting the declining state of transatlantic

[115] NATO, C-R(74)1, "Summary record of a meeting of the Council held at the NATO
     Headquarters, Brussels, on Wednesday, 9th January, 1974 at 10:15 a.m.," January 29,
     1974.
[116] NATO, C-R(74)11, "Summary record of a meeting of the Council held at the NATO
     Headquarters, Brussels, on Thursday, 14th March, 1974 at 10:15 a.m.," March 14,
     1974.
[117] Jacques Ogliastro, *Le Monde*, June 20, 1974.
[118] *FRUS*, 1969–1976, Volume E-15, Part 2, 50.

relations that they had observed in opposition during the preceding year. They were also not opposed to the United States maintaining an observer position at EC meetings (often Helmut Sonnenfeldt or Arthur Hartman), which further sped up the negotiations process. The United States took advantage of more pragmatic and pro-American European leaders by calling a meeting with EC political directors over March 11–12. Kissinger announced that the conclusion of the meetings would "facilitate a visit to Western Europe by President Nixon in the second half of April."[119] A complete draft EC resolution was completed on March 5, 1974.[120]

Despite the arrival of a new government, some French remained bitter toward Henry Kissinger, especially Henri Pierre, the Washington correspondent for *Le Monde*. In addition, Michel Jobert may have departed the Quai d'Orsay, but he remained a popular figure and did not hide his future national political ambitions. "Mr. Kissinger often reacts like many European immigrants who have become American citizens. Without renouncing European culture, with which he is imbued, but retaining with good reason some grievance towards Europe, he remains suspicious and takes his distance with regard to Europe," Pierre wrote.[121] Kissinger struck back at the French. According to Arthur Burns, Kissinger called Burns and asked if there was anything the Federal Reserve could do to damage Michel Jobert. "Henry at times strikes me as a madman; a genius, yes, but he has a lust for power – a good pupil of Nixon's and Haldeman's, or perhaps one of their teachers? What outrageous thinking on his part!" Burns recorded in his diary.[122] "What do you think of these fucking Europeans?" Kissinger asked White House Chief of Staff Alexander Haig. "They can't be right and I think the French will get isolated," Haig responded, noting that Nixon was just as upset. "I was told to get 'the football'[123] at 2:30 [p.m.]."[124]

---

[119] RMN, NSC, Box 688, Telegram from American Embassy Bonn to Secretary of State, "US/EC Declaration: Commentary by German Political Director," March 5, 1974, Bonn 3538.

[120] NARA, RG 59, CFPF, Telegram from American Embassy Bonn to Secretary of State, "FRG Press Reaction to Latest Dispute Between U.S. and EC Nine," March 7, 1974, Bonn 3685.

[121] NARA, RG 59, CFPF, Telegram from American Embassy Paris to Secretary of State, "French Press and Secretary's Remarks to Congressional Wives," March 12, 1974, Paris 6189.

[122] GRF, Papers of Arthur Burns, Handwritten Journals, 1969–1974, Box 1, April 19, 1974.

[123] The "nuclear football" is a briefcase from which the President of the United States can authorize a nuclear attack.

[124] RMN, HAK Telcons, Box 25, March 16, 1974.

Joe Kraft devoted his March 26 *Washington Post* column to transatlantic relations. "The Year of Europe is going to come out all right after all. The president and Dr. Kissinger are backing off their demand for a statement of overall principles."[125] On April 6, President Nixon and Chancellor Brandt met in Paris, a somber occasion because both men were in Paris to attend the funeral of President Pompidou.[126] Nixon noted that the growing isolationist trend in the United States worried him and that it was one reason why the Year of Europe must be wrapped up soon. Nixon said that there were no problems in bilateral relations between the United States and Germany and that cooperation between these two nations, along with the United Kingdom, should be sufficient to bring closure to the current discussions related to the declarations.[127] Privately, the Americans had concluded that "the death of President Pompidou and the French elections offer an opportunity to advance U.S. interests by putting relations with France and Europe on a better footing."[128]

An unlikely catalyst, the Canadian government helped to push negotiations along. Ottawa was the host for the upcoming NATO summit on June 16–19, and the Canadian government hoped that the NATO declaration could be signed by NATO foreign ministers there.[129] "The NATO meeting here in Ottawa has gone extremely well, with the new Foreign Ministers from Britain, France, and Germany all contributing to a far more constructive mood than last December," Kissinger reported to his staff.[130] The title that American Ambassador to NATO Donald Rumsfeld had suggested for the document, the "Declaration on Atlantic Relations," was the titled formally adopted.[131] Following the meeting of the NATO foreign ministers, that would leave only the final step of the signing by heads of state in Brussels on June 26, 1974. On the second communiqué, drafted by the EC, the Germans noted that the EC foreign ministers had

[125] NARA, RG 59, CFPF, Telegram from Secretary of State to American Embassy Moscow, "Press Material," March 27, 1974, State 60840.

[126] PRO, FCO 46–558, Memorandum from British Embassy Paris to Foreign and Commonwealth Office, "The Death of President Pompidou," April 17, 1974.

[127] *AAPD* 1974, Gespräch des Bundeskanzlers Brandt mit Präsident Nixon in Paris, April 6, 1974, 115.

[128] RMN, NSC Box 680, telegram from American Embassy Paris to Secretary of State, "U.S.-European Relations," May 8, 1974, Paris 11128.

[129] NARA, RG 59, CFPF, Telegram from American Embassy Ottawa to Secretary of State, "NATO Declaration: Canadian Views on British Text," May 22, 1974, Ottawa 1554,

[130] *FRUS*, 1969–1976, Volume E-15, Part 2, 60.

[131] NARA, RG 59, CFPF, Telegram from Secretary of State to American Embassy Jidda, "Title of NATO Declaration," June 15, 1974, State 128360.

reached a "Gentlemen's Agreement on consultations with the United States in order to conclude the declaration," even though it would not be ready in time for the signing of the NATO document.[132] The delay on the EC document did not upset Kissinger, who seemed quite happy to let it fail so that the EC could be blamed. "At a minimum we should so toughen the EC Declaration that it will fail," he suggested to his staff.[133] Sonnenfeldt liked the idea. "We can tell the Nine that they have been naughty and are not ready for a mature relationship," he said.[134]

The new French government, led by forty-one-year-old Prime Minister Jacques Chirac, was not as troublesome as past French leaders. Chirac "represents two things: a new generation of politicians who are not direct heirs of de Gaulle and are therefore relatively uninhibited by Gaullist rhetoric and past positions," the U.S. Embassy in Paris summarized.[135] The Chirac government quickly set to repairing the damage done to transatlantic relations in the past. "We are friends and allies. ... I really do feel that all these discussions run into the category of artificial problems," French Foreign Minister Sauvagnargues told U.S. Ambassador to Paris John Irwin.[136] "Sauvagnargues and [Valéry] Giscard [d'Estaing] are probably more disposed to work with the United States than any combination of president and foreign minister since the Fourth Republic," Irwin said.[137] In fact, the biggest remaining trouble over concluding the EC and NATO declarations came from an unlikely source: the United Kingdom. Foreign Secretary Callaghan refused to sign any document that referred to "European Union."[138] Such difficulty foreshadowed a larger problem on the horizon for the EC.

The Brussels summit on June 26 came off as planned, ending months of gridlock. References to "European Union" had been expunged, replaced by "European region." "I am tired of a crisis with them every six months," Kissinger said.[139] The declaration was much weaker

[132] *AAPD* 1974, Aufzeichnung des Referats 204, June 14, 1974, 171.

[133] *FRUS*, 1969–1976, Volume E-15, Part 2, 50.

[134] *FRUS*, 1969–1976, Volume E-15, Part 2, 51.

[135] NARA, RG 59, CFPF, Telegram from American Embassy Paris to Secretary of State, "Jacques Chirac, New Prime Minister of France," May 29, 1974, Paris 13007.

[136] RMN, NSC, Box 680, Telegram from American Embassy Paris to Secretary of State, "Meeting with Foreign Minister Sauvagnargues," June 7, 1974, Paris 13847.

[137] RMN, NSC, Box 680, Telegram from American Embassy Paris to Secretary of State, "Your Meeting in Ottawa with Foreign Minister Sauvagnargues," June 14, 1974, Paris 14541.

[138] RMN, NSC, Box 688, Telegram from American Embassy Bonn to Secretary of State, "Atlantic Declaration: the European Union Question," June 7, 1974, Bonn 9055.

[139] *FRUS*, 1969–1976, Volume E-15, Part 2, 51.

than the United States originally had in mind, but at least it affirmed the importance of the Atlantic alliance on the twenty-fifth anniversary of NATO. Secretary General Joseph Luns opened the summit and then turned the floor over to President Nixon. "When the treaty was signed in Washington twenty-five years ago, Paul Henri-Spaak called it 'an act of faith in the destiny of Western civilizations.' The Declaration on Atlantic Relations which we will sign today is a reaffirmation of that faith," Nixon said.[140] There was unanimous endorsement of the president's speech, almost as if the attendees knew it was Nixon's last major foreign policy address. Prime Minister Wilson compared the success of the Atlantic Declaration to the deep anxieties felt twenty-five years earlier. German Chancellor Schmidt, the bona fide economics expert at the summit, took a more precautionary view, noting the emerging economic strains facing the alliance, including inflation and increased prices of oil and raw materials.[141] He noted that, for the first time, major industrial nations might not report an income increase for their workers, a problem started by the erosion in confidence in Bretton Woods.[142] There was no official French response because France was a no longer a member of the North Atlantic Council. It was fitting that an initiative begun in late 1972 with American rhetoric, German caution, and French isolation ended much the same way.

The second communiqué, drafted in the EC, did not come to closure as easily. "We have no objection to leaving the U.S.-EC declaration in abeyance," Nixon said to Prime Minister Wilson.[143] In fact, it would not be until the resignation of Richard Nixon that European leaders completed the second communiqué that addressed the political and economic aspects of transatlantic relations. As both outgoing Nixon advisors and incoming Ford advisors predicted, it would take until 1975 to complete what started as the EC half of the Year of Europe. In a speech by Senator Henry M. Jackson to the Pilgrims of Great Britain on November 11, 1974, Jackson stated: "Apart, we will find neither solutions to nor sanctuary from our common peril. When the Pilgrims gathered a year ago

[140] RMN, NSC, Box 669, Telegram from American Embassy Brussels to Secretary of State, "Text of President's Opening Statement to NAC, June 26, 1974," June 26, 1974, Brussels 4583.

[141] RMN, NSC, Box 669, Telegram from American Embassy Brussels to Secretary of State, "Summary of NAC Plenary Discussion, June 26, 1974," June 26, 1974, Brussels 4584.

[142] *FRUS*, 1969–1976, Volume E-15, Part 2, 281.

[143] RMN, NSC, Box 54, briefing book for President's meeting with British Prime Minister Harold Wilson, Residence of the U.S. Ambassador, Brussels, June 26, 1974.

to hear Secretary of State Kissinger, the Western alliance ... proceeded to march off in as many directions as there were marchers."[144]

The EC drafts related to the Year of Europe and European identity were eventually folded into the Helsinki Accords, long after the Year of Europe was forgotten and Richard Nixon was forced into early retirement in California. The Helsinki Accords, signed on August 1, 1975, by thirty-five nations set in motion the beginning of the G-7 – then the United States, United Kingdom, France, Japan, Italy, Germany, and Canada. The G-7 first met during November 1975 to coordinate the economic policies of the major industrial democracies, meetings that continue to the present day.

* * *

The Year of Europe was an ambitious foreign policy initiative that took place in the shadows of the Vietnam War, Soviet-American arms talks, rapprochement with China, the Yom Kippur War, EC expansion and integration, and an escalation of the Watergate investigation. The transatlantic relationship had simply experienced too much trauma in too short a time period. For Europeans, the feeling of rejection was still too fresh following the way they had been treated during the dismantling of the Bretton Woods system, starting in 1971. For the United States, Nixon and Kissinger came to believe that Europeans were too self-absorbed with the European integration movement and that they had subordinated the Atlantic alliance in the process.

These events simultaneously caused a breakdown in the European integration movement and transatlantic relations. It remains perhaps the greatest lost opportunity of Nixon foreign policy, and something Henry Kissinger regrets even decades later. As Alistair Horne summarized, the Year of Europe was Kissinger's least successful initiative, "even though, with his special European interests, it was one closest to his heart."[145] All of the governments of the major nations involved – United States, France, Germany, and the United Kingdom – fell in 1974 within a span of six months. After tensions had been reduced between the United States and the Soviet Union and China in Nixon's first term, by 1973, the need to overhaul transatlantic relations was long overdue. "A healthy U.S.-European relationship is the best way to keep the Soviet Union and China

[144] NARA, RG 59, CFPF, Telegram from American Embassy London to Secretary of State, "Address by Senator Henry M. Jackson to the Pilgrims of Great Britain," November 11, 1974, London 14680.
[145] Horne, 121.

in line," Nixon said on numerous occasions.[146] The Year of Europe was intended to be just as bold an American diplomatic maneuver as were American negotiations with China and the Soviet Union.

The Year of Europe failed due to four main obstacles. First, although Britain was traditionally a close ally of the United States, with its adhesion to the EC, the British FCO did not know how to mesh its American policy with its newly created European policy. The FCO did not receive proper leadership from 10 Downing Street. Publicly, the British government was pro-Europe, but privately the FCO under Alec Douglas-Home sought closer ties with the United States after he realized the flaws in the Heath foreign policy of trying to have the best of both the Atlantic and European alliances. Second, the French were publicly against most of the Year of Europe initiative, especially anything that dictated a timetable for closer European cooperation or had to do with defense cooperation. Bilaterally, the French were interested in discussing both defense and economic cooperation with the United States, as long as progress on these subjects was not linked to other topics. Third, the German government under the Social Democratic Party had foreign policy ambitions in the area of détente with the Soviet Union and these were incompatible with closer bilateral relations with the United States as long as both sides feared what the other might be doing. These *Ostpolitik* overtures also caused a rupture in the Franco-German relationship that had been rooted in the EC since 1963, a closeness that was temporarily replaced by the Anglo-French relationship. This dramatic shift was, as Prime Minister Heath himself noted, sealed in a secret agreement between himself and French Foreign Minister Michel Jobert "in the garden of Number 10."

Finally, for the United States, the failure to achieve a Vietnam ceasefire agreement and the decision to escalate bombing in December to promulgate a January 1973 ceasefire caused an irreversible loss of credibility with European allies. Too much time was lost between mid-November and mid-January, when Nixon planned to launch his European initiative. When the Year of Europe was again jumpstarted in the spring of 1973, the lack of presidential leadership that led to Kissinger's misfired April speech resulted in an entire summer of additional lost time. The speech should have been given by President Nixon, not by the presidential assistant Europeans considered suspicious for negotiating so secretly and

---

[146] RMN, NSC Box 1028, Memorandum of conversation among President Nixon, Henry Kissinger, George Shultz, William Simon, and Brent Scowcroft, San Clemente, February 9, 1974.

extensively with the Soviets and Chinese. This was not to say that Kissinger could not have delivered an appropriate and effective April speech, but oversights in language that insulted the Europeans confirmed that they could never compete for American attention alongside the Soviet Union or China. Kissinger's excuse that he was "short on time" when he prepared the April speech only brought confirmation of this view.

Once these delays extended into the fall of 1973, numerous Congressional constraints were put on Nixon's foreign policy. He was a foreign policy president whose control of that area was in permanent decline. In an era of increasing American insularity, as well as the increasing scrutiny placed on the Nixon White House, Congress attempted to take the reins of foreign policy making. The Watergate investigation intensified, the three major European governments all fell in the first half of 1974, and fresh efforts to improve transatlantic relations could not be revived again until after Nixon's resignation. Although the Year of Europe was the most ambitious plan to improve Atlantic unity since the Marshall Plan, its failure resulted in the lowest point in transatlantic relations since World War II. The failure of the Year of Europe cannot be separated from the scandal that doomed it – Watergate. Like Alistair Horne, today we, too, can wonder: "What Kissinger might have achieved but for that lowering cloud we cannot know with any certainty."[147]

[147] Horne, 399.

6

Britain is out

The year 1974 was the most turbulent in Nixon-era transatlantic relations. U.S.–European ties were at the lowest point since World War II
after the failure of the Year of Europe. The Anglo-American "special
relationship" was threadbare. The Franco-German *moteur* that had
driven European integration since the 1957 Treaty of Rome was stalled.
The British, French, and German governments all fell in the first half of
the year. President Nixon's resignation in August brought a relative
unknown to the White House. The major industrialized nations did
not seem to have an answer to the challenges of the 1970s, including
stagflation, rising energy prices, and food shortages. Cumulative unad-
dressed problems in the areas of defense, trade, and monetary policy
created a bleak outlook for another disappointing year in transatlantic
relations.

However, by mid-1975, the situation was significantly improved. The
process of European integration was relaunched as a result of a revitalized
Franco-German commitment rooted in the friendship between Valéry
Giscard d'Estaing and Helmut Schmidt. Giscard, Schmidt, and Secretary
of the Treasury George Shultz developed an extremely close and productive relationship, one that had no parallel in earlier history. The U.S.-UK
relationship, strengthened in large part by the efforts of Harold Wilson
and James Callaghan on the one side, but also by the continuity into the
Ford administration of Secretary of State Henry Kissinger on the other,
was again closer than it had been for a decade. The year 1975 marked
the beginning of a time of more harmonious bilateral political relations
between the United States and France, Germany, and the United
Kingdom. In this sense, perhaps détente was not the complete failure

that it was so quickly labeled to have been: the Ford years did enjoy transatlantic dividends rooted in the tumult of the Nixon years.[1]

The key to the transformation of and amelioration in transatlantic relations was the successful renegotiation of British membership of the European Community (EC). It is a subject that has been largely ignored by scholars even though it was extremely vital to the Anglo-American "special relationship," European integration, and transatlantic relations in general. It brought an unknown leader, Margaret Thatcher, to the head of the Conservative Party. At a time of Watergate and escalating domestic political crisis in the United States, the process of British renegotiation of membership in the EC also resulted in a sustained, intense period of diplomatic communication between the American Embassy in London and the Department of State in Washington. Top U.S. policy makers learned a valuable lesson from the experience of the Year of Europe: do not push the EC to act before Europeans reach their collective position. The United States acted much more cautiously during British renegotiation, especially since the stakes were higher. American diplomats in Europe provided weekly and sometimes even daily updates for Washington.

The seventeen-month sequence of summits and high-level political meetings held between January 1974 and June 1975 came dangerously close to ending Britain's alliance with Europe, and at least one other nation – Denmark – planned to follow the United Kingdom out of the EC. Prominent Europeans and Americans stated that if Britain were to exit the EC, the result could have splintered the entire Western alliance. An isolated postcolonial Great Britain would have been forced to restructure all of its major alliances in Europe – political, military, and economic. If such an outcome had come to fruition, the United States was prepared to sever the "special relationship." "No special relations," Nixon said to Kissinger. Instead, "they'll have the relation[ship] with the French."[2] American contingency planning concluded that a weakened Britain could become a "drain" in a "lop-sided" alliance. However, American policy makers and influentials such as Henry Kissinger and John McCloy avoided such a rupture at all costs. Unlike during the Year of Europe, when these and other policy makers were publicly skeptical about the future of European integration (and privately concluded that further

---

[1] In a recent essay, N. Piers Ludlow also explores these questions. See N. Piers Ludlow, "The Real Years of Europe? U.S.-West European Relations during the Ford Administration," *Journal of Cold War Studies* 15:3 (Summer 2013): 136–161.

[2] *FRUS*, 1969–1976, Volume E-15, Part 2, 31.

integration was no longer in American interests), during British renegotiation they tried to publicly remain distant from an issue they considered to
be a European affair of the heart, even while, privately, American leaders
tried to exert influence on the outcome.

At the eleventh hour, when cooler heads prevailed and all sides realized
the potential consequences of a British exit not just for the EC, but also for
NATO and more broadly for transatlantic relations, critical budgetary
concessions by the EC – backed by Germany – compelled the United
Kingdom to soften its secessionist rhetoric. Progress toward European
integration has always come on the back of crisis, but the case of British
renegotiation was the greatest, most prolonged crisis in the history of
the EC up to that point. Once the matter was resolved, by mid-1975, the
solution set a future pattern of British behavior within the EC – the
budgetary concessions that were the main result of the renegotiations
represented the first of numerous subsequent British EC budget
"rebates" – that has persisted to this day. Bilateral allied relationships
emerged stronger, and a system of consultation was established that
guided European nations and a weaker form of European integration
through the remaining difficult years of the 1970s, until EC expansion
and integration once again appeared on the agenda under the leadership
of European Commission President Jacques Delors in the 1980s.

* * *

At the beginning of 1974, the United Kingdom was in the midst of that
nation's most serious economic crisis since World War II. After joining the
EC in triumph a year earlier, on January 1, 1973, after two previous failed
attempts in 1963 and 1967, the remainder of the year witnessed sharp
increases in the prices of basic commodities such as food and energy,
which caused ballooning domestic inflation and a significantly worsened
national economic outlook. The Yom Kippur War resulted in a quadrupling of oil prices virtually overnight, forcing the government to enact
severe spending cuts that were already causing problems with the trade
unions, most notably the miners, who refused to accept wage discipline.
The problem came to a head during December, when Heath's Tory
government declared a state of emergency, reduced the work week to
three days to save electricity, and Chancellor Barber described the fiscal
situation as "the gravest since the war."[3]

[3] Bernard Donoughue, *Downing Street Diary: With Harold Wilson in No. 10* (London:
Random House UK, 2005), 4.

Much of the British electorate and opposition parliamentarians incorrectly blamed the newly acquired membership of the EC, the *acquis communautaires*,[4] and a perception of lost sovereignty over the administration of domestic policy. It was too coincidental that Britain's vanishing economic strength occurred in parallel with the governing Conservative Party's policy of establishing closer ties with the Six. Tory efforts under Edward Heath placed Britain on a road to full membership in the EC beginning in the late 1960s. Ireland and Denmark joined with the United Kingdom in the EC's first wave of expansion in January 1973. The process of gaining full membership fundamentally reoriented British foreign policy. After the failure of the first attempt to join the EC in 1963, in which Heath, as Lord Privy Seal, was a major figure under then Prime Minister Harold MacMillan, the Conservative government fell and brought the Labor Party and Euro-skeptic Harold Wilson to power from 1964 to 1970. De Gaulle came away from the negotiations impressed by Heath, about whom de Gaulle said "it is he who will bring Britain into Europe."[5] Rejected by Europe, Britain under Labor was forced to accept increased dependence upon the United States.[6] Heath, as opposition leader, remained pro-Europe, even while the second British attempt to join the EC failed in 1967, again condemned by the veto pen of French President Charles de Gaulle.

Then came the parliamentary elections of June 18, 1970. A disinterested electorate returned Edward Heath and the Conservative Party to power, and thus the "Britain in Europe" campaign once again returned to the national agenda. Heath was convinced that the third attempt to join the EC would succeed, especially after its greatest barrier to entry was removed: French President Charles de Gaulle resigned in April 1969. His successor, Georges Pompidou, was more moderate in his views toward Europe and British membership. Pompidou was eager to demonstrate his own policy and distanced himself from de Gaulle, whom he had served as Prime Minister since 1962. Heath signaled an interest in joining Europe even before the 1970 election returned him to power:

In the next year or two there may be another opportunity for Britain to join in this process. If this effort is to succeed it must be most carefully prepared, for public

---

[4] The *acquis communautaire* is term for the accumulated legislation, legal acts, and court decisions that together are considered the body of European Union law.

[5] RMN, White House Special Files, President's Personal File, Box 84, "Fact Sheet: Prime Minister Heath."

[6] Kathleen Burk and Melvyn Stokes, eds., *The United States and the European Alliance since 1945* (Oxford: Berg, 1999), 119.

opinion in Britain could not tolerate a third failure. Britain's application to join the EEC [European Economic Community] remains on the table with those of the other applicant countries. The next step so far as Britain is concerned must be for the Six to signify that they are all ready to begin negotiations on our application.[7]

After de Gaulle's death in 1970 and the arrival of new leadership in both France and Germany, Heath had the window of opportunity he needed. "The time has come to establish that British policies are determined by British interests," he said.[8]

Once in power, Heath had difficulty implementing his vision of a Britain with equally strong ties to both the United States and Europe. Such difficulty was rooted in his government's poor job of communicating to the British electorate and key allies such as the United States his decision to finally and determinedly enter the EC, and at nearly any cost. Some observers claimed that the Heath government lacked skilled communicators. The government's reputation became tarnished by a "gratuitously abrasive style," both at home and abroad.[9] Whereas U.S. President Richard Nixon clearly placed emphasis on the maintenance of the Anglo-American "special relationship," Heath was more distant, which caused the perception of disagreement with his Foreign Secretary, Alec Douglas-Home. The United Kingdom no longer held the position it once did in Washington, and, in London, American views no longer assumed first place in British calculations either. "I declared that I did not favor the suggestion of a 'special relationship' between our two countries," Heath said to Nixon during a White House visit in December 1970.[10]

This alarmed U.S. policy makers, who had heretofore been traditional supporters of European integration. If the prospect of further European integration and the subsequent accession of the United Kingdom to the EC meant a degradation of transatlantic ties, then European integration was not something seen as desirable in Washington.[11] Heath soldiered on, convinced that joining Europe was the best vehicle for Britain to remain a

---

[7] Edward Heath, "Realism in British Foreign Policy." *Foreign Affairs* 48 (October 1969), 42–43.

[8] NARA, RG 59, CFPF, Telegram from American Embassy London to Secretary of State, "The Changing Anglo-American Relationship," November 28, 1973, London 13892.

[9] David Butler and Dennis Kavanagh, *The British General Election of February 1974* (New York: St. Martin's Press, 1974), 10–11.

[10] Edward Heath, *The Course of My Life: My Autobiography* (London: Hodder & Stoughton, 1998), 472.

[11] David P. Calleo, "The European Coalition in a Fragmenting World." *Foreign Affairs* 54 (1975), 98.

great power. "In a world of growing powers Britain has been shrinking in her influence even in comparison with those countries of like size and like potential," Douglas-Home commented.[12] Britain's best hope was to exert leadership and influence from within the EC. This view was consistent with American policy at the time, although Nixon changed his mind later. "It was a horrible mistake that we pushed them into Europe," he confided to Henry Kissinger.[13] At the same time, both Nixon and Kissinger believed it was essential that a British role in Europe prevent a Franco-German polarization within the EC. It was insoluble position.

Once achieved, British membership in the EC was more beneficial for Europe than for Britain. Contemporaneous records of the EC indicate that Britain would experience some "economic and monetary problems" after joining Europe, including a negative balance of payments, movements of capital, and investment.[14] British participation in the Common Agricultural Policy meant higher food prices in the United Kingdom. Heath himself complained that "price levels agreed upon for a community of Six are not necessarily right for a community of Nine."[15] In July 1973, the British Mission to the EC sent a damning assessment of the first seven months of British membership to the Foreign and Commonwealth Office (FCO). The assessment was quoted at length in the *Sunday Times* on July 29. "All the evidence of seven months' membership suggests that EEC is a disaster for Britain," the report summarized.[16] Within the British government, only the FCO remained loyal to the original decision to join Europe as the weakened British economy continued to subsidize the Common Market while getting very little in return. The U.S. Mission to the EC concluded that the challenges of enlargement for the EC meant that there had been delays toward further integration, improving the odds of a "crisis."[17] Heath became isolated both within his own government and the Conservative Party.

---

[12] Alec Douglas-Home, "Our European Destiny" (London: Conservative Group for Europe, 1971), 3–4.

[13] *FRUS*, 1969–1976, Volume E-15, Part 2, 31.

[14] HAEU, Papers of Emanuele Gazzo, Box 127, Report from European Commission, "L'Elargissement de la Communiaute Europeenne," January 22, 1973.

[15] NARA, RG 59, CFPF, Telegram from American Embassy London to Secretary of State, "Heath Speech on the European Community," May 17, 1973, London 05814.

[16] NARA, RG 59, CFPF, Telegram from American Embassy London to Secretary of State, "Press Reports of HMG Dissatisfaction with Common Market," August 1, 1973, London 08883.

[17] NARA, RG 59, CFPF, Telegram from U.S. Mission to the European Community to Secretary of State, "The European Community Seven Months after Enlargement – An Assessment," August 14, 1973, EC Brussels 04686.

American policy makers were partially to blame. "U.S. proposals concerning the Year of Europe are forcing the EC members to concentrate their efforts on seeking to establish a European identity, but this internal EC process is a slow one."[18] The pressure to respond to the proposal for a Year of Europe distracted Europeans from addressing internal EC problems. Meanwhile, the British government was informed that its contributions to the EC budget would increase from around US$312.5 million to an estimated US$395 million during 1974.[19] Heath went on the defensive, giving a long interview to *The Guardian* on November 2 designed to highlight the ways in which Britain benefited from membership in the EC.[20] He blamed the Labor Party for disparaging his effort to secure British membership in the EC. Heath said that withdrawal from the Community was not an option.

Former Prime Minister and Labor Party leader Harold Wilson increasingly designed himself as the "anti-Heath" alternative, which also, by extension, meant he was the anti-Europe alternative; this even though Wilson joked while eating a lunch of a plate of ham and a can of beer with French mustard that he was clearly "not anti-foreigner."[21] At its October all-party conference, Labor committed to calling for a general "renegotiation" of the terms of British entry to the EC if it were brought back to power. Labor also committed to a popular referendum on continued British membership in the EC, which was controversial since it meant the consensus of Parliament would not be sufficient to settle the matter. Such a threat was not taken very seriously by Heath. Wilson had his chance at governance from 1964–1970 and was democratically removed from power by a dissatisfied electorate. Surely the British people would not flip-flop again. And surely Wilson would not make Europe the primary issue of his party's platform. The issue split the Labor party in the 1972 vote on entry to the EC, and pro-Europe Roy Jenkins was forced to resign over the issue.[22]

---

[18] NARA, RG 59, CFPF, Telegram from American Embassy London to Secretary of State, "Britain and the European Community at the Summer Break," August 17, 1973, London 09538.

[19] NARA, RG 59, CFPF, Telegram from American Embassy London to Secretary of State, "Britain and the European Community at the Summer Break," August 17, 1973, London 09538.

[20] NARA, RG 59, CFPF, Telegram from American Embassy London to Secretary of State, "Heath Interview on the Benefits of EC Membership," November 2, 1973, London 12863.

[21] Donoughue, 21.

[22] Donoughue, 6.

The new Labor platform gained the backing of the Trade Union Congress (TUC), a significant endorsement that helped to ensure that renegotiation of British membership in the EC would be taken up by more than a fringe subset of the Labor Party. With Heath maintaining his unpopular pro-Europe stance, the Labor Party's anti-Marketeers fanned the flames of opposition. Heath continued to regard British entry into Europe as his principal contribution to history. However, since entry, the Labor Party refused to take up its allocation of British seats in the European Parliament and opposed EC policies such as the CAP, which raised domestic food prices in order to pay agricultural subsidies to European farmers. Polls in early 1974 showed that the average Briton was noticeably less enthusiastic about the EC and was primarily concerned about the rising costs of energy and food since British entry the year before. The EC could not be blamed for everything, but the coincidence in timing of the economic downturn did not bode well for Heath. The prices of industrial raw materials also increased, and this led to industrial action by British miners that reduced coal output by 30–40 percent. The quadrupling of oil prices as a result of the 1973 Yom Kippur War resulted in a significant check on the Western shift away from coal to oil, which had been under way since the end of World War II.[23] The initial euphoria following Britain's entry into the EC was quickly muted.

More unpopular than ever, by mid-January 1974, the British media rumored that Heath would call an early election.[24] He considered using the snap election to gain a new mandate in his struggle with the miners, following a vote of 81 percent of the members of the National Union of Mineworkers for a strike on February 4.[25] If the Conservatives were to have any chance of remaining in power for the long term, they needed to win a snap election quickly, while the Labor Party was still divided in its official stance with respect to British membership in the EC. Heath hoped he would be returned with a slightly increased majority and, thus, a mandate to remain in power for an additional full five-year term. He wrongly assumed that others would agree with his view that long-term EC membership could solve Britain's short-term economic problems.

[23] NARA, RG 59, CFPF, Telegram from American Embassy London to Secretary of State, "Britain's First Year in the European Community," January 11, 1974, London 00491.
[24] NARA, RG 59, CFPF, Telegram from American Embassy London to Secretary of State, "Prospects of an Early General Election Appear Closer," January 14, 1974, London 00612.
[25] Möckli, 303.

That might have been a convincing assumption a decade earlier when he worked on the first British application in 1963, but, by 1974, the EC itself was facing many of the same economic challenges as Britain. Life in the EC was not nearly as rosy as Heath promised it would be. His public cozying up to the EC also came at a considerable cost to the Anglo-American alliance. This worried those who depended on close U.S.-UK ties, especially those in the defense sector.

Speaking at the Reform Club in London on January 25, NATO Secretary General Joseph Luns said that unless the trend of lessened British interest in close ties with the U.S. was reversed, special ties could disappear altogether.[26] German Finance Minister Helmut Schmidt said at the Royal Institute of International Affairs in London that the EC had found itself in its current economic crisis after positioning itself in opposition to the United States over the previous year. The EC took on more simultaneous reforms than it could handle. "We wish to achieve everything too rapidly, considering the uphill task to be accomplished before solutions can be reached," Schmidt said.[27]

By February 1974, oil now cost US$10 a barrel, up from US$2.50, causing a devastating combination of inflation and recession.[28] Washington hosted an energy conference of all of the major Western heads of state on February 4 to discuss rising energy costs. All EC heads of state were in attendance, except France, which sent Foreign Minister Michel Jobert out of protest over what it saw as American meddling in European affairs. "The French arrived at the Washington Energy Conference determined to block a major U.S. initiative to unite the leading industrialized countries in a cooperative approach to the energy crisis," Helmut Sonnenfeldt reported to Henry Kissinger.[29] France was not opposed to cooperation on energy, but the twofold problem was yielding to American leadership and giving imprimatur to the multilateral forum blessed by the conference.

The conference marked the beginning of the end for Jobert, who lost credibility with his European colleagues as a result of his performance

---

[26] NARA, RG 59, CFPF, Telegram from American Embassy London to Secretary of State, "Speech By NATO Secretary General Luns to Reform Club, London," January 29, 1974, London 01299.

[27] NARA, RG 59, CFPF, Telegram from American Embassy London to Secretary of State, "Speech by FRG Finance Minister Schmidt on the Current State of the EC," February 4, 1974, London 01590.

[28] Grosser, 278.

[29] *FRUS*, 1969–1976, Volume E-15, Part 2, 48.

during the conference.[30] "In the end the other eight Community members abandoned the French and a common EC position when France proved unyielding. The Conference then endorsed an essentially U.S. position," Sonnenfeldt reported.[31] At that very moment, when the EC had the opportunity to speak with one voice on economic policy, one of its stated the key objectives during the Year of Europe, the disarray in the EC was evident to all.[32] Secretary of State Henry Kissinger took advantage of the disarray and placed the blame on the British. The Heath government, in his view, had gone too far to please the French. "There is a feeling in this government that Heath is some kind of decadent Gaullist. The French poison everybody's well, and that's not good company to be in," he said.[33] Kissinger got exactly what he wanted from the conference. "I don't give a damn about energy; that is not the issue," he said. "The issue is to break the other Europeans away from the French."[34]

A few days after the energy conference, the timetable for the British election was set for February 28, with the provocative theme of "Who Governs Britain?" Media commentary was that the campaign would be the most bitter and divisive in living memory.[35] Both major political parties were nearly evenly divided in the House of Commons, and the opinion polls on the final weekend before the election were as tight as could be.[36] Each projected significant numbers of open seats due to retirements, including thirty-four Conservatives and twenty-six Labor MPs, which meant that Labor actually needed fewer votes to win the general election of 1974 than the Tories needed to win in 1970. It was also the only postwar general election to have been called in a time of emergency. The election also had another unusual element of uncertainty: the largest redrawing of House of Commons constituencies since 1950, which resulted in a massive redistribution of parliamentary seats. Of the 630 constituencies, major changes were made in 311, and minor adjustments were made in another 124.[37]

---

[30] Weisbrode, 264.

[31] *FRUS*, 1969–1976, Volume E-15, Part 2, 48.

[32] Grosser, 281.

[33] NARA, RG 59, CFPF, Telegram from Secretary of State to American Embassy London, "News Article on US-UK Relations," February 4, 1974, State 023197.

[34] *FRUS*, 1969–1976, Volume E-15, Part 2, 50.

[35] NARA, RG 59, CFPF, Telegram from American Embassy London to Secretary of State, "British General Election: Opening Salvos," February 8, 1974, London 01817.

[36] Donoughue, 33.

[37] NARA, RG 59, CFPF, Telegram from American Embassy London to Secretary of State, "Background on British General Election," February 11, 1974, London 01890.

Harold Wilson presented the Labor Party election manifesto on February 12. He confirmed the rumors that he intended to make renegotiation of the British terms of EC membership a major campaign issue. Until the results of the renegotiation had been approved by the British electorate, he said, Britain would put an immediate stop to further integration into the EC. In a direct attack on Prime Minister Heath, Wilson charged that Britain had been "dragooned into the Common Market on terms dictated by Monsieur Pompidou."[38] The Germans watched the evolution of the British election campaign with interest and also took aim at the French. The gloves were off. They suggested that after Jobert's behavior at the Washington energy conference France should consider taking a "half in/half out" position in the EC, as in NATO.[39] Other Europeans believed that, as President Pompidou's health continued to decline, after secretly having been diagnosed with a rare bone cancer in late 1972, the Foreign Ministry, still staffed by orthodox Gaullists, attempted to retake control of French foreign policy.[40] Michel Jobert struck back at his European critics by remarking at a press conference that the next time he saw his European colleagues, he would greet them with "*bonjour, les traitres!*"[41]

On polling day, February 28, the British electorate marked their ballots with a distinct lack of enthusiasm. With a slipping economy and rising inflation on their minds, they were forced to make a decision between two political parties: the Conservatives led by Edward Heath and Labor led by Harold Wilson. Each had failed to improve the British economy as Prime Minister. Wilson walked around the corner from Labor Party headquarters to the polling booth on Great Smith Street. His office had forgotten to mail his postal vote, so he had to vote in person. Wilson was in high spirits, and a big crowd of journalists trailed him. People along the walk wished him well, including a truck driver of about twenty-five who leaned out of

---

[38] NARA, RG 59, CFPF, Telegram from American Embassy London to Secretary of State, "General Election: Wilson Seeks to Make EC an Issue," February 13, 1974, London 02006.

[39] NARA, RG 59, CFPF, Telegram from American Embassy Bonn to Secretary of State, "FRG, France and Europe: German Bitterness Intensifies," February 14, 1974, Bonn 02461.

[40] NARA, RG 59, CFPF, Telegram from American Embassy Paris to Secretary of State, "Impact of Washington Energy Conference on French European and Atlantic Policies," February 20, 1974, Paris 4444.

[41] NARA, RG 59, CFPF, Telegram from American Embassy Paris to Secretary of State, "Foreign Minister Jobert's Remarks to French Deputies on WEC," February 22, 1974, Paris 04667.

his truck window and enthusiastically shouted, "Good luck, Harold, my old son!"[42]

For the electorate, it was convenient to blame British membership in the EC rather than more nebulous menaces such as stagflation or a growing current account deficit.[43] Turnout was higher than expected, which suggested that working-class voters were motivated to vote, a boon for the Labor Party even though the media treated Wilson as though he would soon be nothing other than a back bench MP.[44] Shortly after the polls closed at 10:00 p.m., it became clear that no single party had emerged with a majority. Although not winning outright, Wilson defied his critics. The Labor Party won a plurality, but most observers agreed that there would be another general election before the end of the year.[45]

This put the British government in an even less admirable position than before the election. It was the first election since 1929 to produce no overall majority or even a majority when adding up the results of the winning party (Labor) and the third party (Liberal). Although the Conservatives polled almost 250,000 more votes than Labor (37.9 to 37.2 percent), Labor held 301 seats to the Tories' 296, with 23 additional seats spread around other parties, including the Liberals with 14 seats and 19.3 percent of the vote.[46] Harold Wilson was invited to form a government, but, lacking a mandate, he was forced to fill his cabinet with moderates. The most ardent anti-Marketeers on the Labor front bench, such as Michael Foot and Peter Shore, were shifted to less visible dossiers for employment and trade, which kept them at arm's length from a direct role in the negotiations over Britain's membership in the EC.[47] The most important result of the election was that former Chancellor of the Exchequer James Callaghan, known for his pro-American and pro-NATO views, became Foreign Secretary.[48]

---

[42] Donoughue, 40.

[43] NARA, RG 59, CFPF, Telegram from American Embassy London to Secretary of State, "Election Day Musings," February 28, 1974, London 02592.

[44] Donoughue, 43.

[45] NARA, RG 59, CFPF, Telegram from American Embassy London to Secretary of State, "General Election: The Morning After," March 1, 1974, London 02639.

[46] NARA, RG 59, CFPF, Telegram from American Embassy London to Secretary of State, "Political Deadlock," March 2, 1974, London 02686.

[47] Depending on one's persuasion, Michael Foot and Peter Shore were the leaders of either the euroskeptics or the eurorealists. See the discussion in Michel Gueldry, "La Grande-Bretagne et l'Europe: du pragmatisme insulaire au partenariat sceptique," *L'Europe en formation no. 353-354 (automne-hiver 2009)*: 93–110.

[48] NARA, RG 59, CFPF, Telegram from American Embassy London to Secretary of State, "The New Labor Cabinet," March 5, 1974, London 02781.

The American government was overjoyed. After suffering through four years of Heath, who prioritized closer relations with France and the EC at the expense of relations with the United States, the new British government was highly skeptical of the EC and placed great value on closer transatlantic ties. American Ambassador to London Walter Annenberg saw the window of opportunity and immediately cabled Secretary of State Henry Kissinger. "We should therefore use the time Labor has in office to do some constructive and persuasive work in helping to shape Labor Party attitudes on international issues against the possibility that it might later return to office with a clear majority."[49] The United States benefitted from British membership in the EC and had an interest in keeping Britain in. The White House believed that Britain's view of the world was broader than that of most other European countries, based on its wider and longer experience outside of Europe. Britain's continued dependence on imported food and raw materials meant that the British government blocked the most protectionist ideas of the EC, which was also in the interests of the United States. Britain also prevented EC industrial policy from restricting American investment in Europe, since London also benefitted to such a great degree on substantial inflows of foreign investment.

Henry Kissinger did not wait long to reach out to the new British government. He instructed American Ambassador to London Walter Annenberg to hand deliver a congratulatory message to Foreign Minister Callaghan and request that he receive a delegation of Kissinger's closest aides. "After reading your congratulatory message, Callaghan said he was delighted. As to the second in which you offered to send Messrs. [Helmut] Sonnenfeldt and [Arthur] Hartman to meet him next week, Callaghan said 'the answer is yes,' " Annenberg reported.[50] After Prime Minister Wilson met Annenberg on March 5, Kissinger and Sonnenfeldt agreed that it was "a good thing to have Callaghan in the Foreign Office – he is less volatile than [Home]."[51] Annenberg noted that "he [Wilson] did not wish to criticize the previous British government but he thought the tie with

[49] NARA, RG 59, CFPF, Telegram from American Embassy London to Secretary of State, "The British General Election," March 5, 1974, London 02785.

[50] NARA, RG 59, CFPF, Telegram from American Embassy London to Secretary of State, "Messages from Secretary Kissinger to Foreign Secretary Callaghan," March 6, 1974, London 02889.

[51] RMN, HAK Telcons, Box 25, March 5, 1974, 9:06 a.m.

France had made U.S.-UK relations somewhat uneasy."[52] Word went out from the Foreign Secretary's office that U.S.-UK relations were to have top priority in the new Wilson government.

* * *

While the Americans hastily sought to renew ties with the British government, the French and Germans anxiously awaited the first public statements by Wilson and Callaghan as to the direction the new British government would take with respect to its promise to carry out a renegotiation of the terms of British membership in the EC. On the one hand, the new French government considered that perhaps the Gaullists in the Foreign Ministry had gone too far in recent French foreign policy. On the other hand, the French were not pleased that the Labor Party was forming the new British government, which, if it carried out its platform pledges, would likely reposition Britain closer to traditional views on foreign policy. That included being more critical of French leadership in the EC.

Georges Suffert of the French pro-government weekly *Le Point* was the first to publicly voice such concerns. Even the French media had started to turn on Jobert. In a lengthy March 4 article entitled "Is Michel Jobert Wrong?" Suffert said that Michel Jobert's Gaullist foreign policy placed France in a difficult position. "The consequences of his obstinacy are now becoming apparent," Suffert wrote. "France is beginning again to be disliked abroad, as in the heyday of General de Gaulle." For many long-time observers of French politics, de Gaulle's legacy made his obstinacy more forgivable. As Suffert suggested, "the General's outbursts were more excusable than those of Michel Jobert: One was big, the other is small. That's the whole difference." Despite what many of Jobert's critics said, he was not an orthodox Gaullist. Although the General barely believed in European integration, Jobert claimed to be ardently pro-Europe. De Gaulle probably would have also refused to attend the February Washington energy conference out of his objection to "blocs," whereas Jobert's rationale for not supporting the conference was that Europe should have stood together and spoken with one voice on the subject. Jobert believed that the president of the European Council should have represented all of Europe. Since the presidency of the EC at the time was held by the Germans, that meant that France would have been

---

[52] NARA, RG 59, CFPF, Telegram from American Embassy London to Secretary of State, "Messages to PM Wilson from President Nixon and Secretary Kissinger," March 5, 1974, London 02810.

represented by German Foreign Minister Walter Scheel. That certainly would not have been an orthodox Gaullist position.[53]

To European chagrin, Foreign Secretary Callaghan reassured Labor Party supporters in a public speech on March 9 that "no advice – however well intentioned – will deter the British government from an immediate and fundamental renegotiation of the terms of entry [to the European Community]."[54] This sentiment was then reaffirmed during the Queen's speech a few days later, which opened the new session of parliament.[55] In her speech, Queen Elizabeth II noted that "my government will seek a fundamental renegotiation of the terms of entry to the European Economic Community. After these negotiations have been completed, the results will be put to the British people."[56]

Prime Minister Wilson assembled a kitchen cabinet of advisors on March 13 to begin the process of renegotiation. Since the EC already had an upcoming summit of agriculture ministers scheduled for March 21–22 to discuss farm prices, the British government planned to survey commonwealth countries in advance about their views of continued British membership in the EC. At the summit, the British government would be represented by agriculture minister Fred Peart, a strident anti-Marketeer.[57] Much of this plan was also repeated by Foreign Minister Callaghan to Secretary of State Henry Kissinger's visiting delegation of Helmut Sonnenfeldt and Arthur Hartman on March 15, but with one added twist.

During the meeting, which all major British broadsheets referred to as a Kissinger *mea culpa* in order to rehabilitate Anglo-American relations, Callaghan confirmed he would undertake a renegotiation of British membership in the EC but would not leave an "empty chair" in the EC, a criticism of the French.[58] Callaghan stated that he was "agnostic" over the

---

[53] NARA, RG 59, CFPF, Telegram from American Embassy Paris to Secretary of State, "Le Point Article on Fonmin Jobert," March 7, 1974, Paris 5836.

[54] NARA, RG 59, CFPF, Telegram from American Embassy London to Secretary of State, "Advice by EC Commissioner Thomson on Renegotiating the Terms of Entry," March 11, 1974, London 03082.

[55] NARA, RG 59, CFPF, Telegram from American Embassy London to Secretary of State, "Queen's Speech: Foreign Policy," March 12, 1974, London 03154.

[56] PRO, CAB 129-175, "The Queen's Speech on the Opening of Parliament," March 11, 1974.

[57] NARA, RG 59, CFPF, Telegram from American Embassy London to Secretary of State, "UK Gears Up for EC 'Renegotiations,' " March 14, 1974, London 03249.

[58] NARA, RG 59, CFPF, Telegram from American Embassy London to Secretary of State, "British Press on Secretary's March 14 Remarks on US-European Relations," March 15, 1974, London 03298.

outcome of the renegotiation process, but would ensure that British interests were defended. Specifically, these included (1) continued access to the British market by goods of third countries and (2) reducing Britain's financial contribution to the EC budget. Callaghan, noting past difficulty in U.S.-EC relations during the Year of Europe, stated that, unlike Heath, "we are not interested in an anti-American direction."[59]

On Britain's contribution to the EC budget, the FCO confirmed two days later that it thought British contributions to the EC's budget should be brought in line with Britain's share of EC gross national product. The FCO argued that whereas Britain's economy represented 18 percent of the EC gross national product, Britain was expected to pay 26 percent of the EC budget.[60] Callaghan made these points public in his opening speech in the House of Commons on March 19, which was devoted almost entirely to the topic of the EC. He referred to the EC goal of "European union" by 1980 as "clearly unrealistic" and said that the United Kingdom would firmly oppose any attempt to integrate Europe by means of a confrontation with the United States. He confirmed that the renegotiation would begin with the subject of agriculture because of the decisions that needed to be taken at the March 21–22 summit of EC agriculture ministers. Callaghan stated that if the renegotiation could not take place within the framework of the existing EC treaties and natural working order of the EC, then the British government would be forced to consider whether the treaties themselves – including the Treaty of Rome – would have to be amended.[61] Callaghan shed little light during this or other public addresses on specific British demands but predicted "a hot summer of negotiation."[62]

Callaghan reiterated these thoughts to the eight British ambassadors to EC nations in London on March 20, where he said that although he claimed to be agnostic about the renegotiation and the EC, he thought the Community plans for further integration and economic and

[59] NARA, RG 59, CFPF, Telegram from American Embassy London to Secretary of State, "Sonnenfeldt/Hartman Consultations with Foreign Secretary Callaghan," March 16, 1974, London 03361.
[60] NARA, RG 59, CFPF, Telegram from American Embassy London to Secretary of State, "British View on Renegotiation of Terms of Membership in European Community," March 18, 1974, London 03418.
[61] NARA, RG 59, CFPF, Telegram from American Embassy London to Secretary of State, "Callaghan Speech on the EC and US-European Relations," March 19, 1974, London 03454.
[62] NARA, RG 59, CFPF, Telegram from American Embassy Bonn to Secretary of State, "Callaghan Visit to Bonn – March 21, 22," March 23, 1974, Bonn 04623.

monetary union were "moonshine, just fancy words" and that, as "a simple man," he was "interested primarily in the effect of UK membership on the British housewife."[63] This was his most candid assessment to date. Moreover, "he could not at this stage say whether he preferred that Britain stay in the Community or not ... if after renegotiation the Government felt that the Community corresponded with British interests and the realities of European relations with the United States we should stay in: otherwise we should not."[64] Wilson and Callaghan expected to be taken seriously.

The German government was sympathetic with the British position on renegotiation. "The Community cannot simply reject all of Great Britain's suggestions," Helmut Schmidt admitted.[65] Such a view had something to do with the low point that had been reached in Franco-German relations after the French return to more traditional Gaullist policies. Callaghan expressed essentially the same points to the German Foreign Office on March 21–22 that he had stated earlier on March 15 to Kissinger aides Sonnenfeldt and Hartman. The Germans listened with sympathy and raised no fundamental objections with the British position. Chancellor Brandt stated his willingness to begin high-level discussions to resolve the British concerns "immediately."[66]

The Irish government, also a new member of the EC, expressed sympathy for the British. "The terms of entry negotiated by the Conservative Government insofar as Britain's budgetary contribution was concerned were unfair to Britain," Permanent Representative Brendan Dillon said to Helmut Schmidt.[67] FCO Deputy Under Secretary Oliver Wright credited the cautious approach taken by the British government for the conciliatory German response. Wright suggested that navigating the renegotiation process was like the British Grand National, the grueling annual race infamously known for the

---

[63] NARA, RG 59, CFPF, Telegram from American Embassy Bonn to Secretary of State, "British Government's Views on Europe: Callaghan's Discussion with British Ambassadors to EC Countries," March 26, 1974, Bonn 04807.

[64] PRO, PREM 16–72, "Meeting of Ambassadors to EEC Countries: Wednesday 20 March," March 20, 1974.

[65] PRO, PREM 16–99, Notes of interview by *Le Monde* with Helmut Schmidt, June 11, 1974.

[66] *AAPD* 1974, Gespräch des Bundeskanzlers Brandt mit dem britischen Außenminister Callaghan, March 21, 1974, 99.

[67] PRO, PREM 15–2074, Letter from Michael Palliser, Office of the United Kingdom Permanent Representative to the European Communities to Oliver Wright, FCO, February 25, 1974.

many horses that do not finish due to injury. Like the Grand National, Wright stated, with the EC renegotiations "it was important to take the hurdles one at a time. If you thought about the second hurdle ahead, you might trip over one immediately in front of you." Wright had reason to be hopeful. The meeting of the EC agriculture ministers on March 21–22 had gone better than the British government had expected, which confirmed for some skeptics that it would indeed be possible to complete renegotiation within the EC's normal course of operations.[68] With the Germans in agreement and the French marginalized, British concerns were taken seriously.

Foreign Secretary Callaghan formally opened the process of renegotiation with his April 1 speech to the EC Council of Ministers in Luxembourg. This first meeting between Callaghan and his European colleagues marked the beginning of Britain's policy of "semi-detachment" with Europe, which has continued to the present day.[69] The theme of his address was the undue financial burden imposed upon the United Kingdom to support the EC budget, including support to European farmers.[70] "It will come as no surprise to you that the Labor Government opposes membership of the Community on the terms that were negotiated at the time of our entry in January 1973," he said.[71] "We shall negotiate in good faith and if we are successful in achieving the right terms we shall put them to our people for approval. But if we fail, we shall submit to the British people the reason why we find the terms unacceptable and consult them on the advisability of negotiating the withdrawal of the United Kingdom from the Community."[72] There was not much new revealed in Callaghan's speech. He carefully followed the Labor Party's manifesto from the February election, a course of action that must have indicated that either Wilson and Callaghan had not developed their own positions

[68] NARA, RG 59, CFPF, Telegram from American Embassy London to Secretary of State, "British Views on Callaghan Visit to Bonn," March 26, 1974, London 03819.
[69] Möckli, 302.
[70] NARA, RG 59, CFPF, Telegram from American Embassy London to Secretary of State, "EC Renegotiation," March 28, 1974, London 03905.
[71] PRO, PREM 16–72, "Memorandum from Harold Wilson to Ministers in Charge of Departments," April 1, 1974.
[72] PRO, CAB 129–175, "Renegotiation of the Terms of Entry into the European Economic Community: Text of a Statement delivered by the Secretary of State for Foreign and Commonwealth Affairs in the Council of Ministers of the European Communities in Luxembourg on the 1st of April 1974," April 1, 1974.

yet or that they truly were as agnostic as they claimed to be.[73] Europeans did not know which was more frightening.

* * *

Then, on April 2, 1974, came the first in a series of events that gradually helped to calm the secessionist rhetoric of the British government: the death of French President Georges Pompidou. The German Foreign Office was the first to speculate that Pompidou's death would produce a "cooling off period" that would expose the new British government to "some of the realities in Europe" and help to temper the initial sharp demands for renegotiation.[74] The British slackened the pace of renegotiation, believing that Pompidou's death "added a new element of uncertainty to the problem, more particularly in the timescale."[75] Most importantly for renegotiation, Pompidou's death almost certainly meant the removal of Michel Jobert from the Quai d'Orsay. During a meeting on April 6 between Prime Minister Wilson and Chancellor Brandt while both men were in Paris for Pompidou's funeral, Wilson told Brandt that he thought Pompidou's passing would help improve relations between the EC and the United Kingdom.[76]

Britain also received encouragement from the United States. In Paris for Pompidou's funeral, a scandal-laden Nixon insisted on walking down Rue Saint-Honoré with Wilson. His own domestic political position still fragile, Wilson concluded "that will lose me the election."[77] Although the American government was very pleased thus far with the initial Labor efforts to ameliorate Anglo-American relations, the American Embassy in London noted that "at the same time, we should encourage Britain to view its ties with the U.S. as complimentary to, not a substitute for, its ties with the EC. If Britain remains in the Community, it would be a force for closer U.S.-EC cooperation." This communication from the Embassy was also the first glimpse at American doubt over the role of a United Kingdom outside the EC:

---

[73] John Pinder, "Renegotiation: Britain's Costly Lesson?" *International Affairs* 51.2 (April 1975), 153–154.

[74] NARA, RG 59, CFPF, Telegram from American Embassy Bonn to Secretary of State, "Europe in Aftermath of Pompidou Death: Initial FRG Views," April 3, 1974, Bonn 05429.

[75] PRO, FCO 46–558, Foreign and Commonwealth Office, Diplomatic Report No. 227/74, "The Death of President Pompidou: Her Majesty's Ambassador at Paris to the Secretary of State for Foreign and Commonwealth Affairs," April 17, 1974.

[76] *AAPD* 1974, Gespräch des Bundeskanzlers Brandt mit Premierminister Wilson in Paris, April 6, 1974, 113.

[77] Donoughue, 93.

We also have an interest in preventing a withdrawal that could precipitate a general unraveling of West European relationships, involving the partial or total disintegration of the EC, the revival of rivalries between NATO members, the growth of Nordic neutralism, and various other developments inimical to the preservation of a strong Western alliance. A special relationship with an introspective Britain, cast adrift from Europe and operating from a contracting economic and military base, would be of dubious value to the United States.[78]

The Germans went even further in encouraging the British government to remain in the EC. During Foreign Secretary Callaghan's visit to Bonn on March 21, he had a private discussion with Chancellor Willy Brandt. Although there is no record of the meeting, a leak in the press demonstrated that Brandt apparently reassured Callaghan that the German government would support British renegotiation, but on the condition that "Britain would not spring additional demands late in the negotiations."[79] The Germans knew the EC was divided on many issues and wanted to reduce the chance that Britain could exacerbate tensions further. This was a risky assurance by Brandt, unless, of course, he had advance notice of Pompidou's decline. Otherwise, Franco-German relations had deteriorated to such a degree at that point that Brandt probably no longer had sufficient influence to restrain the French government during the renegotiation process.

Most intriguing was that the leak revealing that Brandt had made such an assurance to Callaghan was not made by a German Foreign Office source, but by the Dutch Foreign Minister, Max van der Stoel. The EC, less France, had already come to terms with the British renegotiation demands and was actively working to determine a position that it could live with, with or without the French. Renegotiation was a process of intrigue, magnified further by the death of Pompidou and the jockeying for influence in the EC that began immediately thereafter. The U.S. Embassy in London observed the process very closely. "Our own view is that Callaghan is engaged in an extraordinarily complicated and delicate operation designed to hold in line both pro- and anti-Marketeers in the Labor Party, at least until the next general election. No one knows where his real sympathies lie or which way he is likely to go when the crunch

[78] NARA, RG 59, CFPF, Telegram from American Embassy London to Secretary of State, "Reflections on US-UK Relations and EC Renegotiation," April 5, 1974, London 04301.
[79] PRO, PREM 16–72, "Reactions to the Foreign and Commonwealth Secretary's statement: Discussion in the Colloquy between the President of the Council, Herr Scheel, and the Political Committee of the European Parliament," April 2, 1974.

comes."[80] In the midst of such turbulence, the EC had no choice but to
make early concessions as long as Wilson's and Callaghan's indifference
to the whole process was believable. Wilson and Callaghan reported to
the House of Commons that the Europeans' response "was clearly
sympathetic."[81]

The French had a different opinion. Although the official beginning of
British renegotiation was delayed due to the death of Pompidou and then
until new French elections could be held, the media was full of commentary on both sides of *la Manche*. The *Financial Times* commented on April
5 that the "death of President Pompidou and Foreign Secretary
Callaghan's speech April 1 on renegotiating terms of entry have brought
Europe to a period more dangerous and confused than any since the mid-
50s. Weak or uncertain governments in Britain, France and Germany;
nationalist bickering, menacing external pressures, both economic and
military, weak American government and energy crisis create a backdrop
for the last act of Gotterdammerung."[82] Many British political observers
concluded that Britain would surely withdraw from a disjointed and
ineffective EC. Frank Giles of the *Sunday Times* referred to Callaghan's
prospects for a successful renegotiation as "a man trying to set up a fried
bacon stall outside a synagogue."[83]

Michel Jobert was clear in his disapproval of the renegotiation process,
even refusing to refer to it using the word "renegotiation." Jobert
suggested that "the EC should not have to buy this horse twice."[84]
Despite the death of Pompidou, he concluded that European integration
could continue without the United Kingdom. "This had already been done
once, and England decided to take the train already in motion, moreover,
with a reduced ticket and with a preferential tariff," he said.[85] The disintegration of Europe could not have been clearer during a meeting on

---

[80] NARA, RG 59, CFPF, Telegram from American Embassy London to Secretary of State,
"Renegotiation among Fraternal Socialists," April 5, 1974, London 04358.

[81] PRO, PREM 16–72, "Statement by the Secretary of State for Foreign and Commonwealth
Affairs, the Right Honorable James Callaghan, MP in the House of Commons on
Wednesday, 3 April 1974," April 3, 1974.

[82] NARA, RG 59, CFPF, Telegram from American Embassy London to Secretary of State,
" 'Financial Times' on Timing of Renegotiation and Next Election," April 5, 1974,
London 04363.

[83] NARA, RG 59, CFPF, Telegram from American Embassy London to Secretary of
State, "Pessimism Over EC Renegotiation," April 8, 1974, London 04406.

[84] NARA, RG 59, CFPF, Telegram from American Embassy Paris to Secretary of State,
"Views of French Official on UK Renegotiation," April 10, 1974, Paris 08879.

[85] NARA, RG 59, CFPF, Telegram from American Embassy Paris to Secretary of State,
"Jobert Statement on French Foreign Policy," April 17, 1974, Paris 09329.

April 22 of the EC foreign ministers. Callaghan conceded that he was not opposed in principle to the idea of a "European union," but he claimed he still did not know what the term meant. When he asked his colleagues to define the concept, it was clear that no one really knew exactly what it meant. German Foreign Minister Walter Scheel, who had been present at the October 1972 Paris Summit during which then President Pompidou had created the term, admitted that "even the fathers of the phrase do not know exactly what it means."[86]

There was yet another setback for European integration. On May 6, German Chancellor Willy Brandt resigned after his Social Democratic Party refused to stand by him in the aftermath of an East German spy scandal, the "Guillaume Affair," in which it was disclosed that Günther Guillaume had gained unauthorized access to classified information. Although Brandt had never been a model of discretion, the idea that the spy also recruited female escorts for Brandt was simply too much to bear.[87] There were also rumors that somehow the episode was related to sexual blackmail against Brandt, which was something that Kissinger reported on in detail to Nixon.[88] That brought Helmut Schmidt to power, a notable turning point not just in the renegotiation of British membership of the EC, but also a capstone to a new generation of European leaders with different views on the future of Europe than their predecessors. Schmidt was also the first German Chancellor who truly excelled in both economic and foreign policy matters.

Only months earlier, Europe had been full of pro-EC leaders: Heath, Pompidou, and Brandt. Now they were ambivalent, or worse: Wilson, Schmidt, and another newcomer to be determined by French elections scheduled later in that month. The FCO panicked. What did Brandt's resignation mean for earlier assurances that Germany would support British renegotiation demands? The day after Brandt's resignation, the FCO North American Department, led by Lord Nicholas Gordon-Lennox, was urgently in touch with the U.S. Embassy in London to make a request for American analysis on the current situation at the earliest possible opportunity. Generally more pro-EC than Wilson or Callaghan,

---

[86] NARA, RG 59, CFPF, Telegram from American Embassy Bonn to Secretary of State, "EC Foreign Ministers Weekend Discussions at Schloss Gymnich – April 20–21," April 23, 1974, Bonn 06405.

[87] Hillenbrand, 334.

[88] *FRUS*, 1969–1976, Volume E-15, Part 2, 280.

the working level of the FCO sought assurance from the United States that it still officially supported European integration, especially while "the Foreign Secretary, who will play a key role in the decision on British membership in the Community, is still forming his own views about the validity of European unity and British cooperation with the continent."[89] Like Callaghan, newly installed German Chancellor Schmidt and Foreign Minister Hans-Dietrich Genscher were expected to place more emphasis on close ties with the United States than with the EC. There was "a general sense that Europe is coming apart at the seams," the U.S. Embassy in Paris commented.[90]

The previous focus of the press on British renegotiation temporarily shifted to the domestic political changes in France and Germany. Wisely, the British government decided that the cabinet subcommittee responsible for renegotiation, the European Community Strategy Committee, should postpone the government's renegotiation proposals until the next meeting of the EC Council of Ministers on June 4.[91] The British adopted a more moderate approach and attempted not to fan the flames in the EC caused by recent European political turbulence. Wilson tried to stay out of the debate between the "antis" and the "pros," not always with complete success. The fact that a Labor Cabinet had to be reminded during a decisive meeting on April 25 that the EC would continue to exist with or without the British was shocking to some who were in the room.[92] Wilson continued to struggle to keep not just his Cabinet in line, but to keep his government and party together.

On the eve of a new French election that would likely result in his exit from the French government, Jobert criticized the pro-Washington views of new Chancellor Helmut Schmidt. In an interview with *France Soir*, Jobert referred to the "customary rudeness" of Schmidt's remarks during the February Washington energy conference. Schmidt was happy to defend himself. "Mr. Jobert can speak of my rudeness, it doesn't embarrass me," he said. "I am surprised that he called it 'customary' as Mr. Jobert does not know me. If you want to know what people

[89] NARA, RG 59, CFPF, Telegram from American Embassy London to Secretary of State, "Interest in US Views on European Unity," May 7, 1974, London 05671.
[90] NARA, RG 59, CFPF, Telegram from American Embassy Paris to Secretary of State, "Brandt's Resignation: Preliminary View from the French Perspective," May 9, 1974, Paris 11318.
[91] NARA, RG 59, CFPF, Telegram from American Embassy London to Secretary of State, "EC Renegotiation," May 8, 1974, London 05741.
[92] Donoughue, 106.

think of me, ask Mr. Giscard d'Estaing or Mr. Michel Debré. They are the friends I have in France."[93] In fact, Valéry Giscard d'Estaing was elected the next president of France on May 19. He was expected to be much less ideological about his approach to the EC, unlike Michel Jobert, and he was expected to rein in the Quai d'Orsay. Giscard had an approach to the EC, relations with the United States and British renegotiation that was similar to that of Helmut Schmidt. Schmidt had never been pro-Europe in the sense that Jean Monnet had been, or even as Willy Brandt or Walter Scheel had been. During Schmidt's first speech as Chancellor he was decidedly cool on the subject. Schmidt had no reservations about throwing the baby (*Ostpolitik*) out with the bathwater (European integration).[94]

The British government carried out a survey of all of the commonwealth nations to gauge whether it was in their interests for the United Kingdom to stay in the EC. A favorite quip of the anti-Marketeers had always been that Britain had severed its international influence by choosing the EC over the commonwealth. However, surprisingly, all commonwealth nations – with the exceptions of Swaziland and Fiji – stated that they were not interested in going back to the old commonwealth and that they preferred that Britain remain in the EC. Rather than expressing concern that their economies had been damaged when their exports had lost preferential access to the British economy upon British entry to the EC, they stated that they had found new markets for their goods and that they liked that they could count on Britain to be a friendly force within the EC.[95]

Although this survey of commonwealth nations was reassuring for the prospects of successful British renegotiation, Gallup public opinion polls as of early June were not. The polls showed that, hypothetically, if at the outcome of renegotiation the British government recommended a negative vote on the referendum, the electorate would choose withdrawal from the EC. On the other hand, the polls showed that if the government supported a referendum vote to remain in the EC, it would be supported by the leadership of the opposition, business representatives, and most of the media. Yet there would still be a real risk that the popular referendum

[93] NARA, RG 59, CFPF, Telegram from American Embassy Paris to Secretary of State, "Brandt's Departure and the French Press," May 9, 1974, Paris 11327.

[94] NARA, RG 59, CFPF, Telegram from American Embassy Bonn to Secretary of State, "The Schmidt Government: A Preliminary Assessment of Domestic and Foreign Policy Problems and Prospects," May 24, 1974, Bonn 08287.

[95] NARA, RG 59, CFPF, Telegram from American Embassy London to Secretary of State, "EC Renegotiation – Commonwealth Trade," May 30, 1974, London 06756.

would fail. The electorate simply remained unconvinced, as shown by the 51 percent of those questioned who thought it had been a mistake for Britain to have joined the EC. Only 33 percent thought it had been right to do so.[96] With new governments getting settled in France and Germany, the difficult process of renegotiation lay ahead.

---

[96] NARA, RG 59, CFPF, Telegram from American Embassy London to Secretary of State, "Prospects for EC Renegotiation," June 4, 1974, London 06973.

7

Britain is in

At the June 4, 1974, European Community (EC) Council of Ministers, the British government officially began renegotiation discussions. The French refused to discuss the British problem in the EC as long as the word "renegotiation" was used because this term suggested revisiting a matter that had been, at least at the time, satisfactorily concluded. French President Giscard d'Estaing stated to German Chancellor Schmidt that his problem with the process was that the "British were not yet psychologically in the EC, and were at best looking in from the outside."[1] German Foreign Minister Genscher came to an agreement with French Foreign Minister Sauvagnargues that a study be created that addressed possible outcomes to the British problem. The study should avoid using the word "renegotiation," substituting "the correcting mechanism."[2]

Foreign Secretary James Callaghan delivered his address, and French Foreign Minister Savarguargues was critical. The British concluded that the French could still impose a veto on the renegotiation process, even with Michel Jobert out of office. In a compromise, Callaghan announced that he was in favor of the German suggestion for an EC-sponsored study that would consider the British problem and make projections through 1980. Before the summit, the French position was to deny that the British even had a legitimate complaint about their contributions to

---

[1] *AAPD* 1974, Botschafter Freiherr von Braun, Paris, an Bundesminister Genscher, June 4, 1974, 157.
[2] NARA, RG 59, CFPF, Telegram from American Embassy Bonn to Secretary of State, "EC Renegotiation," June 5, 1974, Bonn 08926.

the EC budget or any other aspect of EC membership.[3] British demands remained unchanged, including a general review of the CAP that included significant changes in subsidy levels and the products supported. Second, the British demanded that their contribution to the EC budget be substantially reduced and that this should happen as a result of revisiting the formula for determining contributions. British projections showed that whereas their budget contribution was expected to be 300–350 million EUA[4] in 1975, it was to rise to 700–800 million EUA in 1980.[5]

The British government emerged from the June 4 summit encouraged. Roy Hattersley, Minister of State at the Foreign and Commonwealth Office (FCO), believed that the prospects for a successful renegotiation were very good, and for several reasons. First, British demands were consistent with the EC treaties, which allowed for any member nation to recommend adjustments to the functioning of the EC if such operations could be proved to have caused an undue financial burden on a member nation. Second, there was a sufficiently strong commitment among states like Germany to keep Britain in, which meant it was in British interests to stay in the EC. Third, there was no practical alternative for Britain. There was no going back to the old commonwealth or to a European Free Trade Agreement (EFTA) type of arrangement.[6]

At a four-hour private meeting between Foreign Minister Genscher and Foreign Secretary Callaghan at the latter's Dorneywood estate on June 15, Genscher wanted Callaghan to understand that the EC had numerous economic and political problems that, some European colleagues concluded, the British did not fully understand.[7] Genscher explained the difficulty that Europeans such as the French had with the word "renegotiation," to which Callaghan responded that he merely desired a

---

[3] NARA, RG 59, CFPF, Telegram from American Embassy London to Secretary of State, "British View of EC Council of Minister's Meeting June 4," June 6, 1974, London 07087.

[4] At the time of these projections, a European unit of account (EUA), the forerunner to the European currency unit (ECU) and the Euro (EUR), was worth approximately US $1.20635 per EUA. The EUA came into being June 1974 and was equal in value to the previous SDR (Special Drawing Right). The value of the SDR/EUA was equal to one U.S. dollar until the dollar was devalued in December 1971 and subsequently floated in 1973, which caused the SDR/EUA to rise in value against the dollar.

[5] Pinder, 160–161.

[6] NARA, RG 59, CFPF, Telegram from American Embassy London to Secretary of State, "EC Renegotiation: Views of Roy Hattersley," June 13, 1974, London 07474.

[7] *AAPD* 1974, Gespräch des Bundeskanzlers Schmidt mit dem Präsidenten der EG-Kommission, Ortoli, June 11, 1974, 162.

process designed to "have a new look" at the terms of British membership in the European Community.[8] Callaghan added that he was not only no longer opposed to European political cooperation, but was "very much in favor" of it.[9] It helped the British that the Germans shared many criticisms of the EC, especially of the CAP, which had recently been splintered by the increasing number of floating European currencies.[10] Schmidt privately confided in Wilson that "three countries had an essential voice in Community affairs, and that it was the three Governments concerned who really mattered."[11]

When the American Embassy in Bonn was briefed after a long private meeting between Helmut Schmidt and Harold Wilson on June 19, the Embassy learned that Wilson, despite claiming neutrality on the renegotiation issue, "was positive and quite optimistic on renegotiation" and that the British had no intention of recommending changes to the Treaty of Rome.[12] "Renegotiation is now under way ... so far we have not needed to seek a confrontation, but in the months ahead we may have to face a confrontation on some issues. I am ready for that if necessary," Callaghan stated to the Cabinet on June 24.[13]

Meanwhile, in Paris, concerns centered on how the French government would proceed next on the "correcting mechanism," especially now that the French held the rotating presidency of the EC Council for the second half of the year. During a visit by Belgian Prime Minister Leo Tindemans to Paris on July 1–2, it was obvious to him how much different the tone of the Giscard government was as compared to that under Georges Pompidou. Giscard saw the February Washington energy conference as a turning point in French foreign policy. He believed that the energy crisis of 1973–74 was the most serious threat to French economic interests in recent memory. He also saw that the preservation of the CAP and the EC tariff regime were of vital national interest. Giscard believed that the

[8] *AAPD* 1974, Gespräch des Bundesministers Genscher mit dem britischen Außenminister Callaghan in Dorneywood, June 15, 1974, 177.

[9] NARA, RG 59, CFPF, Telegram from American Embassy Bonn to Secretary of State, "Callaghan-Genscher Meeting June 15," June 19, 1974, Bonn 09737.

[10] Pinder, 156–157.

[11] PRO, PREM 16–99, "Record of a Conversation between the Prime Minister and Herr Schmidt, Bonn: 19 June 1974," June 19, 1974.

[12] NARA, RG 59, CFPF, Telegram from American Embassy Bonn to Secretary of State, "Meeting of June 19 Between Chancellor Schmidt and Prime Minister Wilson," June 21, 1974, Bonn 09850.

[13] PRO, CAB 129–177, "Renegotiation and Related European Economic Community Questions: Memorandum by the Secretary of State for Foreign and Commonwealth Affairs," June 24, 1974.

sooner the issue of British renegotiation was over, the better so that more serious EC reforms could be addressed. Unlike Pompidou and Jobert, Giscard was not interested in creating an EC hostile to the United States, and he made it a goal to hold a major summit on these matters during the French term of EC Council leadership.[14]

The French communicated this more conciliatory attitude to the Germans and the British. During the first Franco-German summit between President Giscard and Chancellor Schmidt on July 8–9, they found common ground on pursuing common economic policies that created stability in the EC. The Giscard-Schmidt relationship long predated this meeting; they had established a working relationship during their earlier tenures as finance ministers of their respective nations. In a summit conducted in English, both sides had criticisms of the CAP, yet they agreed that the policy had to be preserved. They agreed that higher food prices were good for both economies.[15] British renegotiation was not a substantive point of discussion.[16]

Meanwhile, Henry Kissinger moved behind the scenes to speed up the renegotiation process, taking advantage of a slate of new European leaders who desired to make progress. "I think there has been a new climate in our relations. In my opinion, many of the differences we have had appeared much greater than the substance in them," President of the European Commission François-Xavier Ortoli said to Kissinger. Kissinger seemed confused over the trough that had been reached in transatlantic relations during the previous year. "When I look back, it is hard to see what it was all about . . . but let's not talk about the past. I agree with you that the climate is now much better."[17]

The positive atmosphere between Giscard and Schmidt carried over into the first official meeting between Wilson and Giscard a week later, on July 18–19. Although Prime Minister Jacques Chirac was not thrilled with the meeting called by the British, Wilson and Callaghan sought to allay French concerns over British renegotiation. The French government, led by Foreign Minister Sauvagnargues, was very firm that the Treaty of Rome not be modified and that the French were not willing to

[14] NARA, RG 59, CFPF, Telegram from American Embassy Paris to Secretary of State, "French European Initiative," July 10, 1974, Paris 16194.

[15] NARA, RG 59, CFPF, Telegram from American Embassy Bonn to Secretary of State, "July 8–9 Franco-German summit," July 10, 1974, Bonn 10941.

[16] *AAPD* 1974, Aufzeichnung des Ministerialdirigenten Fischer, Bundeskanzleramt, July 9, 1974, 206.

[17] RMN, NSC, Box 1029, Memorandum of Conversation between François-Xavier Ortoli and Henry Kissinger, July 4, 1974.

"renegotiate" British entry into the EC.[18] Neither side expected any great result from the meeting, since the intent of the occasion was simply an opportunity to feel out the other side's views on a variety of topics, even though most of the agenda centered on British renegotiation.[19] Neither side was prepared to get into any difficult discussions knowing that the British minority government faced another general election that would produce a new government with a surer mandate to negotiate on such issues.[20]

The date of the second 1974 British general election was fixed for October 10. Both the French and Germans lobbied the British in the hopes that their efforts would produce a more desirable election outcome, with Giscard hosting a "summit dinner" on September 14. In the run-up to the British election, the German government played a clever game with the French president.[21] Schmidt antagonistically suggested a second set of renegotiations, for the CAP. Specifically, he suggested holding "a second Stresa," a reference to the Italian city where the CAP has been originally drawn up in 1958. The French Ministry of Foreign Affairs had concluded that Schmidt – already known as no fan of the CAP – wanted "to tear up the CAP and start all over again."[22]

British opinion polls showed a Labor lead going into polling day. An increasingly desperate Conservative Party under Edward Heath went so far as to suggest, on October 6, that Heath would be willing to create a national coalition government with the Labor Party.[23] Heath's suggestion was a recognition that the Labor Party had successfully positioned itself as a populist government in order to maximize its electoral chances. However, the likelihood that the two old rivals – former Prime Minister Edward Heath and current Prime Minister Harold Wilson – could somehow form a government together seemed unlikely to most observers.

The American government was preparing for every possible outcome from the election, labeled the most important since 1945. Before the

---

[18] NARA, RG 59, CFPF, Telegram from American Embassy Paris to Secretary of State, "Anglo-French Summit, July 19," July 22, 1974, Paris 17810.
[19] NARA, RG 59, CFPF, Telegram from American Embassy London to Secretary of State, "British Views on Anglo-French Summit, July 19," July 25, 1974, London 09446.
[20] NARA, RG 59, CFPF, Telegram from American Embassy Paris to Secretary of State, "Anglo-French Summit, July 19," July 26, 1974, Paris 17810.
[21] *AAPD* 1974, Aufzeichnung des Bundeskanzlers Schmidt, September 3, 1974, 249.
[22] NARA, RG 59, CFPF, Telegram from American Embassy Paris to Secretary of State, "Views of French Official on EC Developments," September 19, 1974, Paris 22144.
[23] NARA, RG 59, CFPF, Telegram from American Embassy London to Secretary of State, "General Election: Three Days to Go," October 7, 1974, London 13030.

resignation of President Nixon, Secretary of State Henry Kissinger and German Foreign Minister Genscher met in San Clemente on July 26. The visit at the president's home capped a busy agenda that included key cabinet members, Senators, and even an inspection of an American B-52 and rocket factory in Grand Forks, North Dakota. Days before his resignation, the president had "aged noticeably," Genscher reported.[24] According to American Ambassador to Bonn Martin Hillenbrand, who escorted the German foreign minister to the Western White House, Nixon "surprised us all by his up-to-date information about issues and ability to articulate his thoughts clearly and precisely. This was not a man who had plunged to the borders of irrationality."[25] Nixon urged the Europeans to work together on British renegotiation and to consider issues of broader significance, such as instability in the Mediterranean caused by East-West tensions.[26]

After President Ford arrived at the White House, the American government cautiously encouraged the British to resolve the renegotiation process as expeditiously as possible. In one of the first summaries of the situation by Henry Kissinger for President Ford, Kissinger suggested that the need for the renegotiation, as well as the decline in transatlantic relations, should be blamed on Edward Heath. Heath, Kissinger noted, was "a doctrinaire person, Gaullist in his outlook, and the only anti-American UK Prime Minister in many years. He is a complex, sensitive man who tends to sulk. At the same time, he is a strong individual not afraid to take hard decisions despite their unpopularity."[27] As Alistair Horne summarized, the arrival of Gerald Ford at the White House was the end of bold American moves. "There would be no exciting new initiatives. It was a time of recuperation, of rehab – of domestic tidying up," he said.[28]

The American Embassy in London recommended "in a discreet and appropriate way" to make "unmistakably clear" to the British government that the United States preferred to see Britain remain in the EC. The alternative was seen to be a grave scenario:

---

[24] PAAA, ZA 101414, "Kabinettsitzung; Reise des Herrn Bundesministeres in die USA," July 30, 1974.

[25] Hillenbrand, 332.

[26] *AAPD* 1974, Botschafter von Staden, Washington, an Auswärtiges Amt, July 27, 1974, 225.

[27] GRF, NSA, Country Files, United Kingdom, Box 15, Memorandum from Henry Kissinger to President Ford, "Meeting with Edward Heath," September 10, 1974.

[28] Horne, 394.

If Britain opts out of Europe, the U.S.-UK relationship could become lop-sided and a drain on the U.S. Adrift from Europe, a progressively enfeebled Britain would find it hard to avoid becoming internationally irrelevant. The U.S. could not gain from such an outcome.

Britain, the American government argued, had in fact benefitted from EC membership. No further proof of this was needed than the fact that Prime Minister Wilson moved from his agnostic view of the EC to "qualified acceptance of British membership." Not only did Britain gain from affiliation with the markets of Europe, but so did the United States. Callaghan made it clear in private that he wanted the United States to retake a more active role in European affairs, after the cooling period that had occurred since the Year of Europe. "The Europeans are ambivalent about the United States. We want you to take the lead ... we welcome your leadership."[29]

The Wilson government came closest to representing American interests by proxy in the Community, with shared views on NATO, the role of U.S. forces stationed in Europe, trade and tariffs, and, more generally, on broader foreign policy questions. Henry Kissinger understood that. When he prepared President Ford for a meeting with Foreign Secretary Callaghan, Kissinger suggested, "at the outset of your meeting with Callaghan while the press is taking pictures, mention the excellent relationship and superb cooperation between our two governments, for which he, Callaghan, deserves much credit ... that would be a nice and harmless gesture for Callaghan at election time." Without Britain in Europe, the American government believed that "its withdrawal ... would set in motion an unraveling of the entire structure of Atlantic cooperation."[30] "If the British people ... opt for a little England solution, it is hard to see how this country can avoid slipping into international irrelevance. In such circumstances, the United States would have to reflect very carefully whether we would wish to carry on any kind of close (let alone 'special') relationship which would become an increasingly lop-sided and probably unacceptable burden," the American Embassy in London reported.[31]

***

[29] GRF, NSA, Memcons, Box 6, Memorandum of Conversation between President Ford and James Callaghan, September 24, 1974.

[30] GRF, NSA, Country Files, United Kingdom, Box 15, Memorandum from Brent Scowcroft to President Ford, September 24, 1974.

[31] NARA, RG 59, CFPF, Telegram from American Embassy London to Secretary of State, "A Declining Britain and the Anglo-American Relationship," October 8, 1974, London 13098.

The British election produced the result polls predicted, a slight majority for the Labor Party. As Henry Kissinger predicted to President Ford before the election, "the state of the British economy has been *the* issue in this election."[32] Although still ambivalent, the British electorate put their trust once again in the Labor Party as the best hope for the future of the economy. There was simply no better option. Even the Wilson team seemed without direction on the very night of their victory.[33] With just 39.2 percent of the vote, the tally represented the lowest of any majority government since 1922. The new House of Commons sat with 319 Labor and 277 Conservative MPs, with 39 additional MPs spread across other political parties. These figures represented a gain of eighteen for Labor and a loss of twenty for the Tories. Prime Minister Wilson got the mandate he wanted, even if he would have to work hard to control deep divisions in his own party.[34]

Henry Kissinger acted quickly to speak about the state of the world following the British election. In a James Reston *New York Times* article on October 13 entitled "Kissinger Sees the World on Verge of Historic Era," Kissinger spoke out just weeks after President Ford had pardoned former President Nixon about what he believed was then "one of the great periods of human creativity." Kissinger summarized the Labor Party's victory for President Ford. "The party has also run against the EC, arguing that the organization is a shambles and pledging a referendum on British membership ... they [the Tories] have also tried to stir the electorate on the EC issue, but, as with most other issues, have failed to arouse voter interest or passion," he said.[35]

Kissinger also reflected on the Nixon administration. "What I regret is that so much of the time had to be spent on the Vietnam War. If we could have got that behind us more rapidly, we could have brought the more positive side of our foreign policy (to the fore) at a time when attitudes were less rigidly formed," he said. "The real tragedy was Watergate, because I believe that at the beginning of President Nixon's second term, we had before us – due to changing conditions – a period of potential creativity. Instead, we had to spend almost all of our energy in preserving what existed, rather than building on the foundations that had been laid.

[32] *FRUS*, 1969–1976, Volume E-15, Part 2, 232.
[33] Donoughue, 217.
[34] GRF, NSA, Subject Files, Box 56, Memorandum from George S. Springsteen to Brent Scowcroft, "UK General Election Results," October 10, 1974.
[35] GRF, NSA, Country Files, United Kingdom, Box 15, Memorandum from Henry Kissinger to President Ford, undated.

Even the Year of Europe could have gone differently in a different environment. But you never know what opportunities may have been lost."[36] The time spent on Watergate victimized many opportunities.

Prime Minister Wilson returned to power with an enhanced majority. He benefitted from a secret American guarantee, communicated by back-channel on September 24, that no matter the outcome of the election, should Britain's economy or currency be affected negatively, President Ford stood willing to intervene. "I fully agree that, should such a contingency arise, it should receive our cooperative attention," Ford said.[37] The Queen opened the new session of Parliament on October 29, giving a speech that contained many of the points contained in her previous address earlier in the year at the opening of the short parliament. "My Government will energetically continue their renegotiation of the terms of the United Kingdom's membership of the European Economic Community. Within twelve months the British people will be given the opportunity to decide whether, in the light of the outcome of the negotiations, this country should retain its membership."[38] Wilson believed that his small majority in the House of Commons would enable him to restrain the left wing led by the anti-Marketeers through the process of the renegotiation and the referendum that was intended to follow.[39]

The German government called the Queen's speech a "positive presentation." The Germans recognized their own financial interests in achieving a positive outcome of British renegotiation and the British contribution to the EC budget.[40] The French remained skeptical, especially since the world economic situation had worsened, with higher inflation levels and energy prices. John Hunt, Secretary of the British Cabinet, stated that despite the British election, "renegotiation is taking place against a very different economic and political background from the earlier negotiations for entry."[41] Jean Dufourcq, Deputy Director for

[36] NARA, RG 59, CFPF, Telegram from Secretary of State to American Embassy Cairo, "Press Material," October 13, 1974, State 226130.

[37] GRF, NSA, Chronological Files, Box 1, "From the President to the Prime Minister, via Cabinet Line," September 24, 1974.

[38] PRO, CAB 129–179, "The Queen's Speech on the Opening of Parliament: Note by the Secretary of the Cabinet," October 24, 1974.

[39] NARA, RG 59, CFPF, Telegram from American Embassy Bonn to Secretary of State, "FRG Reaction to British Election Results," October 16, 1974, Bonn 16251.

[40] PAAA, ZA 105612, "Gegenwärtiger Stand der britischen Europapolitik," October 27, 1974.

[41] PRO, CAB 129–179, "Strategy and Priorities: Note by the Secretary of the Cabinet," October 14, 1974.

Western Europe at the French Ministry of Foreign Affairs, concluded that
it was too early to tell what the outcome of the British election would be
until the British government publicly declared whether it intended to
remain in the EC or not.[42]

Retiring American Ambassador to London Walter Annenberg had his
own views: "There was a perceptible disposition to diverge from the
United States during the Conservative government." The recent October
election that returned the Labor Party to power "should ensure the maintenance of easy, constructive relations with the United States." Annenberg
cautioned the State Department, though, that Britain was a nation with
"little sense of direction or national purpose." Annenberg argued that the
root of the problem was that the nation had not yet decided whether it saw
its future within or without the EC. "Continued British membership of the
European Community, in my view, is vital to Britain. It is also in the
interests of the United States. In Europe, Britain will help promote the
kind of open, cooperative relationships which we wish to see with
Western Europe. British withdrawal, however, would undermine our
policy in Europe and weaken the common defense."[43]

On November 20, former German Chancellor Willy Brandt resurfaced
and made a controversial suggestion that set a future pattern for EC
integration and enlargement. His suggestion was a two-tiered system of
EC membership. Rather than scrapping either existing or proposed EC
policies when trouble arose for one or more nations that were not ready to
take part – such as a common currency, a customs union, or the CAP –
those countries that were ready to press ahead should do so, and the
abstaining nations could catch up later. The Germans had long been
fond of a two-tier system of EC membership. Chancellor Kiesinger had
once suggested the idea to Henry Kissinger, noting, "two European bodies
are needed, a smaller political one and a larger one for economic
purposes."[44] Brandt's idea was that such a system would act as a compromise when the EC found itself in a stalemate. Given the timing of
Brandt's suggestion with the process of British renegotiation, the French
reacted as though Brandt proposed a mechanism for Britain to opt out of

---

[42] NARA, RG 59, CFPF, Telegram from American Embassy Paris to Secretary of State,
"French Reaction to UK Elections," October 23, 1974, Paris 25013.
[43] NARA, RG 59, CFPF, Telegram from American Embassy London to Secretary of State,
"For the President and the Secretary: United States Relations with the United Kingdom –
Ambassador's Retrospective," October 23, 1974, London 13818.
[44] RMN, NSC, Box 1023, Memorandum of Conversation between Chancellor Kiesinger
and President Nixon, August 8, 1969.

EC initiatives as it chose to do so. The French concluded that the proposal was hardly compatible with the concept of an increasingly united Europe.[45]

The French government called for an EC heads of state summit in Paris on December 9–10, 1974, during which the major topic of discussion was expected to be the "correcting mechanism." This kept with Giscard's wishes that the French would hold a major summit as a capstone to the French presidency of the EC in the second half of 1974. Giscard invited Wilson to Paris on December 3 for an opportunity to determine what could be achieved during the upcoming summit.[46] The Germans had already arranged their negotiating position with the British in advance during a mini Anglo-German summit in London over November 30–December 1. In a meeting at Chequers, Wilson and Callaghan reassured the visiting Germans, led by Chancellor Schmidt, that the United Kingdom intended to remain in the EC as long as agreement could be met on the remaining points under consideration, in particular the British contribution to the EC budget.[47] For the Germans, it was especially important to have British demands with respect to agriculture clarified, so that the Germans could start negotiating with the French.[48] Schmidt gave private assurance to Wilson that, should Britain stay in the EC, they "could count on the Germans, on the Dutch, on the Danish, and probably the Irish, in every field where he wanted to replace bureaucratic processes with political decisions made by political animals."[49] The Germans were more inclined to make concessions to the British because of the "estrangement" that had developed between Schmidt and Giscard, in particular over the French reaction to Brandt's two-tier membership proposal.[50]

In the process of this pre-summit positioning, the German government made a significant concession. They agreed to the creation of an EC regional fund designed to aid developing areas of the EC. Britain would

---

[45] NARA, RG 59, CFPF, Telegram from American Embassy Paris to Secretary of State, "Brandt's Speech on Europe's Future," November 20, 1974, Paris 27778.

[46] NARA, RG 59, CFPF, Telegram from American Embassy Paris to Secretary of State, "Wilson-Giscard Meeting December 3," December 3, 1974, Paris 28885.

[47] *AAPD* 1974, Botschafter von Hase, London, an Bundesminister Genscher, December 1, 1974, 346.

[48] PAAA, ZA 105613, "Schreiben vom PM Wilson an den Bundeskanzler vom 5.12.1974," December 13, 1974.

[49] PRO, PREM 16–77, Record of a Conversation at Chequers on Saturday 30 November 1974 at 10:15 p.m., November 30, 1974.

[50] PRO, PREM 16–77, Note of Talk with Herr Schmidt on Sunday 1 December 1974, 9:30 a.m.–10:00 a.m., December 1, 1974.

be a major beneficiary whereas Germany would not.[51] The German gesture also pleased France, which had overseas territories likely to benefit. Giscard still sought assurance before the upcoming summit that the British government was determined to remain in the EC before additional concessions were made. The French would not tolerate a situation in which the EC reached a compromise with the United Kingdom only to have the whole plan voted down by the British government after the summit was over. Wilson privately stated that "he was feeling a good deal happier about the possibility of an acceptable outcome to the renegotiation of the terms of British membership of the European Community."[52]

Opinion throughout the EC on the renegotiation was divided. Denmark, which joined with Britain in 1973, was sympathetic, noting "the difficulty new member states had in getting accustomed to the Community." The Belgians believed that if a solution was not found soon "an unacceptable solution could develop." The Netherlands stated that it was "pleased" with the way Britain presented its demands in terms of a "correcting mechanism." Luxembourg stated its continued preference "to find a solution within the context of the development of the Community." The Italians took the French side in that a solution was desirable only within the existing framework of the EC and that additional demands must not be raised. The Irish agreed with the proposed solution brokered by the Germans, but wanted to avoid "traps" in the negotiation process.[53]

The French conceded that budget adjustments would indeed be needed for Great Britain, especially for budget contributions planned for 1978 and 1979. Although the Germans were unhappy about the prospect of paying more to the EC budget, their primary concern was controlling inflation. In addition, the Germans sought to arrive at a solution with the British while the French maintained a "loosened attitude."[54] Although the British claimed they were within their rights to invoke the Luxembourg Compromise, a reference to de Gaulle's insistence to veto EC decisions that conflicted with vital national interests, British Prime Minister Harold

---

[51] PAAA, ZA 105612, Report by Auswärtiges Amt, "Vorbereitung des Treffens der Regierungschefs einschl. Frage des britischen Wunsches betr. Finanzlasten," November 26, 1974.

[52] PRO, PREM 16–77, Note for the Record, December 1, 1974.

[53] *AAPD* 1974, Botschafter Lebsanft, Brüssel (EG), an das Auswärtige Amt, December 3, 1974, 350.

[54] PAAA, ZA 101248, "Thematik und Ausgangslage des Treffens," December 6, 1974.

Wilson was told he did not have that right. The EC decided that retaining de Gaulle's 1966 precedent would hopelessly weaken the EC. Other EC nations would not tolerate remaking the British Prime Minister into "a kind of latter-day de Gaulle."[55]

At the Paris summit on December 9–10, which included the EC heads of state and EC Commission President François-Xavier Ortoli, German Chancellor Helmut Schmidt took on the role of "providing push" in the triangular relationship among himself, Wilson, and Giscard. Even the French President optimistically referred to the meeting as "the final summit," expecting closure on renegotiation.[56] Whereas many of the British demands were at least "partly fulfilled," there was work to be done on the budget and various agricultural policies and prices.[57] It was clear to the smaller EC nations that the three big nations had choreographed their positions in advance when an interim agreement was made between the French and Germans on the EC regional fund in exchange for British agreement on more flexible voting procedures.[58]

Over British disagreement, the rest of the EC moved forward with the requirement that EC parliamentarians be elected no later than 1980, which began the transition of the legislature away from bring an appointed body. The regional fund took effect beginning January 1, 1975, endowed with 300 million EUA in 1975, and 500 million EUA in 1976 and 1977. The fund itself was not a point of controversy, but who paid for it was. In another concession by the Germans, payments to the fund would be based on gross national product (GNP) per capita. The major beneficiaries of the fund were France at 15 percent, Italy at 40 percent, and the United Kingdom and Ireland at 34 percent combined. The remainder was spread over the remaining countries, including Germany, which would receive 6.4 percent.

Most importantly, the EC recognized Britain's right to renegotiate its terms of membership. "If unacceptable situations were to arise [for any EC nation], the very life of the Community would make it imperative for the institutions to find equitable solutions." The institutions of the

---

[55] NARA, RG 59, CFPF, Telegram from American Embassy Bonn to Secretary of State, "FRG Views on EC Summit," December 4, 1974, Bonn 18762.

[56] *AAPD* 1974, Runderlaß des Vortragenden Legationsrats I. Klasse Dohms, December 12, 1974, 369.

[57] PAAA, ZA 105613, "Britische EG-Mitgliedschaft," December 2, 1974.

[58] NARA, RG 59, CFPF, Telegram from American Embassy Paris to Secretary of State, "EC Summit: The View from Paris," December 6, 1974, Paris 29347.

Community, including the Council and the Commission, were tasked with developing:

a correcting mechanism of a general application which, in the framework of the system of "own resources" and in harmony with its normal functioning, based on objective criteria and taking into consideration in particular the suggestions made to this effect by the British Government, could prevent during the period of convergence of the economies of the Member States, the possible development of situations unacceptable for a Member States and incompatible with the smooth working of the Community.[59]

The prospects for concluding British renegotiation were better than ever following the Paris summit. The Schmidt-Wilson-Giscard chemistry was credited for clearing the way for progress on the regional fund and renegotiation. A key question remained whether Wilson would drop his public neutrality and openly support British membership in the EC.[60] It was clear that the British had achieved considerable results in almost every category of the renegotiation process.[61] Privately, Wilson was beginning to see that Britain simply had no viable alternative outside of the rest of Europe.[62]

Wilson still had problems at home. The anti-Marketeer wing of the Labor party, led by Tony Benn, adopted a position that continued British EC membership was an unacceptable loss of national sovereignty. Roy Hattersley, third in rank at the FCO, struck back at Benn and his pursuit of "a Victorian chimera" in which Britain ran the world from London. Hattersley argued that the pooling of sovereignty in the EC actually yielded more, not less, economic strength and greater power to influence decisions taken abroad that affected Britain's vital interests.[63] Cabinet meetings were becoming increasingly tense, yet Wilson did little to rein in the rebels.

* * *

On January 17, 1975, the British government discussed planning for the referendum, including the ballot layout, how the question was to be

---

[59] *Meeting of the Heads of Government, December 9–10, 1974* (Brussels: Bulletin of the European Communities, No. 12, 1974).

[60] NARA, RG 59, CFPF, Telegram from American Embassy Paris to Secretary of State, "EC Summit: An Initial Analysis," December 11, 1974, Paris 29779.

[61] PAAA, ZA 105613, "Deutsch-britishe Konsultationen: Bilanz der britischen Forderungen nach 'Neuverhandlung der Beitrittsbedingungen' und ihrer Erfuellung," December 11, 1974.

[62] Donoughue, 240.

[63] NARA, RG 59, CFPF, Telegram from American Embassy London to Secretary of State, "EC Membership: Sovereignty Issue," January 7, 1975, London 00219.

worded, and how to manage the media and public relations aspects of the national vote. Wilson and Callaghan visited Washington on January 29 to brief President Ford on the details of the planned referendum.[64] After a harrowing journey from Ottawa in a winter storm, the British landed with a full schedule of events at the White House, the State Department, and the Senate Foreign Relations Committee.[65] The Americans continued to monitor the situation very carefully. Even the Central Intelligence Agency prepared a study in order to brief Ford. The CIA's conclusion was consistent with prior thinking by Kissinger, Nixon, and Ford: "Staying in the EC means Britain would have a larger voice, especially in European affairs, while pulling out would probably deprive Britain of financial assistance from the other Eight."[66] At times, the impression of the visiting Wilson party was that Britain mattered less to the United States than ever before.

Ford gave the British maximum assurance of American support. "As I very recently said in my state of the union address, if we act imaginatively and boldly to deal with our present problems, as we acted after World War II, then this period will in retrospect be seen as one of the great creative moments in our history," Ford said during Wilson's arrival ceremony in Washington.[67] Wilson and Callaghan understood that the Americans wanted the British to remain in the EC. "I would imagine that it would be, from all I've heard, their hope that we shall be in a position to help the generation of outward-looking policies in Europe," they said in their joint press conference.[68] At the same time, the United States was prepared for either scenario. "We cannot make British membership in the EC our decision (or our quarrel), wherever our sympathies lie," wrote Winston Lord to Henry Kissinger. "But we should continue to do what we can to encourage the British political establishment and public opinion to remain committed to an active international role."

Prime Minister Wilson gave into the growing demand by cabinet members Michael Foot, Tony Benn, and Peter Shore that they be

---

[64] Alvin Shuster, "Ford and Wilson to Discuss Europe," *The New York Times*, January 27, 1975, 5.

[65] Donoughue, 302.

[66] *FRUS*, 1969–1976, Volume E-15, Part 2, 235.

[67] GRF, NSA, Presidential Speeches, Box 5, "Arrival Remarks, Prime Minister Wilson, Thursday, January 30, 1975."

[68] LOC, Papers of Elliot P. Richardson Box I-304, "Text of Press Conference by the Rt. Hon. Harold Wilson and the Rt. Hon. James Callaghan at the British embassy, Washington, D.C., May 7, 1975."

permitted to "express their convictions publicly parallel with their accepted right to record them privately, in the polling stations."[69] Privately, Wilson prepared a propaganda machine to counter any negativism that came out of his cabinet.[70] "There is also a need to consider the possibility of introducing machinery for controlling the information and propaganda activities of outside partisans of both sides," a confidential summary by the Lord President of the Privy Council said. The stakes of the referendum were so high that the British government regulated free speech and the media. Funds were channeled to media outlets that supported the government's position. "Either in place of or in addition to attempting to control propaganda activities, the Government might wish to consider providing public finance to the protagonists. Any such provision could be controversial," the report said. To avoid accusations of tampering with the referendum, funds were laundered through a third party. "An alternative would be to use an independent agency, which might be combined with the information role discussed earlier."[71] The Cabinet argued that "the Government should undertake an information effort." In addition, "a special interdepartmental unit should be established in the Cabinet Office," a confidential Cabinet report concluded. "Informal contact with the Chairmen of the British Broadcasting Corporation and the Independent Broadcasting Authority for the purpose of consultation about the arrangements they will be making in order to maintain the fair balance [is] required."[72]

At an EC Council of foreign ministers meeting in Brussels on January 20, the British government reiterated its desire to make progress as quickly as possible on the remaining renegotiation issues so that plans could be made for the referendum. The hope was that final issues could be nearly resolved by the next EC Council heads of state meeting scheduled for March 10–11.[73] The British Cabinet agreed during a meeting the morning of January 21 that a referendum would be put to the British people on

---

[69] PRO, PREM 16–558, Letter from Prime Minister to Tony Benn, January 6, 1975.
[70] PRO, PREM 16–558, Letter from Michael Foot, Tony Benn, and Peter Shore to Harold Wilson, November 27, 1974.
[71] PRO, CAB 129–181, "Practical Implications of Holding a Referendum on European Community Membership – Report by Official Working Party: Note by the Lord President of the Council," January 17, 1975.
[72] PRO, CAB 129–181, "European Community Referendum: Immediate Decisions," January 22, 1975.
[73] NARA, RG 59, CFPF, Telegram from U.S. Mission to the European Community to Secretary of State, "EC Foreign Ministers Council, January 20, 1975; Highlights Cable," January 21, 1975, EC Brussels 00540.

continued British membership in the EC once the renegotiations were completed. The Labor Party then announced that it would introduce the legislation that permitted a referendum on renegotiation to the House of Commons on April 8. Members of the Cabinet would be free to campaign as they wished once the Cabinet itself had agreed on the mode of holding the referendum.[74] All Labor MPs were also free to campaign either for or against the government's recommendation as long as they refrained from taking part in a "major publicity campaign" or speaking out officially on the issue from the House of Commons front bench.[75] Although Wilson had not yet set the date for a proposed referendum, he suggested that it be held in June. He assured the House of Commons that it would have the opportunity for a full debate and vote on the matter before the binding referendum was held.[76] "This Government will find time for a debate on the White Paper in this House before the Easter recess," Wilson said.[77]

At the end of January, the EC study on British renegotiation requested during the December Paris summit was published. The findings of the study were not a surprise and confirmed the views of the French in December.[78] On the main issue, how a "correcting mechanism" could be applied to Britain's claims that it had paid more than its fair share of the EC budget, the report recommended that where it was found that any EC nation contributed at least 10 percent more than prescribed to the EC budget, up to two-thirds of the excess contributions could be refunded to the nation in question.[79] Britain, upon its accession to the EC, was in fact placed at an economic disadvantage because "the existing members of the Community had already established a system to which Britain had still to become accustomed, and to do so in a much less favorable climate for international trade." Therefore, the study found that Britain did have a right to a "correcting mechanism."[80] Shifting to a system of EC budget

[74] PRO, CAB 128–56, "Conclusion of a Meeting of the Cabinet held at 10 Downing Street on Tuesday 21 January 1975," January 22, 1975.
[75] NARA, RG 59, CFPF, Telegram from American Embassy London to Secretary of State, "Labor's Plans for EC Referendum Begin to Unfold," January 23, 1975, London 01101.
[76] NARA, RG 59, CFPF, Telegram from American Embassy London to Secretary of State, "Wilson Outlines Referendum Plan," January 24, 1975, London 01157.
[77] PRO, CAB 129–181, "Referendum on EEC Membership: Note by the Prime Minister," January 22, 1975.
[78] *AAPD* 1975, Runderlaß des Vortragenden Legationsrats Engels, January 23, 1975, 15.
[79] Commission of the European Community. "The Unacceptable Situation and the Correcting Mechanism." Document COM(75)40, January 30, 1975.
[80] "The Effects on the United Kingdom of Membership of the European Communities." European Parliament: Directorate General for Research and Documentation, February 1975.

financing based on EC member state GNPs moved more of the budget burden to Germany, but Chancellor Schmidt assured French President Giscard that he was prepared to live with that during a meeting between the two heads of state over February 3–4, 1975.[81] Although the French continued to be skeptical that concessions offered to the British would result in a positive referendum result, Giscard made it clear that he supported keeping Britain in the EC. However, he was not willing to pay "any price" to do so, especially absent any strong effort by Wilson to support Britain's continued EC membership.[82]

The FCO agreed that the EC's findings were "pretty close" to their own. "I am sure the Commission Report, with some relatively minor changes, gives the best basis for a solution," British Chancellor of the Exchequer Denis Healey said to German Minister for Finance Hans Apel.[83] According to David Colvin, spokesman for the European Integration Department at the FCO, the EC findings were also fair because the new framework for determining EC budget contributions and the correcting mechanism were intended to apply to all member states, not just the United Kingdom. However, the British saw no reason why the amount of the budget rebate should be limited to two-thirds of the excess budget contributions.[84] In addition, there was a concern over how to control the counting process of referendum ballots so as to limit embarrassment to the government in case it failed. "In discussion it was argued that the real purpose of a central count would be, and would be seen to be, to conceal from different parts of the United Kingdom knowledge of how they voted, because of the political embarrassment which the voting results could create," Cabinet minutes recorded. "Different results for different parts of the United Kingdom would sharpen the divisions within the United Kingdom and even within England. The Government's policies on devolution could be put at risk, and the nationalist parties would be given a continuing grievance to exploit."[85]

[81] PAAA, ZA 105613, "Korrekturmechanismus für britische Finanzbelastung durch den EG-Haushalt," January 27, 1975.

[82] NARA, RG 59, CFPF, Telegram from American Embassy Paris to Secretary of State, "EC Renegotiation: The Budget Issue," January 30, 1975, Paris 02612.

[83] PAAA, ZA 105613, "Gespräch des Herrn Staatssekretärs mit dem britischen Botschafter am 28.2., 11 Uhr," February 28, 1975.

[84] NARA, RG 59, CFPF, Telegram from American Embassy London to Secretary of State, "EC Renegotiation – UK: Reaction to the Commission Paper on the Budget," February 3, 1975, London 01649.

[85] PRO, CAB 128–56, "Conclusions of a Meeting of the Cabinet held at 10 Downing Street on Thursday 6 February 1975," February 6, 1975.

Prime Minister Wilson was confident that the remaining renegotiation issues could be resolved at the March 10–11 EC heads of state meeting in Dublin. Therefore, the attention of the British government shifted toward conducting the referendum. Privately, the burdens of public office were beginning to weigh more heavily on Wilson. He was tired of the personal attacks aimed at him and of serving as a referee for his Cabinet. The late nights, threats of resignation, leaks in the press, obstinacy in the civil service, rebellion in the trade unions, and the Tories all began to affect him. His inner circle wondered whether he was drinking too heavily.[86]

Treasury conducted a study of the potential effects of the referendum on the British economy. Published in part in the London *Times* on February 24, the study concluded that, should the referendum fail, there could be a run on the pound and a substantial withdrawal of foreign capital from London. One senior civil servant noted "the referendum campaign will not be good for the pound ... if the referendum says no, the currency will go bang."[87] Secretary of State Henry Kissinger raised this point during a February 16 discussion with Chancellor Schmidt.[88] Kissinger requested that the CIA conduct a study of the impact of Irish leadership of the EC and their role as host of the summit that would determine whether Britain remained in the EC.[89] Kissinger doubted that Prime Minister Wilson could survive the referendum, no matter the outcome. "His assignment will be challenging," Kissinger said to newly appointed Ambassador to London Elliot Richardson.[90] The referendum "is likely to split the pro and anti-Marketeer factions of the Labor Party. All of Wilson's legendary political skill will be needed to hold the two groups together, and to obtain a favorable vote on continued membership – to which he is now evidently committed."[91]

[86] Donoughue, 309.
[87] NARA, RG 59, CFPF, Telegram from American Embassy London to Secretary of State, "London Times Article on Whitehall Concern over Financial Effects if Referendum Goes Against EC Membership," February 25, 1975, London 02893.
[88] *AAPD* 1975, Aufzeichnung des Ministerialdirektors van Well, February 17, 1975, 28.
[89] GRF, NSA, Country Files, Ireland, Box 7, Memorandum from A. Denis Clift to Henry Kissinger, "Prospects for the Irish EC Presidency," December 18, 1974.
[90] GRF, NSA, Country Files, United Kingdom, Box 15, Memorandum from Henry Kissinger to President, "Meeting with Elliot L. Richardson, U.S. Ambassador to the United Kingdom," February 27, 1975.
[91] GRF, NSA, Subject Files, Box 56, "Department of State Briefing Paper: Current UK Political Situation," undated.

In advance of the EC heads of state meeting in Dublin, March 10–11, the EC foreign ministers met on March 3–4. Little progress was made. The British proposed the elimination of the proposal that only two-thirds of excess budget contributions could be refunded. When the Germans seemed hesitant to grant an open-ended rebate, the British raised the stakes by requesting preferential treatment of New Zealand dairy products, in violation of the previous Anglo-German agreement not to raise additional renegotiation issues late in the negotiating process. Wilson had given a secret assurance to New Zealand Prime Minister Wallace Edward Rowling that "in terms of our renegotiation aims, we were committed to improving New Zealand's position. It would be very difficult to say that we had fulfilled the [Labor Party] Manifesto commitment if we were to fail in respect of the New Zealand requirement."[92]

French President Giscard and Chancellor Schmidt spoke about the issue immediately following the conclusion of the foreign ministers' meeting. Both leaders agreed that there would be no further concessions to the British.[93] However, rather than raising just one new issue at this late stage of renegotiation, that of access for New Zealand dairy products, Wilson considered that there were in fact *four* remaining issues: finalizing British EC budget contributions, determining the fate of New Zealand dairy products, finalizing the EC regional fund, and determining the future of EC industrial policy. Privately, the Germans were told that, of the four remaining issues, the only one the British insisted on was "the size of the refund ... all the other matters are subsidiary."[94] On the issue of New Zealand, the United Kingdom proposed a three-year guarantee for butter imports after 1977, but admitted privately that it was willing to settle for less. On EC industrial policy, the United Kingdom raised new concerns about some provisions of the European Coal and Steel Treaty that could restrict the British steel industry. The FCO admitted privately that this issue would probably not be part of the main renegotiation, but would be discussed at some later point as a part of normal EC business. On EC regional policy, the United Kingdom was concerned that the EC would place restrictions on how the regional fund could be used, as well as whether

[92] PRO, PREM 16–408, Record of a Meeting between the Prime Minister and the Prime Minister of New Zealand at Chequers at 2:30 p.m. on Monday 10 February 1975.

[93] *AAPD* 1975, Aufzeichnung des Legationsrats I. Klasse Leonberger, Bundeskanzleramt, March 4, 1974, 42.

[94] PAAA, ZA 105614, "Tagung des Rats der Regierungschefs und Außenminister in Dublin am 10./11. März 1975," March 6, 1975.

it would somehow restrict an individual nation's autonomy to direct the aid toward regions it felt needed the aid.[95]

The EC summit in Dublin over March 10–11 was the most critical of the entire process of British renegotiation. It was also the first summit hosted by Ireland, which had joined the EC alongside Britain on January 1, 1973. The U.S. Embassy in Dublin was briefed by Irish Deputy Political Director John Campbell on the summit preparations. Renegotiation and solving the budget impasse were the main items on the agenda. The Irish expected the summit to be a "cliff-hanger," with last-minute drama from both the French and British. Ireland supported a successful renegotiation and keeping Britain in the EC. However, that did not mean that the Irish were not critical of the British. As Campbell pointed out, it was a mistake for Wilson to have raised the additional issues such as New Zealand dairy imports and modifications to the Coal and Steel treaties. By doing so, the British were threatening to "renegotiate after the renegotiations are over."[96]

* * *

The EC heads of government began their meeting at 3:00 p.m. on Monday, March 10, in Dublin. This entire afternoon was devoted to British renegotiation, which carried into the morning of March 11. Seated in alphabetical order, it was a boon for the British that the French and Germans were next to each other, since any deadlock likely could only be overcome by them. In another German concession, Chancellor Schmidt – who was recovering from pneumonia and appeared in Dublin against the wishes of his doctors – proposed that the two-thirds reimbursement limit be removed but insisted on capping the total amount that any member could be refunded from the EC budget at 250 million EUA[97] Schmidt also went along with a diluted form of Britain's demand for EC access for New Zealand dairy products. Without any significant opposition from French President Giscard, the British agreed. These were the most critical remaining issues of British renegotiation, which were decided at 8:00 p.m. on March 11.[98]

---

[95] NARA, RG 59, CFPF, Telegram from American Embassy London to Secretary of State, "EC Renegotiation: The Home Stretch," March 3, 1975, London 03266.
[96] NARA, RG 59, CFPF, Telegram from American Embassy Dublin to Secretary of State, "EC Summit Agenda: British Renegotiation," March 6, 1975, Dublin 00424.
[97] NARA, RG 59, CFPF, Telegram from American Embassy Dublin to Secretary of State, "EC Summit: First Afternoon," March 10, 1975, Dublin 00449.
[98] NARA, RG 59, CFPF, Telegram from American Embassy Dublin to Secretary of State, "EC Summit: Agreement Reached on British Renegotiation," March 11, 1975, Dublin 00462.

Wilson said he was personally satisfied at the outcome of the negotiations and that he would say as much to his Cabinet at its next scheduled meeting on March 18.[99] British renegotiation, for all intents and purposes, was concluded. He provided his assurance that he would "not remain neutral" during the upcoming referendum as long as the British cabinet approved of the result. When the gathering broke up for good just before one in the morning, Wilson was surprised with a chorus of "Happy Birthday." How could he have forgotten? He was now 59 years old.[100]

Attention turned to Wilson's conduct of the British referendum. The British press on March 12 welcomed the conclusion of the Dublin summit, using language such as "a tense climax" and a "ritual table-thumping" to describe the final agreement. In that span of only a year, Wilson had not only secured what many felt was the best possible outcome for Britain, but he had also kept the Labor Party intact, revitalized the special relationship with the United States, and achieved a working relationship with his European counterparts.[101] While the summit itself was taking place, the House of Commons held a debate on the government's proposed referendum bill, which survived a procedural vote with a margin of fifty. The highlight of the debate was new Conservative Party leader Margaret Thatcher's first major speech in the House of Commons since she had assumed opposition leadership. Against all odds, she had won the Tory leadership, defying Henry Kissinger's assertion that "the chances are slim that she could muster sufficient support to become the first woman to lead a major political party in Britain."[102] Kissinger told President Ford that Thatcher was a "great gal, but she is not experienced at all in foreign policy."[103] Even after she won the first round of voting for Conservative leadership, the Americans still believed that "it is doubtful that Mrs. Thatcher will win on the second ballot. A more likely victor is popular Willie

---

[99]   PAAA, ZA 105614, "Tagung der Regierungschefs und Außenminister in Dublin am 10./11. März 1975," March 7, 1975.

[100] Donoughue, 330.

[101] NARA, RG 59, CFPF, Telegram from American Embassy London to Secretary of State, "Initial UK Reaction to the Dublin Summit," March 12, 1975, London 03863.

[102] GRF, NSA, Country Files, United Kingdom, Box 15, Memorandum from Henry Kissinger to President Ford, "Prospects for Edward Heath and the Tories," December 2, 1974.

[103] GRF, NSA, MemCons, Box 9, Memorandum of Conversation among President Ford, Henry Kissinger, and Elliot Richardson, February 27, 1975.

Whitelaw."[104] During her maiden leadership speech, Thatcher raised the shaky constitutional precedent set by holding such a referendum, to the delight of a roaring Tory backbench. However, her argument was devastated when former Labor Foreign Secretary Michael Stewart pointed to the shaky constitutionality earlier in the century of introducing women's suffrage.

For Prime Minister Wilson, the successful conclusion of renegotiation in Dublin removed the greatest obstacle to his June referendum timetable. Wilson had nothing but thanks for Chancellor Schmidt. "This has been evident to me from our talks at Chequers in December, and it was evident again in your determination to come to Dublin and play your full part in our discussions there. . . . I recognize that, and I am thankful," he said.[105] The cabinet was expected to support him, and although he expected the House of Commons vote on renegotiation to divide his own party, he was assured of the support of the vast majority of the Conservative Party, given the continued public presence of its pro-EC elder statesman, Edward Heath.[106] As much as the Conservatives would have been overjoyed to have taken down the Wilson government, and they surely could have, they did not do so.[107] The stakes were too high for the nation.

American analysts were not nearly as convinced that the referendum would secure Britain's future in the EC, and contingency plans were drafted in the State Department in case of British withdrawal from the EC. The U.S. reports concluded that "following a decisive vote in June against EC membership, the United Kingdom would probably withdraw immediately from the EC institutions. It would presumably then look for alternatives to membership in the Community." In seeking such an arrangement, perhaps like the former European Free Trade Agreement (EFTA), a desperate Britain would have a very weak negotiating position. The United Kingdom would be faced with a huge confluence of legal and economic adjustments in the process of untangling the nation from the *acquis communautaire*. Britain would then be forced to define its new world role, and, "at best, it could become a fairly prosperous

[104] GRF, NSA, Subject File, Box 56, Memorandum from George S. Springsteen to Brent Scowcroft, "Ted Heath Defeated as Opposition Leader," February 4, 1975.
[105] PAAA, ZA 105614, Memorandum from the Chancellor's Office to the Foreign Office, March 26, 1975.
[106] PRO, CAB 129–182, "EEC: Renegotiation Stocktaking: Memorandum by the Secretary of State for Foreign and Commonwealth Affairs," March 14, 1975.
[107] NARA, RG 59, CFPF, Telegram from American Embassy London to Secretary of State, "EC Membership: Progress toward Referendum," March 12, 1975, London 03812.

oil-producing European economy. It would continue to be tied to the rest of Europe through NATO and the OECD [Organization for Economic Cooperation and Development], and would exercise positive – if limited – influence in world affairs."[108] The State Department worried that the British government was doing no contingency planning, although the risk of any leaks that such efforts were taking place was also recognized. Even the Germans were creating contingency plans, in which they hypothetically agreed to support the United Kingdom if, after withdrawal, the British chose to set up an EFTA type arrangement. The Germans showed support for the initiative that kept the United Kingdom closest to the EC.[109]

On March 18, Prime Minister Wilson told a packed House of Commons that, a day earlier, his cabinet had approved the renegotiation results by a vote of 16 to 7, despite the fact that more than 100 Labor MPs, including a large number of junior ministers, had tried to spoil Wilson's speech by introducing anti-EC legislation on the same day with designs to stop the upcoming referendum.[110] "The Government has now made its recommendation on the results of the renegotiation of our terms of membership of the European Community," he said. "The Cabinet could not however reach unanimous agreement on this and, given the unique circumstances of a referendum on this long-standing issue which cuts across party lines, has agreed that those Ministers – whether members of the Cabinet or not – who do not agree with the Government's recommendation should be free to advocate a different view during the referendum campaign."[111] Individual positions in the Cabinet shifted right up until the vote was taken, which was why Callaghan was particularly pleased that Wilson took his suggestion: to go around the table twice. The first time around was an opportunity to express views, with the second time being the vote. When some of the ambivalent ones, like Healey, saw that others, like Peart, had become pro EC, that helped to produce a decisive vote on the final time around the Cabinet table.[112]

---

[108] NARA, RG 59, CFPF, Telegram from American Embassy London to Secretary of State, "What Happens If Britain Leaves the European Community?" March 14, 1975, London 04010.

[109] NARA, RG 59, CFPF, Telegram from American Embassy Bonn to Secretary of State, "Britain and the Community," March 25, 1975, Bonn 04913.

[110] NARA, RG 59, CFPF, Telegram from American Embassy London to Secretary of State, "Government Recommends Continued EC Membership," March 19, 1975, London 04235.

[111] PRO, CAB 129–182, "EEC Referendum: Guidance on Procedure Between Announcement of Government Recommendation and Referendum," March 18, 1975.

[112] Donoughue, 334.

Wilson introduced the government's forty-page white paper on the results of renegotiation to the House of Commons on March 27. Much to the chagrin of the anti-Marketeers, the paper spoke extensively of the wider considerations of British membership in the EC, including spillover benefits to Anglo-American relations and NATO, and that a cohesive Europe is "an essential pillar of the Atlantic partnership."[113] After reading the white paper, one came to the conclusion that not supporting the government on the referendum was unpatriotic and un-British. Wilson laid out the procedures for a three-day debate on the government's white paper in the House of Commons, to conclude with a critical vote on April 9. The House of Commons vote on approving a referendum was scheduled on April 10, with the referendum proposed for June 5. Although Wilson expected House of Commons endorsement of the government's white paper and the referendum, he did not know how large the Labor Party rebellion would be.

No sooner did Wilson lay out his agenda to the House of Commons did the nationwide discussion about the future of Britain begin. On the Conservative side, although many prominent Tories supported British membership in the EC, Harold Macmillan emerged to condemn Prime Minister Wilson. "Supermac," as he was known, attacked the "constitutionally dangerous" referendum and charged that the Labor Party's left wing opposed EC membership because "they wanted to convert the UK into a communist country, and they saw EC membership as an obstacle to that objective."[114] With the prominent leaders of Britain's three largest political parties – Labor, the Conservatives, and the Liberals – all supporting continued British membership in the EC, opinion polls showed a swing in favor of staying in. According to one poll published in the *Evening Standard* on April 18, 60 percent of those asked said that they would vote in favor of staying in if the referendum were held that day. Twenty-eight percent said they would vote "no," and 12 percent said that they "don't know."[115]

---

[113] NARA, RG 59, CFPF, Telegram from American Embassy London to Secretary of State, "White Paper on Renegotiation Presented to Parliament," April 1, 1975, London 04918.

[114] NARA, RG 59, CFPF, Telegram from American Embassy London to Secretary of State, "EC Membership: Weekend Developments and Outlook," April 7, 1975, London 05215.

[115] NARA, RG 59, CFPF, Telegram from American Embassy London to Secretary of State, "British Opinion Continues to Swing in Favor of EC Membership," April 23, 1975, London 06149.

After the House of Commons voted on April 9 in favor of the
government's white paper by a margin of 396 to 170, the real testing
ground for Wilson and Callaghan came during an April 26 Labor
Party all-party vote on continued British membership of the EC.[116]
The result demonstrated just how divided their own political party
was. Although not binding on the government, the Labor Party overwhelmingly voted against continued British membership by a vote of
3.7 million to 2.0 million votes, nearly a 2 to 1 margin, led primarily
by the biggest unions, the Transport Workers and the Engineering
Workers.[117] Some blamed Wilson for permitting too much dissent,
but even Wilson never expected members of his own Cabinet to
vote against him.[118] The political division, combined with the weak
British economy, worried the American government. "This is clearly a
very dangerous situation," Alan Greenspan reported to President
Ford.[119]

Following the Labor Party vote, Wilson was propped up when the
leader of the Trade Union Congress, Len Murray, admitted that there
was no sense in letting the party "tear itself to pieces" over the EC.
Advising unions to abstain on the referendum, Murray commented
that "we are not getting our knickers in a twist" over the EC issue.[120]
On May 11, Wilson gave two nationwide television interviews.
He indicated that collective cabinet responsibility was waived until
the June 5 referendum – which allowed Labor MPs and government
ministers to campaign for or against the referendum as they pleased –
but that Wilson would expect cabinet loyalty again beginning June 6.
After that time, he said, any cabinet minister who cannot accept the
decisions of the cabinet will retire to the "full and satisfying life of a
backbencher." Wilson's appearance on nationwide television and

---

[116] NARA, RG 59, CFPF, Telegram from American Embassy London to Secretary of State,
"British Opinion Continues to Swing in Favor of EC Membership," April 23, 1975,
London 06149.
[117] NARA, RG 59, CFPF, Telegram from American Embassy London to Secretary of
State, "EC Membership: Labor Party Conference Votes against EC," April 28, 1975,
London 06350.
[118] Donoughue, 348.
[119] GRF, NSA, Subject File, Box 56, Memorandum from Alan Greenspan to President Ford,
April 23, 1975.
[120] NARA, RG 59, CFPF, Telegram from American Embassy London to Secretary of State,
"Len Murray on the EC: 'We're Not Getting Our Knickers in a Twist,' " May 2, 1975,
London 06680.

radio at a difficult time reassured the British public that his government was still able to deal with the problems that the nation faced.[121]

There was another twist in the referendum campaign. A Danish poll taken late in April 1975 indicated that, should the United Kingdom decide to withdrawal from the EC, 74 percent of Danes would be opposed to continued Danish membership in the EC. The stakes were now even higher for the British referendum.[122] However, many commentators surmised that the British government's pro-Europe stance clearly had the edge in the polls. The government's side had bigger endorsements from a cross-section of political leaders, were better financed, and had superior organizational support and broader media coverage. The referendum had the endorsement of the leadership of the Labor, Conservative, and Liberal parties.[123] Despite the divisions in the Labor Party, the Euroskeptic trade unions stayed true to their word and remained neutral.

There must have been at least a little doubt within Wilson's government. The FCO conducted some basic contingency plans should Britain leave the EC.[124] The government's pro-EC campaign was not helped by continued anti-Marketeer efforts. On May 22, five anti-EC members of the British government jumped on words spoken by French President Giscard during a press conference that they claimed had "effectively repudiated the terms" of Britain's renegotiation conditions of membership. Giscard had been somewhat dismissive in answering a question in which his response suggested that, should the British referendum fail, the other EC nations would continue pushing ahead with integration efforts.[125]

---

[121] NARA, RG 59, CFPF, Telegram from American Embassy London to Secretary of State, "Wilson Seeks to Assert Control and Restore Confidence," May 12, 1975, London 07181.

[122] NARA, RG 59, CFPF, Telegram from American Embassy Copenhagen to Secretary of State, "Gallup Poll Indicates Large Majority of Danes Prefer Following UK If It Withdraws from EC," May 15, 1975, Copenhagen 01387.

[123] NARA, RG 59, CFPF, Telegram from American Embassy London to Secretary of State, "EC Referendum Campaign: A General Wrap-Up," May 16, 1975, London 07423.

[124] NARA, RG 59, CFPF, Telegram from American Embassy London to Secretary of State, "EC Referendum – More Comment on the Consequences of a Yes or No Vote," May 16, 1975, London 07451.

[125] NARA, RG 59, CFPF, Telegram from American Embassy London to Secretary of State, "EC Referendum Campaign: Anti-Marketeers Exploit Giscard Statements," May 23, 1975, London 07876. According to a transcript of the press conference, President Giscard actually stated that should the British referendum fail, " ... je crois que ce seriat une erreur de croire que les autres ne doivent pas poursuivre leur progression des lors qu'il s'agit de mechanisms déjà appliqués et des lors que leur conjuncture leur permet de poursuivre l'objectif d'union economique et monetaire." The entire text can be found in

As the campaign wound down, the British public seemed to lack any further interest in the referendum. Although the British government continued to argue its case with support from leading public figures, the rhetoric of the anti-Marketeers became even more dramatic, making the front pages of even respectable newspapers almost every day. The campaign was led by Tony Benn, who claimed continued British membership in the EC would cost Britain 500,000 jobs. As the U.S. Embassy in London commented, "this comedy provides almost endless grist for the speculative mills of political journalists . . . it is a strange and almost unreal atmosphere in which to resolve a question of such importance to the future of the UK."[126] The British government was also aided by unlikely spokesmen. Before jumping over thirteen single-decker London buses at Wembley Stadium on May 19, daredevil Evel Knievel's endorsement of continued British membership in the EC was drowned out by catcalls and cheers. Knievel's campaign for the EC dramatically came to an end only minutes later after his crash landing on the other side of the buses, which left him with a crushed vertebra, fractured hand, damaged spine, and a firm determination never to jump again.[127]

The polls from the final week of the referendum continued to show the government assured of victory on the referendum. "I notice the polls indicate you will prevail on the EC poll," President Ford reassured Wilson and Callaghan. "I think so. We are keeping a low profile. But the polls are unanimous that it's more than 2–1," Wilson responded.[128] Conservative Party leaders Margaret Thatcher – in Kissinger's words, "a reluctant debutante" – and Edward Heath also campaigned for the government's position.[129] President Ford even spoke up to endorse the British referendum. "My Administration believes strongly in a strong Europe, and I believe strongly in close relations between the EC and the

CFPF, Telegram from American Embassy Paris to Secretary of State, "EC Referendum Campaign," May 27, 1975, Paris 13523.

[126] NARA, RG 59, CFPF, Telegram from American Embassy London to Secretary of State, "EC Referendum Campaign: Reflections on a Stifled Yawn," May 29, 1975, London 08134.

[127] NARA, RG 59, CFPF, Telegram from American Embassy London to Secretary of State, "With Evel Knieval on the Pro-Market Side, How Can They Lose?" May 28, 1975, London 08064.

[128] GRF, NSA, Memcons, Box 11, Memorandum of Conversation among President Ford, Henry Kissinger, Harold Wilson, and James Callaghan, May 7, 1975.

[129] GRF, NSA, Memcons, Box 16, Memorandum of Conversation among President Ford, Henry Kissinger, Harold Wilson, and James Callaghan, May 30, 1975.

United States."[130] The impression that some in Wilson's inner circle had was that the Americans were awfully nice, and willing to be as helpful as they could be, but they did not have a great understanding of either the British domestic situation or an appreciation of the challenges related to Britain's place in Europe.[131]

Chancellor Schmidt was asked by the BBC to give a public statement the night of the referendum, anticipating a positive result. Wilson was so desperate for this last-minute support that he secretly assured Schmidt that the Labor Party would send delegates to the European Parliament, which up until then it had refused to do.[132] The American Embassy in London conducted a full study in terms of which British politicians stood to gain or lose whatever the outcome of the referendum would be. Although the American analysts assumed Wilson would be victorious, they recognized the sensitivity of predicting the winners and losers of a referendum that had not yet taken place, especially the damage that could be done to bilateral relations should such a document leak. The Embassy was careful to note at the end of the study that "if the polls are monumentally in error, and Britain votes no on June 5, please destroy all copies of this cable, and look for a revised assessment next week."[133]

The Conservative Party under Margaret Thatcher wound down its referendum campaign during a press conference on June 3, recommending to the British electorate that the United Kingdom remain in Europe. Thatcher, who had a "terrible" voice according to Wilson, stressed that Conservative Party leaders since Churchill had been supportive of Europe.[134] Under her leadership, her party had voted 249 to 8 with 18 abstentions during the House of Commons vote on the referendum, even while much of Wilson's own party had not supported him.[135] Henry Kissinger rethought his earlier conclusions on Thatcher. Giving her credit for the way she handled herself and her party during the renegotiation process, Kissinger reported to President Ford, "she has succeeded in broadening the range of Conservative views in the Shadow Cabinet,

[130] GRF, NSA, Memcons, Box 16, Memorandum of Conversation among President Ford, Henry Kissinger, Francis-Xavier Ortoli, and Christopher Soames, May 30, 1975.
[131] Donoughue, 374.
[132] *AAPD* 1975, Gespräch des Bundeskanzlers Schmidt mit Premierminister Wilson in Brüssel, May 29, 1975, 140.
[133] NARA, RG 59, CFPF, Telegram from American Embassy London to Secretary of State, "EC Referendum: An Assessment of the Political Fallout," June 2, 1975, London 08305.
[134] Donoughue, 357.
[135] NARA, RG 59, CFPF, Telegram from American Embassy London to Secretary of State, "Tories Wind Up Referendum Campaign," June 4, 1975, London 08421.

making significant changes in party headquarters, initiating a comprehensive review of Tory policies, and all the while keeping the support of some Heath followers."[136] Perhaps she had a political future after all, Kissinger thought.

Prime Minister Wilson puffed on his pipe and tried to stay out of the final days of fighting. "It's good for them to let off steam," he said. The public opinion polls looked strongly in their favor.[137] Wilson left the details of the referendum almost completely to Callaghan. At the end of the campaign, he and Foreign Secretary Callaghan stated that they had weighed all the evidence and had come to the conclusion that Britain would be better able to tackle the problems it faced if it remained in the EC.[138] Commentators at the U.S. Embassy in London focused on the bigger picture:

[T]he business of government goes on but without the sense of urgency that the times demand. British government members feel bewildered. But they are not alone. The present leaders of Western Europe are confused men, baffled by problems for which they do not have solutions. British politicians share the Secretary [of State Henry Kissinger]'s view that the West lacks a theory to cope with simultaneous unemployment and inflation.[139]

* * *

On June 5, 1975, the British electorate went to the polls to decide the future of their nation. Early referendum returns through 2:00 p.m. indicated that the British people had overwhelmingly endorsed the Wilson government's recommendation that the UK remain in the EC.[140] By 6:00 p.m., it was clear that the vote was a "yes." With 69.4 percent of total votes counted, 68.4 percent had voted for continued EC membership. Wilson did not wait for the final results. Feeling confident, he scheduled his televised address to thank the British people that same evening.[141] President Ford immediately cabled a

---

[136] GRF, NSA, Memcons, Box 15, Memorandum from Henry Kissinger to President Ford, "Meeting with Mrs. Margaret Thatcher, Leader of the British Conservative Party," September 18, 1975.

[137] Donoughue, 396.

[138] NARA, RG 59, CFPF, Telegram from American Embassy London to Secretary of State, "EC Referendum: The Dark Side of the Moon," June 4, 1975, London 08435.

[139] NARA, RG 59, CFPF, Telegram from American Embassy London to Secretary of State, "Britain in Crisis," June 5, 1975, London 08537.

[140] NARA, RG 59, CFPF, Telegram from American Embassy London to Secretary of State, "EC Referendum: Britain Votes to Stay In," June 6, 1975, London 08611.

[141] NARA, RG 59, CFPF, Telegram from American Embassy London to Secretary of State, "EC Referendum: Britain Stays in Market," June 6, 1975, London 08666.

congratulatory message. "At this historic moment, I want to congratulate you and the people of Great Britain on the outcome of the EC referendum ... the United States looks forward to continued and growing cooperation with Great Britain as part of a vital, unified Europe." Wilson was appreciative. "Thank you very much for your message on the outcome of the referendum and for your congratulations. It is a great satisfaction that the British people should have given so decisive a verdict."[142]

The final tally was 67.2 percent in favor and 32.8 percent opposed. Even the *Daily Telegraph* admitted it was a triumph for Wilson.[143] When President of the European Commission Ortoli heard the news, he expressed delight at what appeared to be such an overwhelming victory for the EC and noted that "we must now look to the future. Today represents a new point of departure. A whole people had just demonstrated their confidence in Europe. We must not disappoint them."[144] The greatest sigh of relief came not from Brussels, but from Copenhagen. More pro-EC than the electorate, the Danish government was relieved that it would not have to hold a referendum of its own. In that sense, the successful British referendum also served as a test of continued Danish membership of the EC.[145]

Prime Minister Wilson declared in the House of Commons on June 9 that Her Majesty's government would now play a full, constructive role in the EC. He acknowledged the assistance he had received from Edward Heath, Liberal Party leader Jeremy Thorpe, and others. Within Wilson's inner circle, the belief was that he had always been at least mildly anti-European, but he was pragmatic enough to understand that Britain's best future opportunities were inside Europe. Staying in the EC also gave the Labor Party the best odds of holding together.[146] Wilson signaled that the Labor Party would begin the process of selecting its delegates to the European Parliament, taking up seats that, until then, had been empty

[142] GRF, NSA, Presidential Correspondence, Box 5, Memorandum from Harold Wilson to President Ford, June 12, 1975.

[143] Donoughue, 403.

[144] NARA, RG 59, CFPF, Telegram from U.S. Mission to the European Community Brussels to Secretary of State, "Reaction to British Vote to Stay in EC," June 9, 1975, EC Brussels 05107.

[145] NARA, RG 59, CFPF, Telegram from American Embassy Copenhagen to Secretary of State, "Denmark Sighs with Relief at Favorable UK Referendum," June 9, 1975, Copenhagen 01631.

[146] Donoughue, 402.

due to the previous Labor Party refusal to take part in any EC legislative body seen as compromising the authority of the British parliament.[147]

Wilson also commended the support of the British people. A poll taken June 12, one week after the referendum, showed 61 percent with favorable views of the EC, whereas only 31 percent remained opposed, a radical shift in little more than a year. That meant that the numbers those in favor of the EC in the June 1975 poll were even greater than the 57 percent in favor during an October 1972 poll conducted immediately before British entry into the EC.[148] The French and German governments were delighted that renegotiation was in the past. In a Franco-German summit meeting between German Foreign Minister Genscher and French Minister of Foreign Affairs Sauvagnargues on June 13, they were in agreement over enhancing Labor Party support for the European Parliament. Now that Britain's membership in the EC was no longer in question, Britain would have to be pushed to keep its side of the agreement.[149]

Callaghan was able to thank his European colleagues during the EC Council of foreign ministers held in Luxembourg on June 24–25. He confirmed that Labor Party representatives would soon be taking up their seats in the European Parliament and that British trade union representatives would soon take up their places in the EC economic and social committee. The EC Council meeting also marked the end of the six-month Irish presidency of the EC during the first half of 1975, which was one of the most critical presidencies in the history of the European integration movement. One senior European Commission official, who had been observing the Council for more than fifteen years, remarked that the Irish presidency would be sorely missed.[150]

* * *

Harold Wilson, first in opposition and then elected twice as Prime Minister in one year, took a political party and a British electorate firmly opposed to continued British membership in the EC and convinced them

---

[147] NARA, RG 59, CFPF, Telegram from American Embassy London to Secretary of State, "Wilson Reports to Parliament on EC Referendum," June 10, 1975, London 08799.

[148] NARA, RG 59, CFPF, Telegram from American Embassy Copenhagen to Secretary of State, "British Referendum Strengthened Danish Popular Support of EC Membership," June 19, 1975, Copenhagen 01725.

[149] NARA, RG 59, CFPF, Telegram from American Embassy Bonn to Secretary of State, "Genscher-Sauvagnargues Talks in Paris, June 13," June 20, 1975, Bonn 10007.

[150] NARA, RG 59, CFPF, Telegram from U.S. Mission to the European Community Brussels to Secretary of State, "EC Foreign Ministers' Council Meeting, June 24–25: Highlights," June 25, 1975, EC Brussels 05746.

that Britain had no other choice but to remain in Europe. He did this despite the odds against him, the unfavorable terms of original entry into the EC, the political turbulence in Europe during 1974, and the failure of the Year of Europe. Rather than be bogged down in the negativity that was so common at each stage in the renegotiation process, Wilson remained above the fray, above politics itself, and bridged the support of political leaders past and present from all major political parties in doing what he was convinced was right for the nation. Wilson admitted to the American government later that he intentionally played a very clever game with the EC throughout the negotiation process. "We played it cool, acted as though we had to be convinced and only pulled out the stops at the end."[151]

Also of critical importance, Wilson and Callaghan acquired German support for the renegotiation effort early on, and they took advantage of a series of events – the death of President Pompidou and the changes in government in France and Germany, as well as in the United States. With German support, Wilson could stand up to France. The German government recognized France's desperate position and took advantage of a brief window of opportunity to push through the necessary EC concessions to keep the British in. Learning their lesson from the Year of Europe, Ford and Kissinger supported Callaghan and refrained from the public commentary and criticism of the EC that had doomed the Year of Europe. Over time, Wilson and Callaghan saw the EC as a friendlier place, and they actively campaigned for Britain to remain in the EC. The alternative, had Britain pulled out of the EC, was simply unthinkable.

---

[151] GRF, NSA, Memcons, Box 14, Memorandum of Conversation among President Ford, Henry Kissinger, Harold Wilson, and James Callaghan, July 30, 1975.

Conclusion

On June 26, 1974, at NATO Headquarters in Brussels, the heads of state of all member nations gathered to celebrate the twenty-fifth anniversary of the Atlantic military alliance. "It took great courage and statesmen to create [the] alliance," Nixon privately noted. "It will take greater [courage] to preserve."[1] Five years earlier, its future was full of doubt, but now, the climate was much improved. Richard Nixon, despite his domestic troubles, could not help but be elated. He may have been called a crook at home, but he was received as a senior statesman overseas throughout a summit-packed summer of 1974.

While planning the Brussels summit, Henry Kissinger reflected on what had been achieved in transatlantic relations during Nixon's five and a half years in the White House. "During the past year, this relationship had been the object of considerable debate, and it should not be forgotten that the debate had started in the expression of the United States' intention to give a new perspective to a valuable Alliance, in order to allow it to continue to serve as a vital instrument for peace and progress."[2] The summit marked the conclusion of a nearly two-year process to revitalize the Atlantic relationship, first via the Year of Europe, and then through the process of British renegotiation. Both processes divided the alliance, but in the end brought it back together again.

The June 1974 meeting marked only the second time the NATO heads of state had ever gathered, thus underscoring the importance of this

---

[1] RMN, White House Special Files, President's Personal File, Box 94, handwritten notes.
[2] NATO, C-R(74)28 Part I, "Summary Record of a meeting of the Council held at the Government Conference Centre, Ottawa, on Tuesday, 18th June, 1974 at 11:00 a.m."

meeting. NATO General Secretary Joseph Luns applauded the American achievement. "A young Harvard Professor, who looks strangely similar to the present Secretary of State, once said that a quest for absolute security by one power leads to the absolute insecurity of the others. We did not need the Yom Kippur War of last autumn to know that our security is not stable and that sudden crises in East-West relations continue to be possible, continue to be likely."[3]

Opening the twenty-fifth anniversary meeting in Brussels on June 26, Luns stated that Nixon "had placed in the very forefront of his policies the ending of confrontation and the opening of an era of negotiation between East and West. Nobody would deny that few statesmen with such tremendous responsibilities had been able to affect so positively, and even dramatically, the international situation." When it was his turn to speak, Nixon also looked back at his contributions to the Atlantic alliance. "Some five years ago – on April 10, 1969 – I urged creation of a NATO committee which 'would explore ways in which the experiences and resources of the Western nations could most effectively be marshaled toward improving the quality of life of our peoples,' " he said in one of his final foreign policy addresses. "The CCMS [Committee on the Challenges of Modern Society] program demonstrates the ability of the NATO nations effectively to broaden the scope of their concern beyond the defense perimeter, to work cooperatively on those problems which face modern technological societies."[4] The CCMS helped to shift the focus of the transatlantic alliance away from simply defense ties to strengthening political relations and considering a broader definition of Western security.

On NATO's twenty-fifth anniversary, the Declaration on Atlantic Relations "laid the groundwork for another quarter century of Atlantic cooperation, solidarity and security."[5] It was a key milestone in the history of NATO, bringing the alliance into the détente era and putting a cap on the tumultuous Year of Europe.

***

The election of Richard Nixon in 1968 sent an immediate signal to Europeans that the United States would soon be able to see beyond

[3] NATO, C-VR(74)28, "Verbatim Record of the Meeting of the Council held on Tuesday, 18th June, 1974, at 11:00 a.m. at the Government Conference Centre, Ottawa."
[4] NATO, C-M(74)35, Tenth Plenary Session of the Committee on the Challenges of Modern Society, August 6, 1974.
[5] NATO, C-R(74)31, "Summary record of a meeting of the Council held at the NATO Headquarters, Brussels, on Wednesday, 26th June, 1974 at 10:30 a.m."

Vietnam, just as he had articulated the need to do so in his *Foreign Affairs* article the year before. Nixon prioritized Europe at the start of his first term, conducting some much needed mending of political relations, especially with French President Charles de Gaulle. Between his tour of Europe a month into his presidency, his NATO twentieth anniversary speech in April, and his speech at Guam – which became known as the Nixon Doctrine – in July, his vision for the world was unveiled in just the first six months of his presidency. In the course of Nixon's five and a half years in the White House, the American commitment to Europe was renewed: politically, it was strengthened; economically, it was shifted commensurate with the détente era; and militarily, NATO was given a new mission with a broader definition of security.

The year 1969 was the most promising for a fresh start in transatlantic relations. Nixon needed Europe, and Europe needed him. Nixon and Kissinger presented themselves as Atlanticists, yet the foreign policy they ultimately became known for was based on attributes that were contrary to Atlanticism: they shifted the focus of American attention and creativity from West to East, they prioritized bilateral diplomacy, they subordinated transatlantic relations to opportunities with adversaries such as China and the Soviet Union, and they sought to preserve American dominance as the world transitioned to a more diffuse place. These efforts seemed contrary to Richard Nixon's training, political upbringing, and long apprenticeship under the most Eastern Establishment of Republicans, Atlanticist Dwight Eisenhower. However, during his presidency it was Nixon – not Eisenhower – who took his party in a new direction, the direction of its future, the direction of the American West. Growing up and coming of age in California, Nixon saw the West – not the East – as America's next window to the world, a Pacific world. All Republicans elected to the presidency since Nixon have been from the West.

Over time, Europeans became frustrated with their diminished place in American foreign policy. They blamed the declining American position caused by Vietnam, as well as rising American isolationism. To Europeans, these trends blinded Nixon from prioritizing Europe, just as Johnson had been similarly distracted by both Vietnam and his Great Society programs.

However, there is another, more plausible reason that transatlantic relations diminished in importance beginning with the Nixon administration, in favor of emerging areas such as China, India, the Middle East, and South America. Throughout the postwar period – in terms of waning political influence, economic stagnation, an aging population, and a lack of military might – the decline of Europe as an American foreign policy priority had more to do with the Nixon reorientation of American foreign policy to the East than the decline of the United States as a result of Vietnam.

Despite the new American priorities, maintaining strong transatlantic ties was important for Richard Nixon in terms of the need to signal unity to American adversaries such as China and the Soviet Union. The shift in foreign policy thinking was necessary, and it was Nixon and Kissinger who came to power with that vision, based on his *Foreign Affairs* article and the Nixon Doctrine. Europe remained an important partner, but the shift to a Pacific strategy forever changed the relationship among the Atlantic allies.

Bibliography

ARCHIVAL SOURCES

Belgium

Historical Archives of the European Commission (HAEC), Brussels:
  Commissions of the European Economic Community, 1957–1975 (BAC)

North Atlantic Treaty Organization (NATO) Archives Division, Brussels:
  North Atlantic Council (C-)
    Verbatim Records (C-VR)
  North Atlantic Military Committee (MC)

France

Centre d'accueil et de recherche des Archives Nationales (CARAN), Paris:
  Papiers des Chefs de l'État:
    Présidence de la République, Georges Pompidou (5 AG 2)
      Entretiens franco-américains, conférences des chefs d'état de la CEE,
      notes, télégrammes, correspondance, voyages officiels, 1969–1974

Council of Europe Archives Division (COE), Strasbourg:
  United Nations (889/031/2)
  United States of America (889/031/1)

Germany

Politisches Archiv des Auswärtigen Amts (PAAA), Berlin:
  Economic Policy: B52, IIIA2
  North American File:
    B31, 1968–1971
    B32, 1955–1969

B32/204, 1971–1975
ZA (various)

Italy

Historical Archives of the European Union (HAEU), Florence:
  Papers of Emanuele Gazzo (EG)
  Papers of Edoardo Martino (EM)
  Papers of Klaus Meyer (KM)
  Papers of Robert Triffin (RT)

United Kingdom

National Archives (Public Record Office), Kew Gardens, Surrey:
  Cabinet Papers (CAB)
  Papers of the Prime Minister (PREM)
  Papers of the Foreign and Commonwealth Office (FCO)

United States

Bentley Historical Library, Ann Arbor, Michigan:
  Papers of Paul W. McCracken

Hoover Institution Archives (HIA), Stanford University, Palo Alto, California:
  Papers of John Ehrlichman
  Papers of Milton Friedman
  Richard M. Nixon Notes (1968 Campaign)

Library of Congress, Washington, D.C.:
  Manuscript Division:
    Papers of Stephen Hess
    Papers of Daniel Patrick Moynihan
    Papers of Elliot Richardson
    Papers of William L. Safire

National Archives and Records Administration (NARA):
  Archives II, College Park, Maryland:
    Record Group 59, State Department: Central Foreign Policy Files (CFPF)

Gerald R. Ford Presidential Library, Ann Arbor, Michigan:
  Papers of Arthur Burns: Handwritten Journals, 1969–1974
  Papers of Melvin Laird
  National Security Adviser:
    Chronological File
    Memoranda of Conversations
    Outside the System Chronological File
    Presidential Correspondence with Foreign Leaders
    Presidential Country Files for Europe and Canada
  Presidential Speeches, Reading Copies:

White House Central Files:
  Name File
  Subject File
White House Photographic Office

Lyndon B. Johnson Presidential Library, Austin, Texas:
National Security File (NSF)
Oral History Interviews

Richard M. Nixon Presidential Library, Yorba Linda, California:
National Security Council Files:
  Henry A. Kissinger Telephone Conversation Transcripts (Telcons)
  Country Files, Europe:
    France
    Germany
    United Kingdom
  Henry A. Kissinger Office Files: Country Files
  Presidential Correspondence
  Presidential/HAK Memcons
  President's Trip Files
  Subject Files:
    European Common Market
    National Security Decision Memoranda
    National Security Study Memoranda
  VIP Visits
  National Security Council Institution Files (H-Files):
    Study Memorandums: National Security Study Memorandums
White House Central Files:
  Name File: Papers of Paul W. McCracken
  Presidential Daily Diaries
White House Photographic Office
White House Special Files:
  President's Office Files
  President's Personal File
White House Tapes (also accessed at http://nixontapes.org)

United States Air Force Museum, MUA Research Division, Wright Patterson
  Air Force Base and Archive, Dayton, Ohio:
Papers of Stanley Goodwin

PUBLISHED GOVERNMENT DOCUMENTS

Akten zur Auswärtigen Politik der Bundesrepublik Deutschland. Munich:
  R. Oldenbourg Verlag, 2000–2006.
  1969: Rainer A Blasius; Franz Eibl; Hubert Zimmermann.
  1971: Ilse Dorothee Pautsch; Martin Koopmann
  1973: Ilse Dorothee Pautsch; Matthias Peter; Hans-Peter Schwarz
  1974: Ilse Dorothee Pautsch; Daniela Taschler; Fabian Hilfrich; Michael Ploetz

1975: Ilse Dorothee Pautsch; Michael Kieninger; Mechthild Lindemann; Daniela Taschler

Ambassade de France. *Address Delivered by Maurice Schumann, French Minister of Foreign Affairs, Before the National Assembly on November 3, 1971.* New York: Service de presse et d'information, 1971.

Burr, William. "U.S. Secret Assistance to the French Nuclear Program, 1969–1975: From 'Fourth Country' to Strategic Partner." Wilson Center Nuclear Proliferation International History Project *Research Update* #2 (2011). Available from http://www.wilsoncenter.org/publication/us-secret-assistance-to-the-french-nuclear-program-1969-1975-fourth-country-to-strategic.

Central Intelligence Agency. Directorate of Intelligence. "Basic Factors and Main Tendencies in Current Soviet Policy." National Intelligence Estimate (NIE) Number 11–69. February 27, 1969.

Central Intelligence Agency. Directorate of Intelligence. "Central Intelligence Bulletin." July 15, 1969.

Central Intelligence Agency. Directorate of Intelligence. "Soviet Nuclear Doctrine: Concepts of Intercontinental and Theater War." National Intelligence Estimate (NIE). July 1973.

Commission of the European Community. "The Unacceptable Situation and the Correcting Mechanism." Document COM(75)40, January 30, 1975.

Digital National Security Archive (DNSA) [online]. Available from http://nsarchive.chadwyck.com/home.do.

"The Effects on the United Kingdom of Membership of the European Communities." European Parliament: Directorate General for Research and Documentation, February 1975.

Elwell, Craig K. "Brief History of the Gold Standard in the United States." Washington, D.C.: Congress Research Service, 2011.

Foreign Relations of the United States (FRUS), *1969–1976.* Washington, D.C.: Government Printing Office.

Volumes
    I: Foundations of Foreign Policy, 1969–1972 (2003)
    III: Foreign Economic Policy, 1969–1972 (2001)
    XLI: Western Europe, NATO, 1969–1972 (2012)
    E–15, Part 2: Documents on Western Europe, 1973–1976 (2014)

Meeting of the Heads of Government, December 9–10, 1974. Brussels: Bulletin of the European Communities, No. 12, 1974.

Merrill, Dennis, and Thomas G. Paterson. *Major Problems in American Foreign Relations: Documents and Essays, Volume II: Since 1914, Sixth Edition.* Boston: Houghton Mifflin Company, 2005.

Myth and Reality: A Reference Manual on US-European Community Relations, 4th Ed. Washington, D.C.: European Community Information Service, 1974.

Nixon: The Fifth Year of His Presidency. Washington, D.C.: Congressional Quarterly, Inc., 1974.

Nixon: The Second Year of His Presidency. Washington, D.C.: Congressional Quarterly, Inc., 1971.

Rumsfeld, Donald. *The Rumsfeld Papers* [online]. Available from: http://www. rumsfeld.com/.

Woolley, John, and Gerhard Peters. *The American Presidency Project* [online]. Santa Barbara: University of California (hosted), Gerhard Peters (database). Available from: http://www.presidency.ucsb.edu/ws?pid=3441.

MEMOIRS

Brandt, Willy. *My Life in Politics*. London: Hamish Hamilton, 1992.

——. *People and Politics: The Years 1960–1975*. London: Collins, 1978.

Connally, John. *In History's Shadow: An American Odyssey*. New York: Hyperion, 1993.

Couve de Murville, Maurice. *Une Politique Étrangère, 1958–1969*. Paris: Plon, 1971.

De Gaulle, Philippe. *De Gaulle Mon Père, Vol. 1: Entretiens avec Michel Tauriac*. Paris: Plon, 2003.

Friedman, Milton, and Rose D. *Two Lucky People: Memoirs*. Chicago: University of Chicago Press, 1998.

Haldeman, H. R. *The Haldeman Diaries: Inside the Nixon White House*. New York: G. P. Putnam's Sons, 1994.

Heath, Edward. *The Course of My Life: My Autobiography*. London: Hodder & Stoughton, 1998.

Hillenbrand, Martin J. *Fragments of Our Time: Memoirs of a Diplomat*. Athens: University of Georgia Press, 1998.

Jobert, Michel. *L'Autre Regard*. Paris: Bernard Grasset, 1976.

Kissinger, Henry. *The White House Years*. Boston: Little, Brown, and Company, 1979.

——. *Years of Upheaval*. Boston: Little, Brown, and Company, 1982.

——. *Years of Renewal: The Concluding Volume of His Memoirs*. New York: Simon and Schuster, 1999.

Nixon, Richard. *RN: The Memoirs of Richard Nixon*. New York: Grosset & Dunlap, 1978.

——. *1999: Victory without War*. New York: Simon and Schuster, 1988.

Safire, William. *Before the Fall: An Inside View of the Pre-Watergate White House*. Garden City, N.Y.: Doubleday & Company, Inc., 1975.

Schmidt, Helmut. *Men and Powers: A Political Perspective*. New York: Random House, 1989.

Volcker, Paul A., and Toyoo Gyohten. *The World's Money and the Threat to American Leadership*. New York: Times Books, 1992.

PERIODICALS

Bergsten, C. Fred. "Reforming the Dollar: An International Monetary Policy for the United States." New York: Council on Foreign Relations, Inc., 1972.

Bossuat, Gérard. "Jean Monnet et le partenariat atlantique des années soixante." *Relations Internationales* 119 (2004): 285–301.

Brzezinski, Zbignew. "America and Europe," *Foreign Affairs* 49 (October 1970): 11–30.

Buchan, Alastair. "Europe and America: From Alliance to Coalition." Paris: The Atlantic Institute for International Affairs, 1973.

Caldwell, Dan. "The Legitimation of the Nixon-Kissinger Grand Design and Grand Strategy." *Diplomatic History* 33:4 (September 2009): 633–652.

Calleo, David P. "The European Coalition in a Fragmenting World." *Foreign Affairs* 54 (October 1975): 98–112.

Chance, James. "The Concert of Europe," *Foreign Affairs* 52 (October 1973): 96–108.

Douglas-Home, Alec. "Our European Destiny." London: Conservative Group for Europe, 1971.

Emminger, Otmar. "The D-Mark in the Conflict Between Internal and External Equilibrium, 1948–1975." Princeton: Essays in International Finance, 1977.

Goldsborough, James O. "France, The European Crisis and the Alliance." *Foreign Affairs* 52 (April 1974): 538–555.

Gray, William Glenn. "Floating the System: Germany, the United States, and the Breakdown of Bretton Woods, 1969–1973." *Diplomatic History* 31, no. 1 (April 2007): 295–323.

Gueldry, Michel. "La Grande-Bretagne et l'Europe: du pragmatisme insulaire au partenariat sceptique." *L'Europe en formation no. 353–354 (automne-hiver 2009)*: 93–110.

Hanhimäki, Jussi M. "Kissinger et l'Europe: entre intégration et autonomie." *Relations Internationales* 119 (2004): 319–332.

Heath, Edward. "Realism in British Foreign Policy." *Foreign Affairs* 48 (October 1969): 39–50.

Kaiser, Karl. "Europe and America: A Critical Phase." *Foreign Affairs* 52 (July 1974): 725–741.

Kimball, Jeffrey. "The Nixon Doctrine: A Saga of Misunderstanding." *Presidential Studies Quarterly*, Vol. 36, No. 1 (March 2006): 59–74.

Ludlow, N. Piers. "The Real Years of Europe? U.S.-West European Relations during the Ford Administration." *Journal of Cold War Studies* 15:3 (Summer 2013): 136–161.

Marhold, Hartmut. "How to Tell the History of European Integration in the 1970s: A Survey of the Literature and Some Proposals." *L'Europe en formation no. 353–354 (automne-hiver 2009)*: 13–38.

Ogliastro, Jacques. *Le Figaro*. June 20, 1974.

Pinder, John. "Renegotiation: Britain's Costly Lesson? *International Affairs* 51 (April 1975): 153–165.

Rowen, Hobart. "Changes Ahead for the Fed?" *Washington Post*. August 5, 1976.

Schmidt, Helmut. "Germany in the Era of Negotiations." *Foreign Affairs* 49 (October 1970): 40–50.

Shuster, Alvin. "Ford and Wilson to Discuss Europe." *The New York Times*. January 27, 1975.

Simonet, Henri. "Energy and the Future of Europe." *Foreign Affairs* 53 (April 1975): 450–463.

Ullman, Richard. "The Covert French Connection." *Foreign Policy* 75 (Summer 1989): 3–33.1

Vaïsse, Maurice. "Les 'relations spéciales' franco-américains au temps de Richard Nixon et Georges Pompidou." *Relations Internationales* 119 (2004): 345–362.

Zeiler, Thomas W. "Requiem for the Common Man: Class, the Nixon Economic Shock, and the Perils of Globalization." *Diplomatic History* 37:1 (January 2013): 1–23.

BOOKS

Beloff, Max. *The Future of British Foreign Policy.* New York: Taplinger Publishing Company, 1969.

Blang, Eugenie M. *Allies at Odds: America, Europe, and Vietnam, 1961–1968.* Lanham, Md.: Rowman & Littlefield Publishers, 2011.

Brands, H. W. *The Wages of Globalism: Lyndon Johnson and the Limits of American Power.* New York: Oxford University Press, 1995.

Brinkley, Douglas, and Richard T. Griffiths, eds. *John F. Kennedy and Europe.* Baton Rouge: Louisiana State University Press, 1999.

Bundy, William. *A Tangled Web: The Making of Foreign Policy in the Nixon Presidency.* New York: Hill and Wang, 1998.

Burk, Kathleen, and Melvyn Stokes, eds. *The United States and the European Alliance since 1945.* Oxford: Berg, 1999.

Butler, David, and Dennis Kavanagh. *The British General Election of February 1974.* New York: St. Martin's Press, 1974.

Calleo, David P. *The Imperious Economy.* Cambridge: Harvard University Press, 1982.

Carreau, Dominique. *Le Système Monétaire International: Aspects Juridiques.* Paris: Librairie Armand Colin, 1972.

Cleveland, Harlan. *NATO: The Transatlantic Bargain.* New York: Harper & Row, 1970.

Cromwell, William C. *The United States and the European Pillar: The Strained Alliance.* New York: St. Martin's Press, 1992.

Dallek, Robert. *Nixon and Kissinger: Partners in Power.* New York: HarperCollins, 2007.

Denizet, Jean. *Le Dollar: Histoire du Système Monétaire International Depuis 1945.* Paris: Fayard, 1985.

Dior, Eric. *Un couple infernal: 200 ans de francophobie et d'antiaméricanisme.* Paris: Perrin, 2003.

Donoughue, Bernard. *Downing Street Diary: With Harold Wilson in No. 10.* London: Random House, 2005.

Ebenstein, Larry. *Milton Friedman, A Biography.* New York: Palgrave Macmillan, 2007.

Eichengreen, Barry. *The European Economy since 1945: Coordinated Capitalism and Beyond.* Princeton: Princeton University Press, 2007.

Emminger, Otmar. *D-Mark, Dollar, Währungskrisen.* Stuttgart: Deutsche Verlags-Anstalt, 1986.

Evans, Rowland, and Robert Novak. *Nixon in the White House: The Frustration of Power*. New York: Random House, 1971.

Frick, Daniel. *Reinventing Richard Nixon: A Cultural History of an American Obsession*. Lawrence: University Press of Kansas, 2008.

Gaddis, John Lewis. *Strategies of Containment: A Critical Appraisal of American National Security Policy during the Cold War*. New York: Oxford University Press, 2005.

Gavin, Francis J. *Gold, Dollars, and Power: The Politics of International Monetary Relations, 1958–1971*. Chapel Hill: University of North Carolina Press, 2004.

Gowa, Joanne S. *Closing the Gold Window: Domestic Politics and the End of Bretton Woods*. Ithaca: Cornell University Press, 1983.

Greider, William. *Secrets of the Temple: How the Federal Reserve Runs the Country*. New York: Simon and Schuster, 1987.

Grosser, Alfred. *The Western Alliance: European-American Relations since 1945*. New York: Continuum, 1980.

Haftendorn, Helga, et al., eds. *The Strategic Triangle: France, Germany, and the United States in the Shaping of the New Europe*. Washington, D.C.: Woodrow Wilson Center Press, 2006.

Hanhimäki, Jussi. *The Flawed Architect: Henry Kissinger and American Foreign Policy*. New York: Oxford University Press, 2004.

Herring, George C. *From Colony to Superpower: U.S. Foreign Relations since 1776*. New York: Oxford University Press, 2008.

Hess, Stephen. *The Professor and the President: Daniel Patrick Moynihan in the Nixon White House*. Washington, D.C.: Brookings Institution Press, 2014.

Hobsbawm, Eric. *Age of Extremes: The Short Twentieth Century, 1914–1991*. New York: Viking, 1994.

Horne, Alistair. *Kissinger: 1973, The Crucial Year*. New York: Simon and Schuster, 2009.

James, Harold. *International Monetary Cooperation since Bretton Woods*. New York: Oxford University Press, 1996.

Judt, Tony. *Postwar: A History of Europe since 1945*. New York: Penguin Press, 2005.

Kagan, Robert. *Of Paradise and Power: America and Europe in the New World Order*. New York: Knopf, 2003.

Kaplan, Lawrence. *NATO and the United States: The Enduring Alliance*. New York: Twayne, 1994.

Kintner, William R., and Richard B. Foster. *National Strategy in a Decade of Change: An Emerging U.S. Policy*. Lexington, Mass.: D.C. Heath and Company, 1973.

Kissinger, Henry. *Nuclear Weapons and Foreign Policy*. New York: Council on Foreign Relations, 1957.

——. *American Foreign Policy: Three Essays*. New York: W. W. Norton & Company, 1969.

——. *Crisis: The Anatomy of Two Major Foreign Policy Crises*. New York: Simon and Schuster, 2003.

Lacouture, Jean. *De Gaulle: The Ruler, 1945–1970*. New York: Norton, 1992.

Logevall, Fredrik, and Andrew Preston, eds., *Nixon in the World: American Foreign Relations, 1969–1974*. New York: Oxford University Press, 2008.

Lundestad, Geir. *"Empire' by Integration: The United States and European Integration, 1945–1997*. New York: Oxford University Press, 1998.

Macmillan, Margaret. *Nixon and Mao: The Week That Changed the World*. New York: Random House, 2007.

Maresca, John J. *To Helsinki: The Conference on Security and Cooperation in Europe, 1973–1975*. Durham, N.C.: Duke University Press, 1987.

Möckli, Daniel. *European Foreign Policy during the Cold War: Heath, Brandt, Pompidou and the Dream of Political Unity*. London: I. B. Tauris, 2009.

Nouailhat, Yves-Henri. *Les Etats-Unis et le monde au 20e siècle*. Deuxième édition. Paris: Armand Colin, 2000.

Perlstein, Rick. *Nixonland: The Rise of a President and the Fracturing of America*. New York: Scribner, 2008.

———, ed. *Richard Nixon: Speeches, Writings, Documents*. Princeton: Princeton University Press, 2008.

Pope, Philip H. "Foundations of Nixonian Foreign Policy: The Pre-Presidential Years of Richard M. Nixon, 1946–1968, Volume I." Ph.D. Dissertation. University of Southern California, 1988.

Reeves, Richard. *President Nixon: Alone in the White House*. New York: Simon & Schuster, 2001.

Reis, Jaime, ed. *International Monetary Systems in Historical Perspective*. New York: St. Martin's Press, 1995.

Schurmann, Franz. *The Foreign Politics of Richard Nixon: The Grand Design*. Berkeley, Calif.: Institute of International Studies, 1987.

Schwartz, Thomas A. *America's Germany: John McCloy and the Federal Republic of Germany*. Cambridge: Harvard University Press, 1991.

———. *Lyndon Johnson and Europe: In the Shadow of Vietnam*. Cambridge: Harvard University Press, 2003.

Sloan, Stanley. *NATO's Future: Toward a New Transatlantic Bargain*. Washington, D.C.: National Defense University Press, 1985.

———. *NATO, the European Union, and the Atlantic Community*. 2nd Ed. Lanham, Md.: Rowman & Littlefield Publishers, 2005.

Steil, Benn. *The Battle of Bretton Woods: John Maynard Keynes, Harry Dexter White, and the Making of a New World Order*. Princeton: Princeton University Press, 2013.

Stein, Herbert. *Presidential Economics: The Making of Economic Policy from Roosevelt to Clinton*. Washington, D.C.: American Enterprise Institute, 1994.

Suri, Jeremi. *Henry Kissinger and the American Century*. Cambridge: Harvard University Press, 2007.

Trachtenberg, Marc, ed. *Empire and Alliance: America and Europe during the Cold War*. Lanham, Md.: Rowman & Littlefield Publishers, 2003.

van der Harst, Jan, ed. *Beyond the Customs Union: The European Community's Quest for Deepening, Widening and Completion, 1969–1975*. Brussels: Bruylant, 2007.

Volcker, Paul A., and Toyoo Gyohten. *The World's Money and the Threat to American Leadership*. New York: Times Books, 1992.

Weisbrode, Kenneth. *The Atlantic Century: Four Generations of Extraordinary Diplomats Who Forged America's Vital Alliance with Europe*. New York: Da Capo Press, 2009.

Wells, Wyatt C. *Economist in an Uncertain World: Arthur F. Burns and the Federal Reserve, 1970–78*. New York: Columbia University Press, 1994.

Wilkens, Andreas, ed. *Willy Brandt et l'unité de l'Europe: de l'objectif de la paix aux solidarités nécessaires*. Bruxelles: P. I. E. Peter Lang, 2011.

Witcover, Jules. *Very Strange Bedfellows: The Short and Unhappy Marriage of Richard Nixon and Spiro Agnew*. New York: Public Affairs, 2007.

Young, David R. "The Presidential Conduct of American Foreign Policy, 1969–1973." Ph.D. Dissertation. Oxford University, 1981.

Index

1972 Presidential Election, 32, 36, 43, 45, 54, 71, 72, 75, 83, 87, 93, 102, 103, 106, 107, 108, 110, 122
26th Amendment, 7

ABM, xiii, 22, 25, 26, *See* Anti-ballistic missile
Acheson, Dean, xvii, 29, 31
Agnew, Spiro, xvii, 143
Allen, George, 91
Alsop, Joe, 117
Andersen, Knud, xvii, 137, 140, 141, 142
Annenberg, Walter, xvii, 96, 170, 192,
Anti-ballistic missile. *See* ABM
Apel, Hans, 200
Atlantic Charter, 4, 14, 105, 117, 119, 133
Azores Summit, 91, 99, 100, 129

Bahr, Egon, xvii, 33, 103, 145
Barber, Anthony, xvii, 75, 160
Barzel, Rainer, xvii, 73
Belgium, 14, 27, 28, 44, 73, 150, 185, 194
Benn, Tony, 196, 197, 210
Berger, Marilyn, 119
Bergsten, Fred, xvii, 87
Berlind, Alan, 17
Bernard, Jean René, 94
Bierrign, Ole, 150
Blancard, Jean, 22
Brandt, Willy, xvii, 8, 16, 33, 45, 46, 73, 97, 105, 108, 111, 112, 118, 119, 122, 133, 137, 142, 144, 145, 150, 152, 174, 176, 177, 179, 181, 192, 193

Bretton Woods, 1, 3, 4, 36, 37, 38, 40, 41, 42, 48, 50, 55, 64, 65, 68, 69, 98, 101, 102, 103, 105, 123, 131, 148, 154, 155
Brezhnev, Leonid, xvii, 110, 133, 134
Brimelow, Thomas, 122,
Britain, 4, 5, 7, 15, 16, 17, 18, 21, 22, 26, 31, 57, 60, 72, 75, 77, 78, 81, 84, 85, 86, 92, 96, 97, 105, 108, 109, 110, 111, 114, 115, 116, 119, 120, 122, 123, 129, 135, 136, 137, 140, 143, 145, 146, 147, 149, 150, 152, 154, 156, 158, 159, 160, 161, 162, 163, 164, 165, 166, 167, 168, 169, 170, 171, 172, 173, 174, 175, 176, 177, 178, 179, 180, 181, 182, 183, 184, 185, 186, 187, 188, 189, 190, 191, 192, 193, 194, 195, 196, 197, 198, 199, 200, 201, 202, 203, 204, 205, 206, 207, 208, 209, 210, 211, 212, 213, 214, 215, 216, *See* Great Britain, Britain, United Kingdom, UK
Brosio, Manlio, xvii, 8, 14, 15
Bundesbank, 45, 46, 68, 90
Bundy, McGeorge, 29, 30
Burns, Arthur, xiii, xvii, 41, 42, 43, 44, 45, 47, 48, 50, 51, 52, 53, 54, 56, 58, 61, 64, 65, 66, 67, 71, 73, 74, 75, 77, 78, 79, 80, 81, 82, 85, 86, 87, 91, 93, 94, 95, 96, 97, 99, 102, 123, 129, 151,

Callaghan, James, xvii, 149, 153, 158, 169, 170, 171, 172, 173, 174, 175, 177, 178, 179, 180, 183, 184, 185, 186, 189, 193, 197, 206, 208, 210, 212, 214, 215,
Campbell, John, 203

Canada, 14, 95, 110, 113, 144, 152, 155
CAP, xiii, 46, 165, 184, 185, 186, 187, 192,
 See Common Agricultural Policy
Carrington, Peter, xvii
CCMS, xiii, 13, 14, 15, 16, 17, 18, 19, 27,
 34, 35, 217, *See* Committee on the
 Challenges of Modern Society
CDU. *See* Christian Democratic Union
Central Intelligence Agency, 197, *See* CIA
Chaban-Delmas, Jacques, xvii
China, 2, 3, 4, 5, 8, 23, 28, 33, 34, 43, 53,
 62, 65, 69, 72, 74, 82, 92, 97, 102, 103,
 104, 105, 106, 108, 109, 113, 114, 115,
 122, 123, 124, 130, 133, 134, 135, 139,
 140, 147, 155, 156, 157, 218, 219
Chirac, Jacques, 153, 186
Christian Democratic Union. *See* CDU
Christmas Bombing, 105, 110, 111, 114,
 115, 116, 124, *See* Operation
 Linebacker II
Churchill, Winston, 4, 105, 115, 148, 211
CIA, 10, 197, 201, *See* Central Intelligence
 Agency
CIEP, 42, *See* Council on International
 Economic Policy
Clean Air Act, 7, 19
Clean Water Act, 7, 19
Cleveland, Harlan, xvii
Clifford, Clark, xvii, 30
Colson, Charles, xvii, 52, 87,
 100
Colvin, David, 200
COMECON. *See* Council for Mutual
 Economic Assistance
Committee on the Challenges of Modern
 Society, 4, 8, 13, *See* CCMS
Common Agricultural Policy, 46, 163, 165,
 See CAP
Conference on Security and Cooperation in
 Europe, 32, *See* CSCE
Connally, Arthur, 81
Connally, John, xvii, 44, 45, 47, 48, 49, 50,
 51, 52, 53, 54, 55, 56, 57, 59, 60, 61, 62,
 63, 65, 69, 70, 71, 72, 73, 74, 75, 76, 77,
 78, 79, 80, 81, 82, 83, 84, 85, 86, 87, 88,
 89, 90, 91, 92, 93, 94, 95, 96, 98, 99, 100,
 101, 102, 103, 104, 107, 109, 113, 131,
 132, 134
Coombs, Charles, xvii, 57, 58
Council for Mutual Economic Assistance,
 110, *See* COMECON

Council of Economic Advisers, 48, 54,
 55, 93
Council of Europe, 13, 18
Council on Environmental Quality, 8, 15, 18
Council on International Economic Policy,
 42, 55, *See* CIEP
Council on Urban Affairs, 8
Couve de Murville, Maurice, xvii
Cox, Archibald, 143
Cromer, Earl of, xvii, 146
CSCE, 32, *See* Conference on Security and
 Cooperation in Europe
Czechoslovakia, 30
Czechoslovakia, Soviet invasion of, 1, 9,
 10, 21

Daane, J. Dewey, xvii, 45
Dahrendorf, Ralf, 16
Davis, Jeanne, xvii
De Gaulle, Charles, xvii, 1, 4, 8, 10, 20, 21,
 22, 26, 27, 38, 126, 128, 153, 161, 162,
 171, 194, 195, 218
de Staercke, André, 150
Dean, John, 119
Debré, Michel, xvii, 27, 181
Declaration on Atlantic Relations, 128, 140,
 147, 149, 152, 154, 217
Delors, Jacques, 160
Denmark, 104, 110, 135, 137, 140, 142,
 150, 159, 161, 193, 194, 209, 213
desegregation, 7
détente, 1, 2, 4, 5, 6, 8, 16, 19, 29, 34, 135,
 147, 150, 156, 158, 217, 218
Dillon, Brendan, 174
Dobrynin, Anatoly, xviii, 73
Douglas-Home, Alec, xviii, 32, 108, 143,
 145, 147, 156, 162, 163
Dufourcq, Jean, 191

Earth Day, 7, 19
EC, xiii, 4, 5, 23, 42, 95, 114, 118, 125,
 126, 127, 128, 132, 134, 137, 138, 139,
 140, 141, 143, 145, 146, 148, 149, 151,
 152, 153, 154, 155, 159, 160, 161, 162,
 163, 164, 165, 166, 167, 168, 169, 170,
 171, 172, 173, 174, 175, 176, 177, 178,
 179, 180, 181, 182, 183, 184, 185, 186,
 187, 188, 189, 190, 191, 192, 193, 194,
 195, 196, 197, 198, 199, 200, 201, 202,
 203, 205, 206, 207, 208, 209, 210, 212,
 213, 214, 215, *See* European Community

EEC, xiii, 13, 18, 69, 70, 72, 76, 104, 162, 163, *See* European Economic Community

Ehrlichman, John, xviii, 48, 49, 51, 52, 87, 119, 139

Eisenhower, Dwight, 7, 38, 147, 218

Eliot, Theodore, xviii

Ellsworth, Robert, xviii, 28, 40

Emminger, Otmar, xviii, 45, 46, 68, 90,

EMU, 45, *See* European Monetary Union

Endangered Species Act, 7

Environmental Protection Agency, 6, 15, 19

Equal Protection Amendment, 7

Erhard, Ludwig, xviii, 42, 48, 90

Ervin, Sam, 131

EU, 19

European Community, 1, 2, 4, 23, 28, 45, 105, 108, 110, 111, 113, 115, 116, 119, 120, 122, 123, 125, 126, 127, 129, 132, 133, 136, 137, 138, 139, 140, 141, 143, 145, 146, 148, 149, 150, 153, 154, 155, 156, 159, 160, 161, 163, 164, 165, 167, 168, 170, 171, 172, 173, 174, 175, 176, 180, 181, 185, 189, 192, 193, 194, 195, 196, 197, 199, 205, 206, 210, 214, 215, *See* EC

European Economic Community, 13, 17, 26, 46, 68, 78, 84, 86, 100, 104, 162, 163, 172, 191, *See* EEC

European Free Trade Agreement, 184, 205, 206

European Monetary Union, 45, 46, 70, *See* EMU

European Security Conference, 32, 33, 110

Evans, Rowland, 117, 140

FCO, xiii, 15, 18, 84, 109, 110, 115, 122, 129, 132, 136, 147, 156, 163, 173, 174, 179, 180, 184, 196, 200, 202, 209, *See* Foreign and Commonwealth Office

Federal Republic of Germany. *See* FRG, Germany, West Germany

Federal Reserve Board, 40, 42, 44, 51, 52, 57, 70, 71, 87, 96, 97, 123, 151

Fiji, 181

Finch, Robert, xviii

Flanigan, Peter, xviii, 49, 87

Flexible Response, 10, 12

Foot, Michael, 169, 197

Ford, Gerald, xiv, xviii, 5, 105, 154, 158, 159, 188, 189, 190, 191, 197, 204, 208, 210, 211, 212, 215

Foreign and Commonwealth Office, 15, 163, *See* FCO

Foster, John, xviii, 23, 25

Fourquet, Michel, xviii, 24

France, xx, 1, 4, 6, 7, 9, 16, 19, 21, 22, 23, 24, 25, 26, 27, 34, 35, 46, 47, 68, 69, 72, 73, 78, 81, 83, 84, 85, 86, 90, 91, 92, 93, 94, 97, 98, 99, 105, 108, 110, 111, 112, 118, 119, 120, 121, 122, 125, 126, 127, 128, 129, 131, 134, 136, 137, 138, 140, 141, 144, 145, 147, 148, 149, 150, 151, 152, 153, 154, 155, 156, 158, 159, 161, 162, 163, 164, 166, 167, 168, 170, 171, 172, 174, 175, 176, 177, 178, 179, 180, 181, 182, 183, 184, 185, 186, 187, 191, 192, 193, 194, 195, 199, 200, 202, 203, 209, 214, 215

FRELOC, xiv, 27

FRG, xiv, xvii, xviii, xix, *See* West Germany, Germany, Federal Republic of Germany

Friedman, Milton, xviii, 40, 41, 42, 47, 83, 84, 87, 97,

Galley, Robert, 120

GATT, xiv, 75, 84, *See* General Agreement on Tariffs and Trade

General Agreement on Tariffs and Trade. *See* GATT

Genscher, Hans-Dietrich, 180, 183, 184, 188, 214

Germany, 14, 16, 17, 25, 30, 32, 33, 34, 39, 43, 44, 45, 46, 47, 48, 68, 70, 72, 73, 75, 78, 81, 84, 85, 86, 87, 90, 91, 92, 97, 98, 99, 103, 105, 107, 108, 109, 110, 111, 112, 118, 122, 123, 127, 129, 134, 137, 140, 141, 142, 145, 147, 149, 150, 152, 154, 155, 156, 158, 160, 162, 163, 166, 168, 171, 172, 174, 175, 176, 177, 178, 179, 180, 182, 183, 184, 185, 186, 187, 188, 191, 192, 193, 194, 195, 200, 202, 203, 206, 214, 215, *See* FRG, West Germany, FRG, Federal Republic of Germany

Giles, Frank, 178

Giscard d'Estaing, Valéry, xviii, 69, 150, 153, 158, 181, 183, 185, 186, 187, 193, 194, 195, 196, 200, 202, 203, 209

Glassboro Summit, 9
gold, 1, 4, 36, 37, 38, 39, 40, 41, 42, 45, 51, 54, 55, 56, 57, 58, 59, 60, 61, 63, 64, 65, 66, 68, 70, 71, 76, 77, 78, 79, 80, 81, 83, 84, 91, 92, 97, 98, 99, 124
Goodpaster, Andrew, xviii, 24, 29, 122
Gordon-Lenox, Nicholas, 179
Great Britain, 159, 213, *See* Britain, United Kingdom, UK
Great Society, 2, 101, 218
Greece, 110
Greenspan, Alan, 208
Gromyko, Andrei, xviii
Guam, 2, 3, 4
Guillaume Affair, 179
Guillaume, Günther, 179

Haig, Alexander, xviii, 87, 151
Haldeman, H. R., xviii, 28, 48, 51, 52, 55, 59, 65, 90, 119, 139, 151
Harmel, Pierre, 9, 10, xviii
Hartman, Arthur, 151, 170, 172, 174
Hattersley, Roy, 184, 196
Healey, Denis, 200, 206
Heath, Edward, xviii, 31, 32, 72, 84, 91, 96, 97, 100, 105, 115, 116, 120, 122, 132, 134, 136, 143, 144, 145, 146, 147, 149, 156, 160, 161, 162, 163, 164, 165, 167, 168, 170, 173, 179, 187, 188, 205, 210, 212, 213
Helms, Richard, xviii
Helsinki Accords, 155
Herter Committee, xiv, 74
Herter, Christian, xiv
Hess, Stephen, 13
Hillenbrand, Martin, xviii, 117, 188
Hitler, Adolf, 30, 115
Hormats, Robert, 109, 113, 116
Humphrey, Hubert, xviii, 83
Hunt, John, 191

ICBM, xiv, *See* Intercontinental ballistic missile
Iceland, 110
IMF, xiv, 58, 95, *See* International Monetary Fund
Intercontinental ballistic missile. *See* ICBM
International Bank for Reconstruction and Development, 37
International Monetary Fund, 37, 54, 65, 84, *See* IMF

Ireland, Northern, 116
Ireland, Republic of, 104, 161, 174, 193, 194, 195, 201, 203, 214
Irwin, John, xviii, 120, 122, 123, 137, 153
Israel, 149
Italy, 7, 68, 91, 97, 98, 110, 140, 155, 187, 194

Jackson, Henry, xviii, 154
Jackson-Nunn Amendment, 138,
Jackson-Vanik Amendment, 139
Japan, 17, 43, 68, 73, 74, 81, 87, 91, 97, 98, 155
Javits, Jacob, xviii, 29, 30
JCS, xiv, *See* Joint Chiefs of Staff
Jenkins, Roy, xviii, 164
Jobert, Michel, xviii, 120, 121, 122, 125, 126, 128, 131, 132, 134, 137, 139, 142, 147, 148, 149, 150, 151, 156, 166, 168, 171, 176, 178, 180, 181, 183, 186
Johnson, Ernest, 49
Johnson, Lyndon, 2, 9, 20, 21, 23, 30, 31, 38, 40, 47, 50, 83, 88, 112, 218
Johnson, U. Alexis, xiv, xviii
Joint Chiefs of Staff. *See* JCS

Katzenbach, Nicholas, xviii, 29
Kennedy, David, xiv, xviii, 41, 42
Kennedy, John F., xviii, 24, 38, 87, 89, 112
Keynes, John Maynard, 37
Kiesinger, Kurt Georg, xviii, 8, 192
Kissinger, Henry, xviii, 2, 4, 5, 10, 11, 12, 13, 22, 23, 24, 25, 26, 27, 28, 29, 30, 31, 33, 34, 35, 39, 41, 49, 66, 67, 69, 72, 73, 76, 81, 82, 84, 85, 86, 87, 88, 89, 90, 91, 93, 94, 95, 96, 97, 99, 103, 104, 105, 106, 107, 108, 109, 111, 112, 114, 115, 116, 117, 118, 119, 120, 121, 122, 123, 125, 126, 127, 128, 129, 130, 131, 132, 133, 134, 135, 136, 137, 138, 139, 140, 141, 142, 143, 144, 145, 146, 147, 148, 149, 150, 151, 152, 153, 155, 156, 157, 158, 159, 163, 166, 167, 170, 172, 174, 179, 186, 188, 189, 190, 192, 197, 201, 204, 210, 211, 212, 215, 216, 218, 219
Knievel, Evel, 210
Kosciusko-Morizet, Jacques, xix, 108
Kosygin, Alexei, xix
Kraft, Joe, 95, 96, 99, 118, 152

Laird, Melvin, xiv, xix, 20, 21, 23, 30, 92
Lemnitzer, Lyman, xix, 29
Lodge, Jr., Henry Cabot, xix, 29
Lord, Winston, 197
Lucet, Charles, xix, 97
Luns, Joseph, xix, 33, 133, 147, 150, 154, 166, 217
Luxembourg, 194
Luxembourg Compromise, 194

Macmillan, Harold, 24, 161, 207
Malraux, André, xix
Malta, 147
Mammal Marine Protection Act, 7
Mansfield Amendment, 29, 46, 122, 138, 146
Mansfield, Michael, xix, 27, 29, 30, 31
Marshall Plan, 2, 38, 74, 117, 135, 157
Marshall, George, 117
MBFR, xiv, 32, 130, 131, *See* Mutual and balance force reductions
McCloy, John, xix, 28, 89, 123, 129, 159
McCracken, Paul, xix, 40, 41, 43, 44, 47, 48, 49, 50, 51, 53, 56, 57, 58, 64, 91, 93
McGovern, George, 106
McNamara, Robert, 20
Messmer, Pierre, 20, 120
Middle East, 115, 143, 147, 218
Mintoff, Dom, 147
Mitchell, John, xix, 66
Monnet, Jean, 100, 111, 121, 127, 181
Moynihan, Daniel Patrick, xix, 8, 14, 15, 16, 17, 18,
Murray, Len, 208
Mutual and balanced force reductions. *See* MBFR

National Oceanic Atmospheric Administration, 15
National Security Council, xx, 13, 34, 41, 54, 89, 106, 112, 116, *See* NSC
Native Americans, 7
NATO, xiv, xvii, xviii, xix, 1, 2, 3, 4, 6, 7, 8, 9, 10, 11, 12, 13, 14, 15, 16, 20, 21, 22, 23, 24, 25, 27, 28, 29, 30, 31, 32, 33, 34, 35, 82, 92, 95, 104, 105, 109, 111, 113, 118, 122, 123, 125, 129, 130, 132, 133, 134, 138, 139, 142, 145, 147, 148, 149, 150, 152, 153, 154, 160, 166, 168, 169, 177, 189, 206, 207, 216, 217, 218, *See* North Atlantic Treaty Organization

Netherlands, The, 7, 44, 73, 86, 110, 177, 193, 194
New Economic Policy, 36, 42, 66, 68, 71, 72, 75, 79, 82, 83, 91, 101
New Zealand, 202, 203
Nixon Doctrine, 3, 4, 5, 11, 13, 21, 29, 34, 35, 36, 43, 48, 49, 50, 71, 79, 104, 124, 128, 136, 218, 219
Nixon, Richard, xv, xix, 1, 2, 3, 4, 5, 6, 7, 8, 9, 10, 11, 12, 13, 14, 15, 16, 17, 18, 20, 21, 22, 23, 24, 25, 26, 27, 28, 29, 30, 31, 32, 33, 34, 36, 40, 41, 42, 43, 44, 45, 46, 47, 48, 49, 50, 51, 52, 53, 54, 55, 56, 57, 58, 59, 60, 61, 62, 63, 64, 65, 66, 67, 68, 69, 70, 71, 72, 74, 75, 76, 77, 78, 79, 80, 81, 82, 83, 84, 85, 86, 87, 88, 89, 90, 91, 92, 93, 94, 95, 96, 97, 98, 99, 100, 101, 102, 103, 104, 105, 106, 107, 108, 109, 110, 111, 112, 114, 115, 116, 117, 118, 119, 120, 121, 122, 123, 124, 125, 127, 128, 129, 130, 131, 132, 133, 134, 135, 136, 137, 138, 139, 140, 142, 143, 144, 145, 148, 149, 151, 152, 154, 155, 156, 157, 158, 159, 162, 163, 176, 179, 188, 190, 197, 216, 217, 218, 219
Non-Proliferation Treaty, xiv, 12, 21, 24, 27, 32
North Atlantic Council, xiv, 13, 14, 18, 28, 109, 150, 154
North Atlantic Treaty of 1949, 1, 7, 9
North Atlantic Treaty Organization. *See* NATO
Norway, 6, 7, 15, 110
Novak, Robert, 140
NSC, xiv, xvii, 49, 55, 89, 106, 109, 113, *See* National Security Council
Nuclear Test Ban Treaty, xiv
Nutter, Warren, xix

OECD, 16, 18, 93, 95, 206, *See* Organization for Economic Cooperation and Development
Office of Environmental Protection, 15
Office of Management and Budget, 48
Organization for Economic Cooperation and Development, 13, 93, 135, *See* OECD
Ortoli, Francois-Xavier, 138, 142, 186, 195, 213
Ostpolitik, 10, 32, 104, 156, 181
Overton, Hugh, 115

Packard, David, xix
Pauls, Rolf, xix, 46, 90, 110
Peart, Fred, 172, 206
Pentagon, 9, 22, 30
Peterson, Peter, xix, 42, 43, 49, 53, 54, 55, 62, 76, 87, 89,
Peyrefitte, Alain, 126
Pierre, Henri, 151
Poher, Alain, xix
Poland, 30
Pompidou, Georges, xix, 20, 22, 23, 24, 25, 26, 27, 69, 73, 81, 91, 92, 93, 94, 96, 97, 99, 100, 105, 112, 119, 120, 121, 127, 128, 129, 133, 145, 149, 150, 152, 161, 168, 176, 177, 178, 179, 185, 186, 215
Portugal, 110
President's Foreign Intelligence Advisory Board, 139

Quadriad, xiv, 50, 53, 55, 62
Quadripartite Agreement, xv, 32, 73,
Queen Elizabeth II, 172, 191

Randers, Gunnar, 16
Resource Recovery Act, 19
Reston, James, 117, 190
Reykjavik Summit, 127, 128
Rhodesia, 116
Richardson, Elliot, xix, 143, 201
Rogers, William, xix, 66, 85, 109, 111, 112, 116, 125, 130
Roosevelt, Franklin D., 4, 105
Rostow, Walt, xix, 31
Rowling, Edward, 202
Rumor, Mariano, 8
Rumsfeld, Donald, xix, 28, 29, 129, 130, 150, 152
Rush, Kenneth, xix, 11, 73, 90, 141

SACEUR, xv, 122, *See* Supreme Allied Commander, Europe
Safire, William, 13, 52, 64, 66
SALT, xv, 32, 103, 109, *See* Strategic Arms Limitation Talks
Samuels, Nathaniel, xix, 48
Sato, Eisaku, xix, 73
Saturday Night Massacre, 143
Sauvagnargues, Jean, 150, 153, 183, 186, 214
Scheel, Walter, xix, 48, 109, 112, 134, 141, 147, 172, 179, 181

Schiller, Karl, xix, 75, 76
Schlesinger, James, 39, 146
Schmidt, Helmut, xix, 107, 150, 154, 158, 166, 174, 179, 180, 181, 183, 185, 186, 187, 193, 195, 196, 200, 201, 202, 203, 205, 211
Schroeder, Gerhard, xix
Schumann, Maurice, xx, 98, 108
Schweitzer, Pierre-Paul, xx, 65
Scowcroft, Brent, xx, 149
Sherman, George, 119
Shore, Peter, 169, 197
Shriver, Sargent, xx,
Shultz, George, xx, 44, 49, 50, 53, 58, 59, 60, 61, 62, 63, 64, 65, 71, 83, 85, 86, 89, 94, 95, 105, 158
Smith, Gerard, xiii, xx
Smithsonian Agreement, 67, 98, 100, 102
Sonnenfeldt, Helmut, xx, 23, 25, 112, 113, 126, 131, 134, 137, 144, 151, 153, 166, 167, 170, 172, 174
Soviet Union, 2, 3, 4, 5, 8, 9, 10, 11, 18, 19, 22, 28, 30, 31, 32, 33, 34, 43, 72, 73, 82, 91, 92, 97, 102, 103, 104, 105, 106, 107, 108, 109, 110, 113, 114, 115, 122, 123, 124, 127, 130, 132, 133, 134, 135, 143, 144, 155, 156, 157, 218, 219
Spaak, Paul Henri, 154
Special Drawing Rights, xv, 40, 80
Special Relationship, 4, 72, 115, 116, 120, 158, 159, 162, 166, 177, 189, 204
Stans, Maurice, xx
Stein, Herbert, xx, 64, 93
Stewart, Michael, 205
Stoessel, Walter, 145
Strategic Arms Limitation Talks. *See* SALT
Strategic Arms Limitation Treaty, 133
Strausz-Hupe, Robert, 28, 141
Suffert, Georges, 171,
Supreme Allied Commander, Europe, xviii, 122, *See* SACEUR
Swaziland, 181
Sweden, 6, 15, 17, 19
Switzerland, 44

Thatcher, Margaret, 159, 204, 205, 210, 211
Thorpe, Jeremy, 213
Tindemans, Leo, 185
Title IX, 7
Tojo, Hideki, 30
Trade Reform Act of 1974, 139

Trade Union Congress, 165, 208
Train, Russell, 8, 18
Trend, Burke, xx, 114, 122, 135
Triffin, Robert, 100
Truman Doctrine, 3
Turkey, 19, 110, 139

UK, 22, 72, 158, 160, 166, 171, 173, 174,
  175, 188, 189, 202, 205, 206, 207, 209,
  210, 211, 212, *See* Great Britain, Britain,
  United Kingdom
UN, xv, 13, *See* United Nations
United Kingdom, xvii, 13, 14, 68, 91, 104,
  115, 116, 120, 127, 136, 152, 153, 155,
  158, 159, 160, 161, 162, 163, 175, 176,
  178, 181, 191, 193, 194, 195, 200, *See*
  Great Britain, Britain, UK
United Nations, 16, *See* UN

van der Stoel, Max, 177
van Lennep, Emile, 135
Vance, Cyrus, xx, 29
Vatican, 28, 110
Vietnam, 2, 3, 8, 139
Vietnam War, 2, 3, 4, 12, 26, 29, 34, 38, 72,
  92, 101, 103, 104, 105, 106, 107, 110,
  111, 112, 114, 115, 116, 117, 118, 123,
  128, 130, 139, 155, 156, 190, 218, 219
Vietnamization, 3
Volcker, Paul, xx, 40, 44, 49, 50, 57, 65, 68,
  69, 71, 76, 82, 83, 85, 86, 98, 99
von Staden, Berndt, 141

Walters, Vernon, xx
War on Cancer, 7
War Powers Act, 139
Warnke, Paul, xx
Warsaw Pact, 8, 10, 21, 30

Washington Energy Conference, 166, 167,
  168, 171, 180, 185
Watergate, xv, 34, 105, 117, 119, 128,
  131, 139, 140, 143, 155, 157, 159,
  190, 191
Watson, Arthur, xx, 90, 91
Wehner, Herbert, 145
Weinberger, Caspar, xx, 48
West Germany, 7, 10, 33, 39, 43, 44, 45, 46,
  73, 110, *See* Germany, Federal Republic
  of Germany, FRG
White, Harry Dexter, 37
Whitelaw, Willie, 205
Wilderness Act, 19
Wilson, Harold, xx, 8, 21, 105, 120, 149,
  154, 158, 161, 164, 168, 169, 170, 171,
  172, 174, 175, 176, 178, 179, 180,
  185, 186, 187, 189, 190, 191, 193, 194,
  195, 196, 197, 198, 199, 200, 201, 202,
  203, 204, 205, 206, 207, 208, 209, 210,
  211, 212, 213, 214, 215
World Bank, 37
Wright, Oliver, 174, 175

Year of Europe, 3, 4, 27, 33, 34, 104,
  105, 106, 107, 109, 112, 114, 115, 116,
  117, 118, 119, 121, 122, 123, 125, 126,
  127, 128, 129, 130, 131, 132, 133, 134,
  135, 137, 138, 139, 140, 142, 144, 146,
  147, 149, 152, 154, 155, 156, 157, 158,
  159, 164, 167, 173, 189, 191, 215,
  216, 217
Yom Kippur War, 105, 149, 155, 160,
  165, 217
Yugoslavia, 17

Ziegler, Ronald, xx, 111
Zijlstra, Jelle, xx, 86

CPSIA information can be obtained
at www.ICGtesting.com
Printed in the USA
LVOW07s0208250517
535635LV00001B/90/P